EDITED BY LEONARD HOLLIS

# The
# Rose
# Annual
# 1974

THE ROYAL NATIONAL
ROSE SOCIETY

Copyright © 1974 Leonard Hollis
Published by
THE ROYAL NATIONAL ROSE SOCIETY
Bone Hill, Chiswell Green Lane, St Albans, Hertfordshire
*Telephone:* St Albans 50461. *Telegrams:* Natiorose, St Albans
Printed and bound in England by
Hazell Watson & Viney Limited
Aylesbury, Buckinghamshire

# Contents

## COLOUR PLATES

Part of the magnificent exhibit of R. Harkness & Co. Ltd. which was awarded the
Autumn Rose Challenge Cup for the best exhibit at the Autumn Show, 1973 and the
Lewis Levy Memorial Cup for the best exhibit over 450 sq. ft

# CONTENTS

## MONOCHROME PLATES

# COMMITTEES FOR 1974

## FINANCE AND GENERAL PURPOSES COMMITTEE

*E. F. Allen
*E. J. Baldwin
*R. C. Balfour
*F. M. Bowen
H. G. Clacy
*E. V. Elwes
*F. Fairbrother
K. E. Fisk

*D. L. Flexman
S. M. Gault
*F. A. Gibson
C. W. Gregory
A. N. Harding
J. L. Harkness
Lord Pilkington
H. N. Raban

Mrs H. Robinson
J. Roscoe
D. H. Scott
J. H. Shotter
S. C. Thomson
Dr J. T. Watts
F. C. H. Witchell

## NEW SEEDLING JUDGING COMMITTEE

*E. F. Allen
*R. C. Balfour
W. K. Bentley
*F. M. Bowen
A. M. Cocker
F. Fairbrother
Miss J. E. Fulford

S. M. Gault
J. L. Harkness
Leonard Hollis
E. B. Le Grice
J. S. Mattock
C. Pawsey
H. N. Raban

C. F. Roberts
Mrs H. Robinson
B. W. W. Sampson
J. H. Shotter
W. E. Tysterman
H. Wheatcroft
H. Williamson

## EXHIBITIONS COMMITTEE

*E. F. Allen
*R. C. Balfour
F. M. Bowen
H. G. Clacy

*E. V. Elwes
Miss J. E. Fulford
S. M. Gault
M. F. Goodchap
C. F. Roberts

J. H. Shotter
Mrs D. Thorn
Dr J. T. Watts
F. C. H. Witchell

## GARDENS MANAGEMENT COMMITTEE

*E. F. Allen
*R. C. Balfour
W. K. Bentley
*F. M. Bowen

*H. G. Clacy
*E. V. Elwes
F. Fairbrother

*S. M. Gault
J. L. Harkness
J. S. Mattock
D. H. Scott

## PUBLICATIONS COMMITTEE

*E. F. Allen
*R. C. Balfour
F. M. Bowen

*E. V. Elwes
J. L. Harkness
A. G. L. Hellyer

R. L. Pallett
H. N. Raban

*Denotes *ex-officio* member.

7

# PRESIDENTS OF THE
# ROYAL NATIONAL ROSE SOCIETY

1877-1904 The Very Rev. DEAN HOLE, V.M.H.

1905-06 CHARLES E. SHEA
1907-08 E. B. LINDSELL
1909-10 Rev. F. PAGE-ROBERTS
1911-12 Rev. J. H. PEMBERTON
1913-14 CHARLES E. SHEA
1915-16 EDWARD MAWLEY, V.M.H.
1917-18 Sir EDWARD HOLLAND
1919-20 H. R. DARLINGTON, V.M.H.
1921-22 Sir EDWARD HOLLAND
1923-24 SYDNEY F. JACKSON
1925-26 C. C. WILLIAMSON
1927-28 H. R. DARLINGTON, V.M.H.
1929-30 ARTHUR JOHNSON
1931-32 HERBERT OPPENHEIMER
1933-34 Dr A. H. WILLIAMS
1935-36 Major A. D. G. SHELLEY, R.E.
1937-38 HERBERT OPPENHEIMER
1939-40 JOHN N. HART, C.B.E.
1941-42 CHARLES H. RIGG

1943-44 HERBERT OPPENHEIMER
1945-46 A. NORMAN ROGERS
1947-48 A. E. GRIFFITH
1949-50 E. J. BALDWIN, O.B.E.
1951-52 D. L. FLEXMAN
1953-54 WILLIAM E. MOORE
1955-56 OLIVER MEE, O.B.E.
1957-58 A. NORMAN
1959-60 F. FAIRBROTHER, M.SC., F.R.I.C.
1961-62 E. ROYALTON KISCH, M.C.
1963-64 Maj.-Gen. R. F. B. NAYLOR, C.B.,
C.B.E., D.S.O., M.C.
1965-66 F. A. GIBSON
1967-68 Maj.-Gen. R. F. B. NAYLOR, C.B.,
C.B.E., D.S.O., M.C.
1969-70 JOHN CLARKE
1971-72 FRANK M. BOWEN, C.ENG.
1973-74 R. C. BALFOUR, M.B.E.


# THE QUEEN MARY COMMEMORATION
# MEDAL AWARDS

1957 & 1973 ALEX DICKSON & SONS LTD
1957 & 1973 SAMUEL McGREDY & SON LTD
1957 & 1973 E. B. LE GRICE (HYBRIDISERS) LTD
1957         HERBERT ROBINSON, M.B.E.
1957         OLIVER MEE, O.B.E.
1957         A. NORMAN

1964 BERTRAM PARK, O.B.E., V.M.H.
1971 C. GREGORY & SON LTD
1973 JAMES COCKER & SONS LTD
1973 R. HARKNESS & CO. LTD
1973 JOHN SANDAY (ROSES) LTD


# THE DEAN HOLE MEDAL AWARDS

1909 Rev. J. H. PEMBERTON
1910 EDWARD MAWLEY, V.M.H.
1912 GEORGE DICKSON, V.M.H.
1914 CHARLES E. SHEA
1917 E. B. LINDSELL
1918 Sir EDWARD HOLLAND
1919 Rev. F. PAGE-ROBERTS
1919 GEORGE PAUL
1920 H. R. DARLINGTON, V.M.H.
1921 S. McGREDY
1923 Miss E. WILLMOTT, F.L.S.
1924 SYDNEY F. JACKSON
1925 COURTNEY PAGE
1926 C. C. WILLIAMSON
1930 Dr J. CAMPBELL HALL
1930 WILLIAM E. NICKERSON
1931 ARTHUR JOHNSON
1933 HERBERT OPPENHEIMER
1935 Dr A. H. WILLIAMS
1935 WALTER EASLEA
1936 ALISTER CLARK
1937 Major A. D. G. SHELLEY, R.E.
1940 JOHN N. HART, C.B.E.
1942 CHARLES H. RIGG
1942 Dr HORACE J. McFARLAND
1945 Dr H. V. TAYLOR, C.B.E.
1947 A. NORMAN ROGERS
1948 Dr G. E. DEACON
1949 W. E. MOORE
1949 A. E. GRIFFITH
1950 JOHN RAMSBOTTOM, O.B.E., Dr. SC., M.A.

1950 F. S. HARVEY-CANT, M.B.E.
1950 E. J. BALDWIN, O.B.E.
1952 D. L. FLEXMAN
1952 BERTRAM PARK, O.B.E., V.M.H ,
Mérite Agri.
1952 Dr A. S. THOMAS, O.B.E., V.M.A.
1954 W. E. HARKNESS
1956 OLIVER MEE, O.B.E.
1958 A. NORMAN
1959 W. J. W. SANDAY
1960 F. FAIRBROTHER, M.SC., F.R.I.C.
1962 H. G. CLACY
1962 E. ROYALTON KISCH, M.C.
1964 G. D. BURCH
1964 Maj.-Gen. R. F. B. NAYLOR, C.B., C.B.E.,
D.S.O., M.C.
1965 H. EDLAND
1965 E. BAINES
1966 EDGAR M. ALLEN, C.M.G.
1966 F. A. GIBSON
1967 ALEX DICKSON
1967 W. KORDES
1969 J. W. MATTOCK
1970 JOHN CLARKE
1971 L. A. ANSTISS
1971 D. BUTCHER
1972 FRANK M. BOWEN, C.ENG.
1973 LEONARD HOLLIS
1973 HARRY WHEATCROFT, V.M.H.

8

# Arrangements 1974

## Shows

*Amateur Spring Competition* 30 April and 1 May.

*Summer Show* 28 and 29 June.

*Autumn Show* 13 and 14 September.

The above shows will be held at The Royal Horticultural Society's Halls, Westminster. The Amateur Spring Competition will be staged at the Flower and Rhododendron Show to which, by courtesy of The Royal Horticultural Society, members will be admitted on production of their membership card. *Northern Show* 16 and 17 July at Roundhay Park, Leeds in conjunction with the Roundhay (Leeds) Horticultural Society.

### Terms of Admission

The Certificate of Membership will admit the holder only to all the above shows.

Members also receive two transferable tickets for the Summer Show and two transferable tickets for the Autumn Show.

Prices of admission for the public will be:

*Summer Show* 28 June 11 a.m. to 5 p.m. 55p, 5 p.m. to 7 p.m. 33p.
 29 June 10 a.m. to 5 p.m. 33p.
*Autumn Show* 13 September 11 a.m. to 7 p.m. 33p.
 14 September 10 a.m. to 5 p.m. 17p.

Members may purchase additional tickets for the Summer and Autumn Shows at half price. Applications accompanied by remittances must be received at the Society's office not less than three days before the show.

*Northern Show* 16 July 11 a.m. to 3 p.m. £1, 3 p.m. to 9 p.m. 50p.
 17 July 10 a.m. to 5 p.m. 30p, 5 p.m. to 8 p.m. 20p.
 Children under 15 15p.

### RNRS Classes at Provincial Shows and Admission Arrangements

By the courtesy of the organisers of the following Shows, members of The Royal National Rose Society are offered special concessions in respect of exhibiting and free admission which the Council acknowledges with thanks. Unless indicated by an asterisk both concessions will apply. Further details of the Shows offering free admission to RNRS members are given on the Membership Certificate:

*Alderley Edge and Wilmslow Horticultural and Rose Society's Show* on 13 July.
*Ashington Rose Society's Show* on 13 July.
*Berwick-upon-Tweed and District Rose Society's Show* on 14 July.
*Bexleyheath and District Rose Society's Show* on 22 June.
*Bournemouth and District Rose Society's Show* on 22 June.
*Bramhall, Cheadle Hulme and Woodford Agricultural and Horticultural Society's Show* on 10 August.
*Bristol and District Group of RNRS Show* on 3 July.
*Bryndorion (Swansea) Rose Society's Show* on 6 July.

*Clevedon and District Horticultural Society's Show* on 23 and 24 August.
*Clontarf Horticultural Society's Show* on 29 June.
*Colchester Rose and Horticultural Society's Show* on 6 and 7 July.
*Congleton and District Horticultural Society's Show* on 13 July.
*Coventry and District Carnation, Rose and Sweet Pea Society's Show* on 6 July.
*Eastleigh and District Rose, Carnation and Sweet Pea Society's Show* on 6 July.
*Federation of Edinburgh and District Allotments and Gardens Association's Show* on 31 August.
*Formby Horticultural and Agricultural Society's Show* on 13 July.
*Glamorgan (Vale of) Agricultural Society's Show* on 21 August.
*Grey Mare Rose Society's Show* on 20 July.
*Hereford and West of England Rose Society's Show* on 6 July.
*Hitchin Horticultural Society's Show* on 22 June.
*Ipswich and East of England Horticultural Society's Show* on 13 and 14 July.
*Isle of Wight Rose, Carnation and Sweet Pea Association's Show* on 22 June.
*Lakeland Rose Show* on 12 and 13 July.
*Lincolnshire Rose Society's Show* on 13 and 14 July.
*Manx Rose Society's Show* on 13 and 14 July.
*Northampton and District Rose Society's Show* on 31 August.
*North of England Rose, Carnation and Sweet Pea Society's Show* on 16 and 17 August.
*North Western Group of RNRS Show* on 7 and 8 September.
*Nottingham Rose Society's Show* on 6 and 7 July.
*Reading Horticultural Federation's Show* on 16 and 17 August.
*Renfrew Horticultural Society's Show* on 21 September.
\**Royal Caledonian Horticultural Society's Show* at The Corn Exchange, Gorgie, Edinburgh on 21 and 22 September (12 noon to 9 p.m. and 12 noon to 6 p.m.). (RNRS classes but *not* free admission.)
*Scottish National Sweet Pea, Rose and Carnation Society's Show* on 3 August.
*Southampton (Royal) Horticultural Society's Show* on 12, 13 and 14 July.
\**Southport Flower Show* in Victoria Park, Southport, on 22, 23 and 24 August (10 a.m. to 9 p.m., 9 a.m. to 9 p.m. and 9 a.m. to 5.30 p.m.). (RNRS classes but *not* free admission.)
*South-West Counties Rose and Sweet Pea Society's Show* on 26 and 27 June.
*Teesside Rose Society's Show* on 6 and 7 July.
*West Cumberland Rose Society's Show* on 20 July.
*West Midlands Rose Society's Show* on 13 and 14 July.

The date of the *Yorkshire Rosarians Group of RNRS Show* had not been fixed at the time of going to press—information may be obtained from the Secretary, Mrs J. Acklam, 10 Kirkstone Drive, Norton Towers, Halifax.

Please note that the Certificate of Membership does not admit to the Royal Caledonian Horticultural Society's Show, Southport Flower Show or any other Show not listed.

For further details and schedules of the aforementioned Shows application should be made to The Secretary, RNRS.

## Display Gardens

Members and their friends are cordially invited to visit the displays of rose varieties that have received awards provided at:

| | |
|---|---|
| Cardiff—Roath Park | Norwich—Heigham Park |
| Edinburgh—Saughton Park | Nottingham—The Arboretum |
| Glasgow—Pollok Park | Southport—Botanic Gardens |

\*Harrogate—Harlow Car                    Taunton—Vivary Park
                                          Teesside—Borough Park, Redcar

\* At Harlow Car, the Gardens of the Northern Horticultural Society, the rose displays occupy a small portion of the ground only and it is hoped that visitors will each be willing to contribute a donation of 10p towards general upkeep.

### International Convention—1974
The International Rose Convention will be held in Chicago, U.S.A. from 7 September to 12 September. Some difficulty has been experienced in arranging a tour in connection with the Convention owing to the high price. Alternative proposals to reduce the cost are now being prepared and details will be available by April. Members interested should write to the Secretary without delay.

A full programme of lectures and outings is being arranged by the American Rose Society and a meeting of the World Federation of Rose Societies will precede the convention.

### Rose Bulletin
*The Rose Bulletin* will be published in October, and all members will receive a copy free of charge. Items of news, topical rose stories and interesting reports from members will be welcomed and should be sent to the Secretary.

### Annual General Meeting
Members are requested to take note that the 98th Annual General Meeting will be held at The Royal Horticultural Society's Hall, Westminster, on Tuesday, 10 December, 1974. Formal agenda for the meeting will be dispatched with *The Rose Bulletin*.

### Judges Examination
The Examination for rose judges will be held at Kendal, Westmorland, on Thursday, 18 July. Applications, which preferably should be endorsed by the Secretary of the local horticultural or rose society, must be received before 31 May, 1974. The number of candidates is limited and selection will be based on area, with preference to applicants from Scotland and the North of England.

### Centenary—1976
Tentative arrangements are being made for the 1976 Centenary International Conference to be held at Oxford from Monday 5 July to Friday 9 July. Information on other activities to mark the Centenary will be published in due course.

### Lecture Aids
The following equipment is intended for use at lectures and, regretfully, it cannot be loaned for private viewing.

*Films*
"Focus on the Rose" is a 16-mm. colour film with sound track. Two spools, running time 77 minutes. Every aspect of rose cultivation is covered and also included are beautiful views of the Society's Garden at St. Albans and shots of the Shows. Hire charge £3.

The Grampian television colour film describing the raising and testing of a new seedling rose is also available for limited circulation. 16-mm. sound, running time approximately 25 minutes. Hire charge £2.

Borrowers are required to indemnify the Society against damage and must undertake to ensure the films will be projected by an experienced operator.

*Slides*
There are sets of slides available covering:
    General cultivation
    Varieties with historical connections

Modern varieties

The Evolution of the Rose—a set prepared by Gordon Rowley of Reading University.

Shrub Roses

Full details of all equipment and booking form may be obtained from the Secretary.

## Library

The library at St Albans contains a comprehensive collection of books on rose growing and is open to members during office hours (Monday to Friday, 9 a.m. to 5 p.m.). Alternatively, books (not more than two at one time) will be despatched by post, subject to postage being paid by the borrower. A list of books available will be sent on application.

## Rose Variety Directory

A directory of rose varieties, compiled from distributors' catalogues, is maintained at the office for the convenience of members wishing to locate a source of supply for particular varieties. It is not possible to give information on varieties no longer in commerce.

## Sales

The following items are available from the office:

*Publications*

Additional copies of the current issues of:

| | |
|---|---|
| *Roses: A Selected List of Varieties* | 25p |
| *Roses: The Cultivation of the Rose* | 25p |
| *The Rose Annual* | 75p |
| *The Rose Bulletin* | 25p |

*Member's tie* made in good quality terylene with three Tudor rose motifs. Available in background colours of brown, maroon, navy blue, medium blue, peach, gold, bottle green and lime green—£1·30.

*Member's badge*, depicting the Tudor rose worked in red and white enamel with either brooch or stud (buttonhole) fitting—33p.

*Postcard* views of the gardens—4p each.

*Plastic car window stickers*—3p each.

*Slides.* Set "A"—eight views of the Gardens at St Albans.
 Set "B"—eight views of the Society's Show.
 Price 72p per set.

## Back editions of The Rose Annual

The Secretary will be pleased to receive any back copies of *The Rose Annual* that may no longer be required. These are often asked for by new members.

## Subscriptions and Resignations

Members are reminded that subscriptions are due and payable on 1 January each year and it would assist the office administration if the reminder form, which is enclosed with *The Rose Bulletin*, is returned with the remittance.

Single subscription £1·75 per annum.

Double subscription, for two resident members of the same household, £2·50 per annum. This provides full privileges of membership for both persons but only one copy of any free publications.

Any member wishing to resign must give notice to the Secretary on or before 1 February, after which date the member will be liable for the subscription for the current year.

## Constitution and Rules

Copies of the Constitution and Rules may be obtained from the office—please enclose stamp for return postage.

# The Society's Gardens

The Society's Gardens at St. Albans are provided for the enjoyment of members and their friends. They are divided into two sections, the Trial Ground and Display Garden.

THE TRIAL GROUND is for new seedlings where some 750 varieties may be seen undergoing merit trial. Varieties are submitted before being introduced into commerce and for this reason the majority will be under number. Adjudication is carried out by the New Seedling Judging Committee and varieties are eligible for the Society's Gold Medal, Certificate of Merit and Trial Ground Certificate awards. The President's International Trophy is awarded annually to the best seedling and the Henry Edland Memorial Medal to the most fragrant variety on trial.

Varieties that have received a trial award since 1963 are planted in a bed around the perimeter of the ground.

THE DISPLAY GARDEN occupies approximately seven acres and contains a comprehensive collection of over 900 historical and modern varieties and species.

## How to get to the Gardens

The Gardens are situated at Chiswell Green, approximately three miles from St Albans Town Hall and off the main Watford-St Albans Road (A412).

By Road—from North or South take M1 and leave by Exit No. 6, turn towards St Albans on A405 and in one mile take left fork (A412) at "Noke" roundabout. From West, M4 to Slough and A412 via Denham, Rickmansworth and Watford. From East join A1 at Hatfield and then A405 (sign-post Watford) to "Noke" roundabout and A412 as above.

By Train—**British Rail** to St Albans City Station (St Pancras) or Watford Junction Station (Euston) or **Underground** (Bakerloo Line) to Watford Junction, thence by 321 bus.

By bus—No. 321 bus, Uxbridge–Watford–Garston–Chiswell Green–St Albans–Luton.

By Green-Line Coach—No. 712 Luton–London (Victoria)–Dorking. No. 724 Romford–St Albans–High Wycombe. Also routes 713 Dorking–London (Victoria)–Dunstable, 714 Dorking–London (Hyde Park Corner)–Luton and 727 Crawley–Heathrow–Luton to St Albans centre and thence by bus No. 321 or 361. Route 727 also connects with No. 321 bus route at Garston Bus Station.

The fare stage at which to alight from bus or coach is The Three Hammers Inn, Chiswell Green. The gardens are half a mile along Chiswell Green Lane which is adjacent to the Inn.

## Visiting Arrangements for 1974

The Gardens will be open from Saturday, 15 June to Saturday, 28 September, at the following times:

> Monday to Saturday  9 a.m. to 5 p.m.
> Sunday  2 p.m. to 6 p.m.

The Gardens will be closed on Monday, 26 August. Members wishing to see the Gardens before 15 June or after 28 September may do so from Monday to Friday only.

## Terms of Admission

Membership certificates and affiliated society certificates, which must be shown at the turnstile, will admit the holder and one guest free of charge and four additional persons at the reduced price of 11p.

*Affiliated Societies* may arrange for a party to visit the Gardens during the above hours. Application must be made in writing to the Secretary at least fourteen days beforehand, stating the number in the party and the proposed date and time of the visit. Holders of Certificates and accompanying guests as specified above will be admitted free of charge; all other members of the party will be admitted at the reduced price of 11p.

*Price of admission* to public, 22p adults, 11p children under 15.

### Refreshments

Tea, coffee, sandwiches, light refreshments, also films may be obtained from the cafeteria at the following times:

|  |  |
|---|---|
| Monday to Friday | 11.30 a.m. to 1.30 p.m. |
| | 2.30 p.m. to 4.30 p.m. |
| Saturday | 11.30 a.m. to 4.30 p.m. |
| Sunday | 2.00 p.m. to 5.30 p.m. |

Picnicking on the lawns is not permitted.

### Car Park

A car park is provided but the Council accepts no responsibility for loss or damage to property or vehicles.

### Disabled or Invalid Members

Two wheel chairs (not self-propelled) are available for the convenience of disabled members. Visitors desirous of using these should make application in advance.

### Guides

An alphabetical list of varieties, giving their location in the Display Garden, may be obtained at the turnstile.

### Photography

Amateur photographers may use cameras in the Gardens but photographs or transparencies must not be used commercially. Professional photographers must obtain written authority from the Secretary.

### General Regulations

Dogs must be kept on a leash at all times.

Entry and exit shall be through the respective turnstiles.

Rose blooms, buds, trees or parts of trees must not in any circumstances be cut, removed or taken from the Grounds.

# Report of the Council

## For the year 1973

### Special General Meeting

A Special General Meeting of members was held on 29 June, the first day of the Summer Show, to consider recommendations put forward by Council to increase the annual subscription. The President explained that in spite of economies the general increase in costs necessitated an increase and the imposition of Value Added Tax on subscriptions meant that we could not delay. The recommendations that the annual subscription be increased to £1·75 per annum and the fee for affiliated societies to £3.00 per annum and that a dual membership for two members of the same household be introduced at £2·50 per annum were approved almost unanimously.

### Membership

During the first ten months of the year 5,200 new members were enrolled. This figure, which is lower than for many years past, is disappointing but not surprising in view of the increase in the subscription for new members. A fall in membership will inevitably follow the increase in the subscription for existing members from the 1 January 1974, but Council feels confident that members will continue to appreciate the exceptional value provided and recommend the Society to their rose-loving friends and neighbours.

The fact that we have maintained the membership at the present level is in no small measure due to the assistance afforded by the rose nurserymen who distribute the Society's leaflets, those who devote so much of their time and travel so far to talk and show films and slides to affiliated and other societies and to members of the press, radio and television who mention the work and activities of the Society whenever possible—to all, Council extends a warm vote of thanks.

### Finance

In spite of economizing on Publications and Shows an excess of Expenditure over Revenue of £521 is shown; this figure is reached after small allocations have been made to reserves to offset a proportion of the costs of improvements at Bone Hill and to increase the provision for future publications and the Centenary. The increased subscription does not take effect for existing members until January 1974, and it is hoped that by further economies and by a drive to increase membership it will be possible to report a more favourable result next year.

### Publications

The Rose Annual was published in the spring as usual and maintained the high standard now expected of this publication. A considerable saving in the cost of publication did not detract from the general appearance of the book. It was, unfortunately, not possible to send out the Rose Bulletin until November but Council hopes that this edition was as welcome as previous ones. Mr Hollis, the Editor, is to be congratulated on these publications.

## Shows

The Spring Competition, held in May, by courtesy of the Royal Horticultural Society, was well staged by the small band of exhibitors who enjoy accepting the challenge of growing their roses under glass and who provide such an attractive display for visitors.

The Summer Show was held at Westminster on the last two days of June. Although space was restricted, to the discomfort of some amateur exhibitors, the standard of the exhibits was extremely high. For the first time for many years the weather had been favourable and the trade exhibitors staged outstanding displays. Mr Edward Heath, the Prime Minister, visited the Show and displayed a keen interest in the Trade stands.

The Northern Show was held at Holker Hall, near Grange-over-Sands, in July where the arrangements made by our hosts, the Lakeland Rose Show, were excellent but incessant rain prior to the show unfortunately prevented many exhibitors, including several nurserymen, from showing. Particularly welcome among the amateur exhibitors were many from Scotland and the quality of their blooms won them a number of prizes.

The Autumn Show in September attracted fewer exhibits than usual but the quality was exceptional.

Congratulations are extended to Mr F. E. Owen of Tamworth, Staffs., who became Amateur Champion for the fourth year in succession.

Appreciation is recorded to the Secretary and staff of the Royal Horticultural Society for their co-operation and untiring assistance in staging the Shows at Westminster.

## Groups

The Yorkshire Rosarians, the newly formed group of Yorkshire members, have set off at a great pace. Not only have they produced a monthly magazine, staged a show and staffed information and enrolment bureaux throughout the area but also, in conjunction with British Rail, organized a competition for the best white rose.

The Bristol and District Group held several meetings during the year and staged a show in July when the quality of the exhibits was of a very high standard.

The conference of the North Western Group, held in June, was well attended and has now become an annual event. The Group is doing much to foster the objects of the Society in the area and members have been particularly helpful in assisting with the Society's bureaux.

## Affiliated Societies

During the year visits have been made to a number of meetings and shows of affiliated societies. The warm welcome extended to the Society's officials on these occasions is greatly appreciated.

'SUNBLEST' (H.T.)
*Parentage unknown*
Raised by Mathias Tantau, Germany
TRIAL GROUND CERTIFICATE 1972
*See 1973 Rose Annual, page 184*

'KORTOR' (floribunda)
'*Europeana*' × '*Marlena*'
Raised by W. Kordes & Son, Germany
CERTIFICATE OF MERIT 1973
*See page* 182

## The Trial Ground, Display Gardens and Offices

The gardens at Bone Hill have been maintained to a high standard which is due in large measure to the Superintendent, Mr Maginnis, and his staff who have achieved this standard in spite of labour shortage. There were more visitors than in the previous year but the number of members who attend is disappointing. The improved catering facilities have been much appreciated by visitors.

The standard of varieties on trial was somewhat lower than in past years and the New Seedling Judging Committee did not award a Gold Medal or the President's International Trophy. The Henry Edland Memorial Medal for fragrance was awarded to 'Compassion', a climber bred by R. Harkness & Co.

## Provincial Display Beds

Arrangements have been made with the City of Nottingham and City and County of Norwich for rose varieties that have received awards at St. Albans to be planted out for the benefit of our members and visitors to their gardens. There are now nine authorities in various parts of the country who provide facilities for these displays.

## Judges Examination

29 candidates attended the judges examination in July at Bone Hill and 9 were awarded the Certificate of Competency. Arrangements are being made for the examination to be held in the North next year thereby giving members in that part of the country a greater opportunity of attending. A Conference for Judges was held during the Summer Show.

## Overseas Visits

A party from the American Rose Society led by their President, Dr Eldon Lyle, attended the Summer Show and paid a brief visit to the Gardens at Bone Hill. Dr A. S. Thomas, the President of the National Rose Society of Australia, and Mr Fred Smith, the President of the National Rose Society of New Zealand, were also welcome visitors.

The President represented the Society at rose trials in Rome, Geneva and at Le Roeulx and Courtrai in Belgium and was elected President of the International Jury at the first and last. He also attended a meeting of Presidents of other European rose societies in Belgium. While on holiday in S. Africa he met Mr Jack Wise, President of the Rose Society of South Africa and gave talks to rosarians in Johannesburg, Pretoria and Cape Town where David Gilad, who is taking a leading part in the formation of a national rose society in Israel, was also a visitor.

Dr R. C. Allen, President of the World Federation of Rose Societies and now President of the American Rose Society visited England while on his world tour. During his visit a series of discussions was held regarding the World Federation and the international Convention to be held in Chicago in 1974.

## Constitution and Rules

The proposed amendments to the Constitution and Rules referred to in last year's Report were ratified by the Annual General Meeting.

(continued on page 21)

# BALANCE SHEET, 30th SEPTEMBER, 1973

| 1972 £ | | £ | £ | £ |
|---|---|---|---|---|
| | **SURPLUS** | | | |
| | Balance I October 1972 .. .. | | 85,404 | |
| | Less Excess of Expenditure over Revenue | | | |
| | for year ended 30 September 1973 | 521 | | |
| | Legacy received 1972, now transferred | | | |
| | to Special Fund .. .. .. | 100 | 621 | |
| 85,404 | | | | 84,783 |
| | **PRIZE FUND (FORMERLY SPECIAL FUND)** | | | |
| | Balance I October 1972 .. .. | | 400 | |
| | Add Frank Naylor Memorial Fund .. | | 100 | |
| 400 | | | | 500 |
| | **RESERVE FOR DEVELOPMENT—TRIAL GROUND, DISPLAY** | | | |
| | **GARDEN AND PROPERTIES** | | | |
| | Balance I October 1972 .. .. | 16,000 | | |
| | Add Charge against Revenue Account .. | 2,214 | | |
| | | 18,214 | | |
| | Less Expenditure during year .. .. .. | 4,214 | | |
| 16,000 | | | | 14,000 |
| | **RESERVE FOR NEW EDITIONS OF PUBLICATIONS, FILM AND** | | | |
| | **CONFERENCE** | | | |
| | Balance I October 1972 .. .. .. | 22,000 | | |
| | Add Charge against Revenue Account .. | 1,500 | | |
| 22,000 | | | | 23,500 |
| 12,000 | **RESERVE FOR PENSIONS** .. .. .. .. | | | 12,000 |
| | **CURRENT LIABILITIES** | | | |
| 4,392 | Sundry Creditors .. .. .. .. | | 4,258 | |
| | Subscriptions received in advance and one quarter | | | |
| | of 1973 subscriptions (excluding life members) | | 24,592 | |
| 27,577 | | | | 28,850 |
| **167,773** | | | | **163,633** |

| 1972 £ | | | £ | £ |
|---|---|---|---|---|
| | **FIXED ASSETS** | | | |
| 33,950 | Freehold Properties .. .. | .. | | 33,950 |
| | Office Equipment, etc. | | | |
| 1,200 | Balance I October 1972 .. | | 1,200 | |
| | Less Amount written off .. | | 400 | 800 |
| | Motor Vehicles, Mowers and Equipment: | | | |
| 2,000 | Balance I October 1972 .. .. | | 2,000 | |
| | Additions less allowance during year .. | | 1,414 | |
| | | | 3,414 | |
| | Less Amount written off .. .. | | 814 | 2,600 |
| 1,650 | Library at Professional Valuation (1967) .. .. | | | 1,650 |
| 38,800 | | | | 39,000 |
| 94,969 | INVESTMENTS at Cost .. .. .. | .. | | 103,800 |
| (106,626) | (Market Value 30 September 1973 £102,810) .. | | | |
| | **CURRENT ASSETS** | | | |
| | Stock of Publications, Badges, etc. as valued by | | | |
| 4,592 | Secretary .. .. .. .. | | 3,714 | |
| 83 | Sundry Debtors for Advertisements, etc. .. | | 1,124 | |
| | Cash at Bank on Deposit and Current Account | | | |
| 25,077 | and Cash in Hand .. .. | | 15,261 | |
| 4,252 | Income Tax recoverable .. .. .. | | 734 | 20,833 |
| **167,773** | | | | **163,633** |

**AUDITORS' REPORT** To the Members, The Royal National Rose Society

We have audited the above Balance Sheet dated 30 September 1973 and Revenue Account for the year ended on that date and have obtained all the information and explanations we have required. In our opinion such Balance Sheet and Revenue Account are properly drawn up so as to exhibit a true and correct view of the state of the Society's affairs according to the best of our information and explanations given us and as shown by the books of the Society. We have verified the Securities representing the investments of your Society at 30 September 1973 and have found the same to be in order.

EVERS & CO., Chartered Accountants, Auditors
SHEPHERD'S FIELD, COURTS HILL ROAD, HASLEMERE, SURREY. 14 November 1973

# REVENUE ACCOUNT FOR THE YEAR ENDED 30th SEPTEMBER, 1973

| 1971/72 | | | £ | £ | £ | | 1971/72 | £ | £ |
|---|---|---|---|---|---|---|---|---|---|
| £ | | | | | | **SUBSCRIPTIONS AND AFFILIATION FEES** | £ | | |
| 32,982 | **PUBLICATIONS** Expenditure.. | | | 29,729 | | Subscriptions | 95,107 | | 94,135 |
| 428 | Less Sales | | 797 | | | Affiliation Fees | 1,512 | | 1,495 |
| 5,648 | Advertising Revenue | | 5,853 | 6,650 | | | 96,619 | | 95,630 |
| 26,906 | | | | | 23,079 | **INCOME FROM INVESTMENTS, etc.** | | | |
| | **SHOWS** | | | | | Gross | 8,240 | | 9,989 |
| 3,158 | Prize Money, Medals and Trophies | | 2,669 | | | SURPLUS ON REALIZATION OF INVESTMENTS | 7 | | — |
| 7,358 | Expenses | | 4,733 | | | LEGACY | 100 | | 521 |
| 10,516 | | | | 7,402 | | BALANCE.—Excess of Expenditure over Revenue for the year | — | | |
| 694 | Less Proceeds | | | 530 | | | | | |
| 9,822 | | | | | 6,872 | | | | |
| 11,020 | **TRIAL GROUND AND DISPLAY GARDEN** | | | | 13,047 | | | | |
| | **ADMINISTRATION** | | | | | | | | |
| 19,757 | Salaries and Assistance, Superannuation Contributions and Supplementary Pensions | | | 20,681 | | | | | |
| 3,018 | Computer | | | 2,692 | | | | | |
| 1,362 | Rates, Lighting, Heating, etc. | | | 1,502 | | | | | |
| 4,363 | Printing and Stationery | | | 5,318 | | | | | |
| 15,825 | Postages | | | 15,393 | | | | | |
| 3,407 | General Expenses, Telephone, Hire of Rooms, etc. | | | 5,302 | | | | | |
| 838 | Repairs and Renewals—office and premises | | | 477 | | | | | |
| 400 | Auditors' Fee | | | 400 | | | | | |
| 1,203 | Bank Charges | | | 1,210 | | | | | |
| 50,373 | | | | | 52,975 | | | | |
| 3,293 | **ADVERTISING AND PUBLICITY** | | | | 3,773 | | | | |
| 164 | **PROVINCIAL DISPLAY GARDENS** | | | | 499 | | | | |
| 400 | **GRANTS TO UNIVERSITIES FOR RESEARCH** | | | | 967 | | | | |
| 1,165 | **RESERVE FOR NEW EDITIONS OF PUBLICATIONS, FILM AND CONFERENCE** | | | | 1,500 | | | | |
| | **RESERVE FOR DEVELOPMENT, TRIAL GROUND, DISPLAY GARDEN AND PROPERTIES** | | | | 2,214 | | | | |
| 876 | **MOTOR VEHICLES, MOWERS AND EQUIPMENT**—Amount written off | | | | 814 | | | | |
| 447 | **OFFICE EQUIPMENT**—Amount written off | | | | 400 | | | | |
| 104,466 | | | | | 106,140 | | | | |
| 500 | **BALANCE**—Excess of Revenue over Expenditure for the year | | | | — | | | | |
| 104,966 | | | | | 106,140 | | | 104,966 | 106,140 |

106,140

# The President's Page

My theme this year is the Rose, the national and international flower.

In this country I have had the great pleasure of meeting so many members at R.N.R.S. and other shows, at the Annual and Special General Meetings of the Society, at meetings of affiliated societies and at Bone Hill. I look forward to meeting many more this year, especially at Bone Hill, where many new beds have been planted in recent years and other changes and improvements made and where refreshments are now available.

I have also met so many other rose lovers in trains and planes, buses and bars, in shops and in the street, not only in this country but in Europe and South Africa, and of so many races and complexions, simply by wearing a rose in my buttonhole. This is a talisman leading to interesting conversations and new friends and is an excellent way of enrolling new members, as I have found both here and abroad.

Internationally, I fulfilled the hope I expressed last year of meeting the Presidents of many other national rose societies. Our friends the Presidents of the American, Australian and New Zealand Societies were all at our Summer Show. In July, in Belgium, I had most stimulating meetings with the Presidents or representatives of most of the European rose societies and in London in the autumn with Ray Allen, President of the World Federation.

In South Africa my wife and I on a holiday visit were most hospitably treated by the President of the South African Society and Mrs Wise and by many other rosarians; we also met there David Gillad who has just established a rose society in Israel.

A R.N.R.S. tour is being arranged, starting on 6 September 1974 and lasting three weeks, which will include the International Rose Conference in Chicago, Banff, Jasper National Park, Vancouver, San Francisco and the Yosemite and Sequoia National Parks. I hope some of you will join us on this tour.

During the next two years we shall be very busy preparing for the celebration of the Society's centenary in 1976 and particularly for the International Conference, which will be held in Oxford in July of that year. We hope this venue will enable a very large number of members to attend and that this will be the highlight for them of our centenary year.

May I wish you all a very successful rose year and ask you again to do your best to enrol new members.

R. C. BALFOUR

Mr R. C. Balfour (centre), President of the RNRS, presided at the Commune di Roma. This photograph was taken at the Banquet

*Rosa gallica versicolor (see page 97)*

'Compassion' (climber), raised by R. Harkness & Co. Ltd. and awarded the Henry Edland Memorial Medal for fragrance, 1973 *(see page 182)*

(continued from page 17)

## Centenary—1976

Provisional arrangements have been made for the Centenary Conference to be held at Oxford from 2 July to 9 July, 1976, and the Conference will be preceded by the Summer Show on 29 and 30 June. Accommodation for those attending the Conference will be available in several colleges as well as nearby hotels.

## Obituary

Just before the Annual General Meeting last year Council learnt with deep regret of the death of John Clarke, D.H.M. Mr Clarke was President in 1969 and 1970 and at the time of his death he was Hon. Treasurer and Chairman of the New Seedling Judging Committee. He devoted untiring energy and considerable time to the Society.

This year the Society lost another great rosarian by the death of John Mattock D.H.M., the head of John Mattock Ltd. Mr Mattock who was elected to Council in 1938 and elected a Vice President in 1964 did a great deal to promote the work of the Society and to raise the standard of exhibiting.

Both these men are sadly missed.

## Dean Hole Medal

Council is pleased to announce the award of the Dean Hole Medal to—

Mr Leonard Hollis, Vice President and Editor, who has contributed so greatly to the work of the Society, especially the publications, since being elected to the Council in 1934.

Mr Harry Wheatcroft, Vice President, who has done so much in popularizing the rose in this country and abroad.

## Queen Mary Commemoration Medal

The Queen Mary Commemoration Medal for successful British hybridists was awarded to A. Dickson & Sons, E. B. Le Grice (Hybridisers) Ltd and S. McGredy & Son for the second time after an interval of 15 years and the award was made for the first time to James Cocker & Son, R. Harkness & Co. and John Sanday (Roses) Ltd.

## Conclusion

In conclusion the Council desires to express its thanks to the Honorary Architect, Honorary Scientific Adviser, Editor, Horticultural Consultant, the Secretary and Staff at Bone Hill for their work during the year.

By order of Council,

R. C. BALFOUR
*President*

# Memories Are Made of This

**F. C. H. WITCHELL**

(*Amateur rose grower*)

One great charm of our hobby of growing the Queen of Flowers is the infinite series of changing scenes with which we are presented. And every one contains something of interest, something to remember.

Unfortunately, Nature has not endowed us with photographic memories, so the majority of these things must be lost beyond recall, or so it would seem. But, no; there is a happy solution to this problem. What we cannot commit to memory, we can commit to film to be recaptured at will and enjoyed to the full in all its original colour and detail.

Now, if you happen to be one of the many people who believe that, to make good pictures, you have to master one of those horribly expensive and frighteningly complicated super cameras, take heart. I will try to convince you that it is just not true.

Our memories can be captured as either still pictures or movies. However, since most of our photography is likely to be of static scenes, it would seem preferable to use a still picture camera. These come in various sizes but I feel that the one most suitable for amateurs is the popular 35 mm size.

The next consideration is whether we want our pictures to be in the form of transparencies or of prints. The former are very much cheaper initially and, subsequently, good prints can be obtained from the transparencies, if required. True, transparencies can be made from good prints but the result may not be very satisfactory and, anyway, it is relatively expensive.

Of course, to view transparencies, a viewer and/or projector are needed. A viewer may cost three or four pounds and a suitable projector will cost from six pounds to around fifty pounds according to the level of sophistication required. Putting the total costs of films and these equipments into perspective, the difference in cost between three rolls of print film and of transparency film will buy a viewer and the difference between four rolls will buy the cheapest currently available projector.

Now let us get on to the business of taking the pictures. The precise sort of still picture that one can take, from a general scene to a close-up of a black spot on a leaf, depends upon two things: how much you are prepared to learn about photography and how much you are prepared to pay for your camera.

Starting at the point of learning and paying as little as possible, you can buy the simplest form of "point and shoot" camera for less than £10. This kind of camera usually has only two controls: one to be set according to whether it is sunny or cloudy and one to take the picture. The lens "sees" a fairly wide area and will bring into reasonable focus all objects situated farther than four or five feet from the camera. Therefore, this very simple camera can be used to record anything from a general garden view down to, say, a group of two or three rose bushes, a single climber on a fence, even a large floral arrangement at a show.

The only skill required to make beautiful pictures with a simple camera is the same skill that will make or mar any picture, however sophisticated the camera being used; skill in composing the picture. Composition means selecting the point from which to take the photograph so that the subject is presented in the most interesting and attractive way and so that any intrusive distractions which would compete with the main subject for attention are excluded. So, having decided that you want to take a picture of, say, a bed in the RNRS gardens, do walk round it a couple of times, looking through the viewfinder at different points until you are satisfied that you have found the spot from which the bed looks most attractive and at which no other objects or groups of colour are intruding into the corners of the picture. With practice and by learning the art of composition from a critical examination of the resultant pictures, it is quite remarkable what can be achieved with elementary equipment.

It is very probable that, after a season or two using a simple camera, you may feel, as I did in my photographic progression, that you would like to impress your personality more effectively on the pictures that you take and to have more direct control of the camera. Thus, you may want to buy yourself a camera equipped with a range-finder and a built-in lightmeter. Do not be put off by this technical jargon; it merely means that, by turning a ring on the lens, you can bring some subjects into sharp focus in the view-finder while throwing, say, the background out of focus and, by turning another ring, or changing the speed of the exposure, you can ensure that the resultant picture will be neither too dark nor too light. By using these controls in combination, you can obtain almost any effect that you require. Some recently introduced models of this kind of camera are fitted with what are called automatic electronic exposure controls, so that all you have to do is to focus the picture and leave the rest to the electronic gubbins to find the right exposure. The best of these cameras have "manual over-ride" facilities so that, if you want to achieve a special effect that would bamboozle the electronic gadgetry, you can do so. Such cameras can be bought for about £30 in the discount shops. From my own experience, one very soon learns how to master the exposure and speed control combinations and I think that you will have much more fun with a camera on which you can over-ride the electronics when you wish than with one on which you cannot.

So far, the cameras I have described are usually fitted with lenses which "see" a quite wide area and so cannot be used easily to take, say, a close-up of a single bloom. This is because the viewfinder that you look through is set beside the lens and is seeing a picture very slightly different from the picture seen by the lens. This effect is called parallax and, for some cameras, gadgets can be obtained to correct it. Even so, for close-up pictures, the most desirable instrument is what is called a single-lens reflex camera. This merely means that you look directly through the lens at the subject you are photo-graphing, so that what you see is what will appear in the resultant picture.

Many single-lens reflex cameras (generally known as SLRs) on the market today are fitted with built-in lightmeters that measure the amount of light actually coming through the lens. These SLRs are identified by the initials TTL which stand for "Through the Lens" metering. This is a kind of camera which I found quite easy to use and most effective for taking close-ups. From a discount shop, one of these "TTL SLRs" (you soon learn to trot out the jargon like an expert!) will cost you around £50.

If you decide that you would like to explore this glorious world of close-up colour, do make sure that the camera you buy has a standard lens (usually 50 mm) that will focus as close as about 0·3 metres. The object of obtaining a lens which focuses as close as 0·3 metres is that it enables one to fill the picture almost completely with a single good-sized hybrid tea rose bloom. The Praktica LTL with a 2·8 Tessar lens will do this and can be bought for the price mentioned above. I happen to use a camera with this particular lens and find it very effective, but I am sure that there are other makes which will do the same thing.

The first attempts to take close-ups of single blooms growing on bushes in one's own or other gardens will reveal two problems not previously encountered. One is to get a picture in which the petals nearest the camera and those farthest away are both in focus at the same time. The distance between them is called "the depth of field" and you will find that the barrel of the camera lens is marked to give an indication of the depth of field which a particular aperture will give. Thus, you learn that you need to set the lens at a small aperture to get the whole of the bloom in focus. The second prob-lem is that you may find that the wind is blowing the flowers about, so that you need to use a very short exposure (usually about a hundred and twenty-fifth of a second) to avoid getting a blurred picture. When faced with the second problem in addition to the first, you soon discover that, unless you use what is called a "fast" film, only in the blazing sun of high noon will there be enough light for you to take a perfect picture. So you will need to use a film such as High Speed Ektachrome. Using this film, I find that one can get good pictures of even dark red roses in all but the worst daylight.

You may well find that, with this sort of camera, the range of memory-capturing possibilities is broad enough to satisfy all your ambitions. On the other hand, you may find that there are situations with which it will not cope; such as, for example, when there is a bloom that you want desperately to photograph but to which you just cannot approach close enough for the flower to fill the picture. If that worries you and you are prepared to fork out about £35 to overcome this kind of difficulty, you can get yourself a close-focusing medium telephoto lens. I possess one called a 135-mm Zeiss Jena "S" which will focus down to just one metre. At that range, it will give me as big a picture of a single bloom as will the 50-mm lens at a third of the distance. Using a close-focusing telephoto lens has additional advantages; because it "sees" through a narrower angle of view and because the "cut off" between what is in clear focus and what is not, is very sudden, it makes it much easier to omit distracting intrusions from edges and corners of the picture. Lastly, the telephoto lens tends to give a better perspective for the single flower picture.

Thus equipped, your memory-capturing capacity is vast indeed. Not only can you record anything from a general view down to an individual flower, but your telephoto lens will enable you to pluck single objects out of the middle distance such as, for example, a cluster of 'Mermaid' from high up on a house gable.

But even this equipment will not enable you to take a big picture of that black spot on a leaf that I mentioned in the beginning of this article. Should you want to do such a thing, for a couple of pounds you can buy what is called a "close-up lens". This is very simple to use. You merely screw it on to the front of your standard SLR camera lens and take your pictures in the normal way. While close-up lenses (they come in several degrees of magnification) enable you to take big pictures of small things, they do possess serious limitations. The problem is that the greater the magnification, the smaller the depth of field. In short, you can only take pictures of very flat objects and, even then, the accuracy of your focusing is critical.

Of course, there are ways of taking well-focused pictures of even microscopic objects, but I feel that they are a little beyond the scope of this article and, in any case, can quickly lead us into the realm of costly specialized equipment.

One topic that I have not mentioned up to now, is the use of flash. Today, even the simplest cameras can be bought with cube flash units already attached. These have their uses and also their limitations. They will do a very good job on subjects situated between four and ten feet from the camera and so can be useful for such tasks as taking pictures of exhibits at shows or of flower arrangements in the home. Their limitations are the restricted distances within which they are effective (they are of no use for general views) and the "flat" sort of picture that they produce. The latter arises because the unit is mounted on the camera and is blasting light straight at the subject.

If one wants to be able to take close-ups of blooms in any light (or even at night) with an SLR camera (remember the jargon?), then an electronic flash unit can be very useful. To avoid "flat" pictures, it must be the sort of unit which enables one to hold the flash head some distance to one side of the camera so that the light strikes across the flower and "models" it. Ordinary electronic flash units are not particularly easy to use for this kind of work. One needs to learn something about "guide numbers" and then take a number of experimental pictures to discover what adjustments to make in order to get the precise effect one needs.

The latest types of "computer flash" (yes, that *is* what they are called) are much easier to use because they are equipped with a sensor device which automatically quenches the flash when enough light has reached the subject to give the correct exposure. They are very clever and the good ones can be rather expensive. If you should think of using one, it is important to acquire a type which allows you to place the flash unit to one side of the camera where it will model the bloom the way you want it.

In this article, it has been my intention to stick to the basics and to keep as simple as possible a subject into which one can very easily introduce a great deal of confusion. So it is that the experts will observe a number of omissions such as references to tubes, bellows, independent meters and tripods. The first two items I have omitted as being hardly relevant. The matter of independent meters is arguable but, many experiences of taking close-ups of blooms in conditions where clouds scudding across the sun have caused the light value to change every few seconds have endeared me to the virtues of the TTL meter. It is certainly especially valuable when one is using a telephoto lens and it makes things much simpler for the less technically minded picture-taker.

The matter of the tripod is one of personal preference. If one has a shaky hand, no doubt it is a necessity. For my own part, I would hate the thought of having to cart around a clumsy object which I consider to have only limited uses.

But to return to the object of these notes, the capture of many beautiful memories; I have hundreds of them. Some were recorded with the simplest of cameras, some with a TTL SLR. They include memories of roses now out of commerce, the histories of our home gardens, views of the old Oaklands Trial Grounds, the many faces of dozens of modern varieties of roses and so on. All of them are valuable memories which my mind could not possibly have retained in any great detail, but which the wonder of photographic technology has captured for me. To be sure, my own extensive library of memories is made of this and perhaps you, too, might be encouraged to make some of your memories return this way in all their glorious original colour and charm.

## TO A YELLOW ROSE

*Fairest of flowers, whose gracious, golden hue*
*Recalls the deepening glow of sunset skies,*
*When twilight's silent dreams of heaven renew,*
*Our hearts with faith and hope, as daylight dies.*

*How sad to think that such pure gifts as thine,*
*Born of that light by which our lives are made,*
*Which make this life akin to the divine,*
*Should, like ourselves, at last in dust be laid!*

*Like those we love, thou shinest for a day,*
*The glory of our gaze, too frail to last;*
*Then comes the darkening hour of swift decay,*
*And thy brave beauty bows before the blast.*

*Yet dost thou leave, abiding in the heart,*
*The vision of a grace that cannot die;*
*Because thy short-lived splendour was a part*
*Of Him, whose radiance lights the earth and sky!*

REV. DAVID R. WILLIAMSON

# Are We Getting Too Many New Roses?

## J. H. SHOTTER

*(Amateur rose grower and successful exhibitor)*

As an Amateur member of Council, I get a considerable number of enquiries from individual members and during questions after talks given to Rose Societies, as to which varieties of new roses I can recommend. No doubt most of our members have some difficulty in deciding which new varieties they should buy for next autumn. All real lovers of roses naturally feel a great urge to try something new in their gardens. As many will know, I grow up to 500 hybrid teas and floribundas, and I have to be very selective in my choice, as some are required for exhibition work, and many purely for garden display. A variety that can combine the two functions is ideal for my purpose, and no doubt many members feel the same way.

The difficulty with the new roses is not only to decide what to buy, but also from whom to obtain them. The annual influx of novelties is quite bewildering, and alas, a large proportion of them seem to disappear without trace after a few years. I say alas, but perhaps the law of supply and demand operates; the nurserymen, having tried a new variety for several years, find perhaps it won't sell, or won't grow properly, or is very prone to disease, and finally decide not to bud it for the following year. What a waste of time and effort! If the so-called "new roses" market were to be drastically curtailed and only really sound and worthwhile cultivars introduced, both the rose-buying public and the rose nurserymen would benefit.

In making your choice, the award-winning varieties from the RNRS trials are a useful yardstick. The Committee dealing with this problem is comprised of members of Council with considerable experience—roughly half are nurserymen and half amateurs—and to get even a Trial Ground Certificate, the variety must have done well under trial, and be recommended by at least a majority of that Committee. Not many members may realize that the RNRS Trial Ground receives between 250 and 300 new cultivars each year. They are not considered for any award for the first year after planting, but even so, of the 500 or more which are carefully examined on a number of visits by the Judging Committee over the whole flowering season in the second and third years of their trials, how many cultivars gain awards? An average of $2\frac{1}{2}$–3 per cent—say around 20 varieties annually. Even that number is far too many for most people, who may have room for perhaps only three or four new varieties. On my many visits to Bone Hill, I try to see all the new varieties under trial—believe me, the vast majority of them should never have been sent at all!

I know the raisers feel they may have likely winners when they send their new seedlings to the Bone Hill Trials—after all they raised them, no doubt are proud of them, and hope that they will impress. Sometimes their behaviour at Bone Hill is nothing like as good as in the raiser's own nursery or garden. I am particularly concerned about the recent tendency of the rose nurserymen to market their new roses even before they go to the Trial Ground, or certainly before the end of the three-years trial period. I am not going to name the culprits—the list is long—but most rose-nurserymen are doing this nowadays, and I would advise members to make a point of seeing that variety growing on the nursery. See it not once, but several times from say the end of June onwards, and note how it grows, flowers, and whether it is disease-resistant, before you order in any quantity.

There is considerable monetary advantage to the raiser, in these days of Plant Protection rights, for those varieties which prove popular, but from whom does the amateur buy them? Almost all the better new roses are currently protected varieties, and each rose nurseryman has to pay the raiser a royalty either on each tree sold, or so much per budding eye. These royalties are complicated, and some raisers insist on a large down payment, plus so much a tree for those sold, which must be specially labelled. As many of the smaller reputable nurserymen cannot afford to pay heavy royalties before they know whether a variety will sell, they do not list that raiser's new cultivars—some of which may be highly desirable, from the Amateur's point of view. While the nurseryman does his best to choose the novelties he thinks he can sell, the poor amateur has to scan all the rose catalogues to find even the award-winning varieties he may wish to try. When he does he will perhaps find one nurseryman may have two new roses; another—very few—may have three or four in his list, but maybe only one novelty in which he is interested. The ordinary amateur, buying his dozen or so new bushes each year (often one bush of each variety) must find this problem frustrating, to say the least. With carriage costs to be included, as well as VAT, and having to pay usually a minimum of 60p per bush, the final cost of buying, say, three bushes of each of four varieties and getting them from several firms, means that the new plants will cost the customer nearly a pound per bush. And then some of them may fail to establish themselves, despite every care taken in preparation and planting.

A careful examination of the rose nurserymen's catalogues—and I get practically everybody's—will show that there is, nowadays, a drastic reduction in the list of cultivars offered. Many nurserymen concentrate very largely on varieties raised by themselves; these are naturally boosted, often in the most fulsome terms, and I can assure you that many of them are "ducklings dressed as swans". Even some of the leading, and what may be termed standard varieties tend to be missing from some catalogues. When talking to rose nurserymen about this they will say they cannot afford to grow a variety unless there is an appreciable demand for it. This I can appreciate, as they are first and foremost businessmen, and cannot grow a variety just to please comparatively few people. One firm I know did this for many years—just grew a few of a very large range of roses that were not really popular—but even they had to discard the practice as unprofitable.

There seems to be far too little in the way of rigorous culling of their seedlings by the raisers in their own trial grounds; very many that are sent to St Albans on trial are no improvement on existing cultivars, and are certainly not disease-resistant. You have only to walk round the Trial Ground at Bone Hill and see the empty spaces where disease-prone varieties have been taken out before the end of their trial period—some in their second year—to prove my point. Normally, no spraying of trial varieties is undertaken during their second and third years. Perhaps the Society should make a charge for each cultivar sent for trial, but unless the fee were to be high, I cannot see that this would stop the malpractice. I must mention that the amateur rose breeder is also guilty of sending his seedlings for test, without a rigorous weeding out of the "also-rans". Alas, the vast majority fall by the wayside, and many of them have to be discarded well before the end of the three-year period.

It will be interesting to see the outcome of the British Association of Rose Breeders' efforts in this field. Most of the U.K. raisers and several from overseas have joined together and as I understand the position, they will run a common licensing system so that the rest of the rose nurserymen can become associates, and can arrange to have new roses from this source. It will be interesting to see whether the Association can persuade these other nurserymen to take sufficient quantities of the really worthwhile new cultivars to sell to the public. It is planned that the member-raisers shall have their own trials, which will be quite distinct from the present RNRS trial ground system.

The Breeders' Association will make perhaps only three awards in any one year, if enough seedlings achieve the standard set. The new cultivar must be viable commercially and be distinct from existing varieties. It must appeal to the general rose-buying public as well as the amateur rose specialist. The decisions will be made by a panel of professional rose nurserymen, and if that panel can act quite independently of the interests of individual members, as I feel sure they can, I for one shall be happy to leave the decision to their expert knowledge. We shall have to wait and see whether the new Association will be an answer to the present problem of too many novelties being introduced, and enable the public to buy what they fancy, perhaps at not too high a cost.

Some people may say I'm prejudiced as I still exhibit at shows, as an amateur, but I love and appreciate purely decorative varieties probably even more than the "box bloom" or the huge sprays of the floribundas mainly used for exhibition purposes. I could name many examples of roses which should never have gone to the Trial Grounds, but do not wish to upset their raisers or the nurserymen who have introduced some of the many poor foreign-raised roses. Many of these novelties are at present on the market, lauded to the skies as wonderful new introductions. There have been quite a number of RNRS award-winning roses too which, after a few years, disappear from commerce—either because they are bad "Black Spotters", suffer severely from mildew, or because the public do not fancy the colour or habit. At last the Council has decided that all the cultivars under trial shall have the raiser's name as well as identifying marks and trial ground number on each batch. There are many thousands of visitors to the St Albans trials each year, and I feel sure that having the raiser's name against the variety may perhaps deter raisers from sending poor varieties for test, as these would not do their reputation any good.

It used to be that, in most industrial areas, disease in roses, apart from powdery mildew, was extremely rare. But, with the spread of clean-air areas, and of course, to all those living in the pure-air country areas, the incidence of Black Spot and mildew, and to some extent Rust, is a serious problem—a burden the rose grower could well do without. The use of sprays to counteract, or to protect against Black Spot and mildew is purely an expedient to be used only until such time as raisers are able to breed new varieties of beautiful form and vigour, and yet of disease-resistance to the order of, say, 'Pink Favourite', and if possible, to have some fragrance. So many of the newest cultivars suffer badly from disease—a point rarely mentioned in rose nurserymen's catalogues generally. I know one or two honest nurserymen do warn buyers that certain varieties may need protection against these troubles, but never in the case of those new varieties they are introducing for the first time! So let's have some really trouble-free roses, please, Mr Raiser! This is a tall order, I know, but necessary if the lover of roses is to feel satisfied that his labours throughout the year will not be in vain.

Summing up, I think there are far too many novelties brought onto the market each year, most of which disappear after only a few years in circulation. Most amateur rose growers would be happy to see a maximum of, say, ten new cultivars introduced annually. Then the larger rose nurserymen would perhaps put at least half of these new roses into their catalogues. The amateur would then need to place his orders with only one or two firms instead of the present four or five from whom he must buy if he wishes to try out most of the award-winning roses in his own garden.

# Foliar Feeding – A Critical Appraisement

**E. F. ALLEN,** M.A., Dip.Agric.(Cantab.), A.I.C.T.A.
(*Gardener, Naturalist, Agronomist and Fruit-Grower*)

One tropical evening some twenty years ago, with the temperature 85° F. and the relative humidity 100 per cent, I sprayed a small block of pineapples with a 20 per cent solution (wt/volume) of a fertilizer mixture made up of urea, potassium nitrate and mono-ammonium phosphate. This near-saturated solution caused no leaf damage and there was a remarkable colour change in the foliage $3\frac{1}{2}$ days later. Thus began my interest in foliar feeding and the striking success of this first trial led me to expect that comparable benefits might be obtainable with other plants and in more temperate climates.

Some ten years ago, during late summer in Suffolk, I sprayed two rows, of four, of celery plants in my own garden with one gallon of a very dilute seaweed emulsion. Once again there was a very remarkable colour change and two weeks later the treated plants had become much darker green in colour than the untreated ones. Furthermore, this colour change was clearly associated with improved growth and yield, although this only became evident after a further two or three weeks.

In subsequent years I carried out a series of replicated trials, mostly on roses, using both commercial foliar feed formulations and my own preparations, these last being based on mixtures of either urea, potassium nitrate and mono-ammonium phosphate or urea, potassium nitrate and Epsom salts.

Soluble phosphate and Epsom salts cannot be dissolved together without adopting chelating techniques such as are used to prepare sequestrenes and these I found unsuitable for foliar feeds, as they caused leaf damage to some plants.

In the conduct of these trials I took care to apply the foliar feeds, both with and without some form of wetting agent, on warm evenings when slow drying conditions prevailed. I was also careful—and this is most important— to water the control unmanured plants with an equivalent amount of rainwater to that applied to the experimental plants. Another precaution taken to ensure lack of bias, in the statistical sense, was to allocate the different plots of each cultivar to the various treatments at random and, so far as possible, to have the same number of bushes in each unit. All rose beds had received a routine application of fertilizer, in March or April, of the order of 2 oz/sq. yd, so my trials were designed to ascertain if the use of foliar feed would give any additional advantage in health or vigour of growth. They were not intended to discover if normal rose fertilizer practice could be replaced by sprays, since no sensible rosarian would wish to burden himself with additional spray applications unless these were associated with major benefits.

Common-sense considerations dictated that most of these foliar feed applications were made in late May or early June, before the onset of flowering, but not before there was sufficient foliage to retain the spray liquid. In some years, however, further applications were made in late July and early August, after most bushes had been dead-headed.

I would be the first to admit that none of these trials was designed to detect small responses, since they all depended on visual assessments of any benefit from the spray treatments. Nevertheless, it is disappointing to record that in not one single instance was I able to detect any benefit in increased vigour of growth from the spray treatments. I therefore concluded that, where roses have been given normal but not heavy fertilizer applications, no major additional benefit can be expected from foliar feeding. This is a somewhat sweeping conclusion, but it is based on many years of trials. However, in one very accurate trial it was possible to demonstrate that a dilute solution of Epsom salts had some slight fungicidal effect in that it helped to control Powdery Mildew. Furthermore, it was frequently clear that trials carried out in July–August were of benefit to all rosebushes, including those receiving only sprays of rainwater and this result merely emphasized the advantage of some irrigation at that time.

Perhaps at this stage I should record that many commercial fruit growers

apply regular applications of various foliar feeds, and there is often an un-
doubted response to such applications, in that the foliage improves in
appearance and increased yields have sometimes been claimed for such a
practice. However, the major response is to nitrogen, applied as urea, although an additional response can sometimes be obtained from Epsom salts
—especially where a slight magnesium deficiency has been induced by heavy
applications of potash fertilizers. I have yet to be convinced that there is any
justification for the addition of soluble phosphates to such spray liquids.

There are two reasons why apple trees should sometimes be more re-
sponsive than roses to foliar nutrition. Firstly, apples are grown in grassed
orchards and the competition for both water and nitrogen from this turf is
considerable in early summer. Secondly, young apple foliage wets much
more readily than do young rose leaves. It is worth noting also that commercial firms that advocate the use of foliar feeds in orchards maintain that
it is chiefly the young leaves which take up the nutrients.

The special use of seaweed emulsions deserves separate mention as they
may sometimes be useful in the vegetable garden. However, on roses, both
outdoors and under glass, I have been unable to detect any benefit at all. It
is perhaps of general interest to gardeners to note that the vegetable crops
which respond to applications of either seaweed sprays or top dressings of
seaweed meal are those which are known to benefit from sodium, even in
the presence of adequate potassium. As far as the home gardener is concerned
these are celery, red beet, turnips and possibly also swedes. Only in the case
of celery have I been able to detect a superior response to seaweed to that
from common salt.

## The Mechanism of Foliar Nutrition

A great deal of research has been conducted into foliar nutrition in recent
years, largely because the physiological disease known as Bitter Pit of apples
can often be prevented by foliar sprays of 1 per cent calcium nitrate solution.
Very little of this work has much obvious practical application to rose
nutrition but anyone interested in the technique should know of its existence.
Thus it appears that these nutrients penetrate the leaf cuticle (outer skin) by
a process of diffusion and that entry via the stomata is discounted. All workers
agree that urea is the most efficient source of nitrogen and it appears that
cations (e.g. bases such as calcium and magnesium) penetrate more readily
than do anions (e.g. a negatively charged group such as $SO_4$). It may well be,
therefore, that efficiency of penetration is affected by choice of wetting agent.

Anyone interested in this subject should study a recent publication on

*The Cuticles of Plants* (Martin, J. T., and Juniper, B.E., 1970, Arnold), not only for its great biological interest but also because of the masterly survey of work in this field. Thus bromeliad growers (Pineapple family) will learn that these plants, which are predominantly epiphytic, have very thick cuticles penetrated by pores and each of these pores is surmounted by a complex cellular structure which acts as a water-absorbing area and non-return valve. For such plants foliar nutrition is likely to be more effective than manuring the rooting zone. It is no surprise, therefore, to find that bromeliads have a central "vase" which acts as a water-collecting unit. However, such specialist developments—although of great interest—have little application to rose cultivation.

Working with tender glasshouse plants I have found that certain delicate seedlings respond very rapidly to very dilute foliar feeds wherein the wetting agent is the skin slime of the rainbow trout. I understand that this substance is of protein origin so can be expected to contain 12 to 16 per cent of nitrogen on a dry-weight basis. Furthermore, where an iron deficiency needs to be corrected, I found that a 0·5 per cent fresh solution of ferrous sulphate (5 grams per litre), with trout skin slime as wetting agent, was more effective as a foliar feed and much less damaging than a comparable solution of a commercial iron sequestrene. It is worth remembering that these sequestrenes were evolved for use in alkaline soils and are much less suitable for foliar application.

## Practical Considerations

Although my own experience with the foliar feeding of roses suggests that this offers no advantage over the application of conventional fertilizers to the soil, I appreciate that many members have reported good results from this practice and they will doubtless wish to continue with it. To these members I commend the following points:

1. Do not use any commercial fertilizer mixture as a foliar feed unless it is expressly recommended for that purpose.

2. So far as possible avoid the use of sequestrenes in foliar feeds.

3. Should you wish to mix your own foliar feeds, then try first (a) 1 per cent urea (10 grams/litre or $1\frac{1}{2}$ oz/gallon) plus a few drops of wetting agent. (b) 1 oz urea plus $\frac{1}{4}$ oz each of potassium nitrate and Epsom salts in a gallon of rainwater plus wetter.

4. Remember that when you dissolve Epsom salts in water you make it hard and any fungicide applied at the same time will be marginally less effective. In practice, however, this effect is a small one.

5. Do not greatly exceed a gross concentration of 1 per cent in a mixed solution in spite of my experience in the humid tropics. Young rose leaves are considerably more delicate than bromeliad foliage. However, with straight urea higher concentrations can be used (vide J. H. Bartram, *Rose Annual* 1971, p. 121).

6. In March 1973, the rooting zone in many English rose beds was dust dry and the application of rose fertilizer had then to be preceded by heavy watering. That was perhaps one special case where foliar feeding might have been justified.

7. Foliar feeding of roses will always involve more work than the application of modern rose fertilizers, especially now that the latter contain slow-release nutrients. Hence foliar feeding should be regarded as a technique to be used in special circumstances and not as a replacement for traditional manuring.

8. Chlorides in solution, such as common salt or muriate of potash, can be expected to be damaging to rose foliage.

## Conclusions

Where roses receive spring applications of a balanced rose fertilizer, my trials suggest that additional applications of foliar nutrients are unlikely to result in large benefits in vigour of growth.

Only in one trial was I able to detect a benefit to plant health and that was a slight reduction of Powdery Mildew from sprays of Epsom salts in the absence of any fungicide. There has been insufficient Rust or Black Spot in my experimental beds to comment on possible effects of foliar nutrition on these two diseases.

> *Eye of the garden, queene of flowers,*
> *Love's cup wherein he nectar pours,*
> *Ingender'd first of nectar;*
> *Sweet nurse-child of the spring's young houres*
> *And beautie's fair charácter.*
>
> *Rose of the Queen, of Love belov'd,*
> *England's great Kings divinely mov'd,*
> *Gave Roses in their banner;*
> *It shewed that beautie's Rose indeed,*
> *Now in this age should them succeed,*
> *And reign in more sweet manner.*

SIR JOHN DAVIES, 1570–1612

# A Case of Poisoning

**E. W. PARNELL,** B.Sc., Ph.D.

(*Amateur rose grower*)

In retrospect, as a chemist and rosarian, I should have known better. But when we moved in 1969 from a noisy main road to a quiet, mature, wooded estate, the house and its setting seemed the most important factors to be considered. It is true that I gave the soil a cursory glance and noted that it seemed rather sandy and contained a fairly large proportion of pebbles in the borders, which were largely occupied by horticultural rubbish. There were some good trees and shrubs, and rhododendrons and heathers flourished. These observations should have sounded a note of warning.

During the first winter, I set about preparing new rose beds and ordered some stocks which were planted in the kitchen garden to be budded the following summer. The new beds were partly cut from lawn and also included parts of old flower-beds. The first thrust of the spade jolted both body and mind and revealed barely six inches of greyish top-soil, somewhat like mineral dust mixed with pebbles, and a hard pan of sub-soil resembling ballast, eminently suitable for the preparation of concrete. Somewhat dismayed, I stripped off the top soil, broke up the sub-soil, mixed it with "compost" from a large heap of rotting remains discovered in a corner of the garden, covered it with inverted turves and replaced the top-soil. The beds were still woefully deficient in organic matter.

In my previous garden I had applied a liberal dressing of sewage sludge with very beneficial results on the clayey soil structure and water-retention properties. As it is a very cheap form of humus-providing material I now applied it very liberally to my new rose beds (50 barrow loads to approximately 80 square yards). The following spring, the beds were planted with a variety of annuals to provide garden colour and to keep the soil in cultivation whilst the roses were being budded. However, something appeared to be wrong; the plants refused to grow properly, became chlorotic and many of them just faded away and died. Even an edging of alyssum, which normally grows like a weed, became stunted and died. I could not understand this at all and foolishly assumed that drought was the probable cause and that nothing was fundamentally wrong. After all, I had prepared the soil in the text-book way.

That autumn, I transplanted my budded stocks, some Laxa and some

Multiflora, into the new beds and headed them back in the usual way in February. They started to grow out normally but then a deterioration became apparent. Nearly all the bushes began to show symptoms of chlorosis and stunted growth. The chlorophyll of some leaves was completely bleached and they became putty-coloured, with a reddish tinge. The youngest shoots were affected the most. The early symptoms resembled those of iron deficiency chlorosis, which was puzzling because this usually occurs on limey, alkaline soils and mine was, from the growth of nearby heathers and rhododendrons, clearly quite acid. However, just in case, I sprayed with iron sequestrene which, of course, made not the slightest difference and the condition progressed. Some bushes were more badly affected than others and some parts of the beds were worse than others. In general, bushes on Multiflora seemed better than those on Laxa.

I was appalled by these results after all my hard work in soil preparation. I read books on soil and plant nutrition, showed samples of affected shoots to various people, and bored my friends with my tale of woe. It wasn't until I explained the situation to a plant physiologist colleague and showed him some samples that an explanation began to take shape. He told me that under very acid conditions, toxicity can arise due to the absorption of *too much* iron or manganese, and although the symptoms did not look quite correct, this was a likely source of the trouble.

At last, I decided to have the soil pH checked. It was 4·5 and needed about 2 lb. of lime per square yard to raise it to the optimum of 6·5! I started to apply lime in increments of 6 oz per square yard during 1971–1972 until a total of 18 oz. had been added and the pH of the top six inches was 5·5. I discovered a relatively cheap source of farmyard manure and applied a heavy dressing in the spring. In 1972 the bushes improved, although a number were still quite sick. I continued to add lime cautiously, not wishing to overdo it, and still asked advice from any likely acquaintance. At last a chance meeting with another specialist threw more light on the problem. He thought that the symptoms resembled those of zinc toxicity in other plants, although he had never seen it in roses. He said that it would certainly be aggravated by an acid soil. But what was the source of the zinc? My suspicions centred on the sewage sludge which had come from an area which included a large number of industrial works. I was finally convinced that zinc, derived from the sewage, was the cause of the trouble when I read the following statement in a book on soil chemistry:[1] "Restriction of plant growth due to an excess

---

[1] *Chemistry of the Soil*, 2nd ed., p. 365. Edited by Firman E. Bear. Van Nostrand Reinhold Co., New York, 1964.

of zinc can arise in acid soils in certain areas, but is more likely to be caused by industrial contamination *or by addition of zinc-rich materials such as sewage sludges. It may be possible to control zinc excess by liming.*" (My italics.) Eureka!

I am continuing to add lime gradually and will carry on until the pH reaches and remains at 6·5. This year (1973), the bushes have mostly grown normally and produced some good exhibition blooms, but some were too far gone to recover and will be replaced, together with the surrounding soil.

This experience has taught me a lot. Because of it I have learned a good deal about plant nutrition and about deficiency and toxicity symptoms through my reading on the subject. If at the outset I had checked and adjusted the pH and used farmyard manure instead of sewage, I would have had no trouble. Although perhaps I might have been excused for not knowing that sewage sludge can contain toxic amounts of zinc, had I not neglected the fundamental question of soil acidity my difficulties would not have arisen.

I hope that this account, the lessons of which are obvious, will help others to avoid similar disappointments, and make them aware of the great importance of pH and the delicate balance between good nutrition and phytotoxicity.

*Footnote by Hon. Scientific Adviser:*

Experience has taught both farmers and growers that sewage sludge from an industrial area can be a very damaging source of organic manure. As Dr Parnell has discovered, the damage is associated with severe leaf chlorosis and poor growth and zinc could well be the culprit. However, unless this has been confirmed by chemical analysis it might be safer to describe the damage as caused by heavy metal toxicity since, in addition to zinc, toxic amounts of copper, nickel, iron and chromium have also been recorded in sewage sludge. Often several of these metals occur together and diagnosis from visual symptoms is not easy.

One other not uncommon source of local zinc toxicity is the use of old tractor or car tyres to start a bonfire. These tyres contain appreciable quantities of zinc and damage to crops on the site of such bonfires can persist for many years.

When a gardener wishes to add large quantities of both organic manure and lime a useful combined source is often spent mushroom compost and this may well be the cheapest and most convenient source.

E.F.A.

# Miss Jekyll's Roses

## GRAHAM THOMAS, V.M.H.

*(Authority on the "Old" roses and Gardens Adviser to The National Trust)*

We spend so much time rushing around these days that it is a good thing to pause sometimes, to take stock of our position and examine our approach to the trends of horticulture. The changes of fashion in our appreciation and use of the rose are mirrored in the Society's Annual and also in the innumerable books that have been written about it through the last 150 years or so, since the Empress Josephine first called attention to its manifold splendours and infinite variety. From those days when the few known species and the group of European once-flowering shrub roses were paramount the picture has gradually changed. The interest engendered by the arrival in Europe of the garden hybrid roses from China, the abundant garden staff, coal and green-houses encouraged many of the wealthy amateurs to consider roses as prize flowers, not plants. They were in danger of losing their graceful vigour through the intermarriage of the two groups. The turning point came when William Robinson and Gertrude Jekyll began to teach us how to use plants in our gardens so that the whole of the plant could be appreciated, and not just its blooms.

Miss Jekyll wrote a book about roses in 1902, with Edward Mawley as co-author; he was a rose exhibitor of considerable experience. It is pretty obvious that Mr Mawley was chosen for his specialized outlook, because Miss Jekyll's part of the book is concerned with roses in the garden and as a cut flower indoors. During a recent "pause" I had occasion to re-read her book and it struck me not only how highly applicable much of her writing is to us today—basic truths can never elude us for long—but that she *lived* in a period of pause. She was, we all know, one who wasted no time but, even so, she approached gardening as an artist and craftswoman of maturity, and experienced through it an overwhelming reverence for the beauty that was hers to use. She also had a desire to teach us all salutary lessons in taste to say nothing of her pioneer work in the use of colour in gardens which is still the basis of most garden schemes.

What would she have thought of our modern roses? I think she would have welcomed even the brightest of them to highlight her most vivid schemes, but can imagine the censorious remarks she would have made when confronted by thoughtless mixtures. "It should be remembered that a Rose

*Above:* 'Céleste' ('Celestial'), a tall-growing Alba rose (*see page* 48)

*Below:* An example of free-grown roses in a formal setting (*see page* 43)

Rambling roses growing freely through low trees and bushes (*see page 43*)

garden can never be called gorgeous: the term is quite unfitting. The gorgeousness or brilliant bloom, fitly arranged, is for other plants and other portions of the garden; here we do not want the mind disturbed or distracted from the beauty and delightfulness of the Rose."

In 1902 the colours of known roses varied from crimson through magenta and pink to white, with a few light yellow and coppery salmon tints. There were no hybrids of full strong yellows, vermilions and flaming reds, only one or two orange tones. Nor was there today's greed for having roses in full spate of flower for some four to five months. In fact, Miss Jekyll had a wholesome love of what was to hand and was quite content to enjoy other flowers at other seasons. Roses to her were one of the glories of the summer months and throughout the pages of her book this deep satisfaction with summer's fullness shines out. Her roses were of gentle tones, cool and charming, needing a dark background for contrast. True to her period and upbringing she abhorred magenta and purplish crimson—like Reginald Farrer—and thus it was obvious she would shy away in the main from the darker Hybrid Perpetuals. It has taken about a hundred years for us to overcome our dislike of this tint, so natural to the rose. Indeed, colour in roses was still traditional until *Rosa foetida* upset it all from 1900 onwards.

Let us see what roses she extolled. The title of her book, *Roses for English Gardens*, published by Country Life, shows her wide approach to the subject and she examined them in her ever logical way. First there were the old garden roses of the previous century, the old French roses, derived from *Rosa gallica* and hybrids with it. Her nomenclature was a bit confused, but we must remember that Miss Willmott's *The Genus Rosa* had not appeared and E. A. Bunyard and Dr C. C. Hurst had not given us of their knowledge. Thus *R. gallica officinalis* is still called Red Damask and the striped sport 'Rosa Mundi', is still confused with 'Cottage Maid' (a Centifolia) and 'York and Lancaster' (a Damask). The Alba roses came in for a generous mead of praise and also 'Blush Boursault', though 'Morlettii' is not mentioned, probably on account of its purplish tint. The Boursault roses add thornlessness to a particularly early flowering habit.

'Blush Gallica' ('Blush Damask') grew well, I remember, in her garden, making a forest of suckers in her sandy soil and she had the same appreciation of the value of *R. spinosissima*, the Burnet or Scots Rose. "By the first week of June the Scotch Briers are in flower, in all their pretty colourings of pink and rose and pale yellow, besides the strongest growing of all, the double white. One of the best and sweetest has become rare. . . . it is of a pale pink colour, . . . the leaves are of a bluish tint and the scent is stronger and sweeter than that of any other." This was, undoubtedly 'Falkland', still inexplicably scarce. Various colour forms, mixed, were used in quantity close by her house, and she devoted a page to their extreme usefulness for sandy soils, for covering banks, for capping a dry wall, and not only for their flowers but also their autumn contribution of soft plum-tinted foliage and shining black heps. The photographs of these roses show how effective they can be for general garden use and also for today's public garden planting where their dense, bushy, prickly growth will control dogs and errant youngsters. In a similar vein the autumn colour of *R. virginiana* is praised; it is the most vivid of all roses at that time. She knew and admired the exquisite double hybrid, the 'Rose d'Amour'. I wish somewhere I could experience the elusive cinnamon scent of *R. cinnamomea*; perhaps, like the musk plant it has lost its fragrance or I have never come across the true plant.

There is quite a lot in her book about China roses and their derivatives with *R. multiflora*—also from the Far East—the dwarf polyanthas. Here her practical mind calls for the abolition of this term, and proposes Pompon: "A French word denoting any kind of upholstered ornament of a roundish tufted form . . . close, bushy, low-growing habit and clustered flowers . . . best in small beds, never in large beds, for here the sense of proportion is at once offended. Or . . . in very narrow beds or borders intended to show only as a wide line or ribbon in the design." These are carefully considered injunctions.

Rugosa roses also did well in her sandy soil, but 'Blanc Double de Coubert' is the favourite—"the whitest rose of any known". This is still true. There is a good photo of 'Schneelicht', a superlative single white which has never been popular, and she mentions the *white* 'Fimbriata' though in my experience this is always blush pink. One glimpse of her delight in flower and foliage is found in the suggestion of a mixture of the common 'Blush China' with rosemary, trained up a sunny wall. Many other species and older varieties are described with pithy words, for instance the use of the prostrate *R. wichuraiana* as an evergreen ground-cover.

The illustrations are monochrome, mostly from photographs, some of them showing remarkable displays. 'Madame Isaac Pereire', for instance, presents an astonishing array of very large double blooms, splendidly full blown. There is a group of 'Paul's Single White Climber' too; this is a perpetual flowerer which I had and distributed some twenty years ago, but have lost and should like to acquire again.

To put it mildly, the illustrations are numerous, and though they cover many aspects of rose culture and many different kinds, there is one great message which Miss Jekyll sought to give. It was not to call attention to specimen blooms from hard-pruned bushes but to pass on the enjoyment she had from the use of shrub and rambling roses as free-grown plants. The whole essence of her thought is provided by some of the captions: "The White Rose on a Cottage Porch"; "the Burnet Rose on a rough garden bank"; "Roses hanging over a Terrace Wall"—and best of all "Roses coming over a wall". Does not this echo completely her thoughts? The roses are not trained up a wall or over a wall; there is no need. The camera caught one of those golden moments when she paused to savour the beauty of one of the little things that mount up to summer's full bounty. Yet again one senses the love of grace and naturalness which can never be attained by the training of plants against their will, but—"coming over a wall".

Miss Jekyll was one of the first to appreciate the grace and abandon of naturally grown plants. Take for instance 'The Garland', one of her favourites; there are several pictures of it. "It is well worth getting up at 4 a.m. on a mid-June morning to see the tender loveliness of the newly opening buds." There was never a rose with a more expressive name for training into trees, a method of enjoying them which she advocated wholeheartedly. Both this and 'Rambling Rector', 'Sanders' White', 'Madame Plantier', 'Albéric Barbier' and others of similar vigour are suitable for use on old fruit trees. It has become customary for some years now to recommend (even to excess) *R. filipes* 'Kiftsgate', *R. longicuspis* and other rampageous species for this purpose but these are suitable only for large trees in full vigour. Some of her photographs of roses in trees can only make us green with envy. Apart from 'The Garland' there is 'Aimée Vibert' some eighteen feet high and completely smothered in bloom; also 'Flora' "growing into a shrub". It is surprising that 'Aimée Vibert' is not grown more today; owing to its close relationship to *R. moschata* it flowers from late summer into autumn, has fully double white flowers in graceful sprays and foliage which in shape and colour can only be described with superlatives. It is best in our warmer counties, and is in fact the only perpetual flowering rambler and deserves the attention of the hybridist. She has a trick for encouraging the plants to entangle the trees gracefully: "When they begin to grow freely among bushes or trees, if it is desired to lead the wayward growths one way rather than another, it is easily done with a long forked stick . . . like painting a picture with an immensely long-handled brush." To this I would add the advisability of planting the rose on the windward side of the object or tree to be covered, if possible. It makes the initial training so much easier.

In common with many gardeners of her time she confused the late-

flowering *R. moschata* with the midsummer *R. brunonii*, whose large trusses
of single, snow-white, incredibly fragrant blooms blend so happily with
long, limp glaucous leaves. Though this is so extremely vigorous, Miss
Jekyll recommends it for pergolas, but we must remember that the pergolas
in great gardens of the Edwardian pause would have had brick piers and
heavy beams atop, and there Brown's rose would be safe. "A Rose pergola
should be placed so that it is well seen from the sides. One whose purpose is
merely to make a shady way is better covered with leafy growths of Vine,
Aristolochia or Virginia Creeper, for if they have not free air and space at
the sides, the Roses will merely rush up and extend skyward where they
cannot be seen." The photograph of *R. brunonii* shows it hanging down the
side of the pillar.

There are chapters about roses on arches, pillars, and swung on garlands;
roses in their carefree abandon clothing sheds and ugly outhouses; roses
trained on supports to act as screens and hedges, and over hedgerows; roses
on pyramid-frames from which they erupt like fountains, or perhaps just
given initial support after which they develop into a mass like a blackberry
bush. A suggestion for a screen is to have a fence covered with a rose with
standards of the same rose at intervals. Though there is so much about their
carefree beauty, Miss Jekyll did not treat their supports in a carefree way; her
practical nature and knowledge of crafts here shine out. "Weather boarding
undefiled by gas-tar" is one of her recommendations, and "for trellis work,
no material is so good as oak, not sawn but split. Split wood lasts much
longer than sawn, as it rends in its natural lines of cleavage and leaves fairly
smooth edges. Sawing cuts cruelly across and across the fibres, leaving a
fringe . . . which catches and holds the wet and invites surface decay." She
recommends winding thick twine or rope around iron supports of metal-
work to avoid frost damage and rubbing. Posts to be inserted in the ground
should have their bases tarred or charred to a foot above soil level to mini-
mize the danger of rotting.

Since with these free-growing species and ramblers any pruning that is
needed should be done immediately after flowering, she revels in the luxury
of being able to cut them for the house. I know full well that six-foot sprays
cut and arranged as they grow are ideal for display in large rooms; for this
purpose free-grown sprays only are of use—those trained up are useless.
"Placed high, on the shoulder of some cabinet about six feet from the floor,
with lovely clusters trending downward, they are charming and beautiful
room ornaments."

It will be seen from the above that her expertise extended to flowers in the home. She was in fact concerned with the whole business of gracious living, but managed to scale down her ideas to small rooms. I think her book *Flower Arrangement* was the first on this subject ever to appear and several of the photographs in her rose book repeat the simple, unaffected, uninhibited care—for care is needed even in this method of decoration. We might caption some of the pictures "Roses brought into a room" or "Roses placed in a jug on a table". Simplicity is at the root of her approach to flowers, gardens and the written word. "Roses arranged for standing high, so as to be seen from below." She does not spare herself in finding out the beauties anew, nor in dropping hints to the Philistine.

To complete the book are chapters on planting, pruning, propagating and exhibiting, and growing roses under glass by Mr Edward Mawley. They contain truths for today. Miss Jekyll herself provides a chapter on the Enemies of the Rose. The pests do not seem to have altered since her day, but it is significant that while mildew and rust occur there is no mention of Black Spot. But of course *R. foetida* had yet to make its susceptibility felt. At the end are lists of recommended roses; they contain many still grown today: 'Mrs John Laing', 'Caroline Testout', 'La France', 'Ulrich Brunner' and 'Fisher Holmes'; some more tender kinds such as 'Niphetos', 'Anna Olivier' and 'Marie van Houtte'; some of the older yellow Tea-Noisettes, 'Gloire de Dijon', 'Claire Jacquier' and 'Alister Stella Gray'; Hybrid Sweet Briars. 'Perle d'Or' is there but her photograph shows another rose; this variety, 'Cécile Brunner' and 'Little White Pet' make a trio of miniatures; 'Souvenir de la Malmaison', 'Mme Alfred Carrière' and 'Gruss an Teplitz' join forces with 'Persian Yellow' and 'Harisonii'.

Many earlier books had been devoted to the artificial culture of the rose; this was the first to extol their natural beauty. From William Robinson and Getrude Jekyll stems the twentieth-century cult of the flowering shrub, and also from them evolves that twentieth-century new English style of gardening epitomized at Hidcote and Sissinghurst, Newby and Tintinhull. Throughout her book we perceive the awe and reverence which should be accorded to plants and flowers. Some fifty years were to pass before plants were to be debased by the term "plant material" by their professional users; this term takes us about as far from Miss Jekyll's ideas and ideals as could be imagined.

# Alba Roses

## TESS ALLEN

*The rose looks faire, but fairer it we deeme*
*For that sweet odor, which doth in it live.*
(WILLIAM SHAKESPEARE 54th sonnet.)

This group has an inappropriate name as in its assemblage of varieties there are pink and cream as well as white roses. All Alba roses are scented; some have become naturalized in parts of Europe, but an Alba rose is not a true species and the pedigree of these very old roses has not been traced by rose genealogists. The theory is that the first Alba roses were natural hybrids between a Gallica rose and *Rosa corymbifera*, which is a Dog-rose with downy leaves.

[1]Alba roses are irregular hexaploids and are thus distinct from the three other groups of Old European roses: Gallicas, Damasks and Centifolias which are considered to be tetraploids. The proven exceptions are: [2]two triploids, a Gallica 'Cardinal de Richelieu' and a Centifolia 'Rose des Peintres' and a [3]pentaploid Damask 'Omar Khayyám'. The majority of us, that is the happy herd, can cheerfully do without these terms. However, empiric rose-hybridists, before planning an unusual cross, ascertain the number of chromosomes in the selected parent plants because triploids and other roses with an odd number of chromosomes are rarely fertile.

The typical old Alba roses are robust, tall, erect-growing shrubs; they have a natural resilience for survival and they also resist the usual strains of rose diseases. The rough, glaucous leaflets are dusted on the upper-surface with soft grey bloom as found on a grape and the under-surface of the leaf is covered with a fine "felt". In the past, when it was the custom to store fresh grapes in the cellar, gardeners took great care not to touch or remove the down on the grapes—otherwise they were attacked by moulds. Possibly the down on Alba leaves serves as a protection against mildew.

Alba roses will tolerate more shade from trees than any other rose with the exception of the purplish-stemmed *Rosa arvensis*; we found this climber growing in a shady glade in Savernake Forest, Wiltshire. Alba's semi-double or double blooms appear usually in June or July, and the oval heps turn scarlet when ripe in October. The thorns are large and slightly curved,

[1] A. P. Wylie, *Journal of the Royal Horticultural Society*, 1954.
[2] G. D. Rowley, *American Rose Annual*, 1960.
[3] C. C. Hurst, *Journal of the Royal Horticultural Society*, 1941.

'TENERIFE' (H.T.)
*'Fragrant Cloud'* × *'Piccadilly'*
Raised by D. T. Bracegirdle
ROSE OF TORRIDGE SILVER SALVER AND TRIAL GROUND CERTIFICATE 1972
*See 1973 Rose Annual, page* 183

ALBA ROSES: on left (pink): 'Céleste'
in centre (creamy-white): *Rosa alba maxima.*
on right (pink): 'Königin von Dänemark'

while the branches are free from the Gallica type of sharp bristles. The shrubs can be left unpruned and some will grow eight to ten feet, or they can be shaped and branches cut out when the bushes become too large.

Friends of ours, the Whitfields, live in one of the oldest inhabited small houses in Suffolk; part of the house dates back to Henry VII. In the forecourt there is a very old suckering shrub of *Rosa alba maxima*, and no one knows how many upheavals in the history of the house the rose has survived. In summer the forecourt is brightened with the shrub's florescence of creamy-white roses; when the double blooms first open the centres are flushed with pink. The shrub is considered to be a double mutant of *Rosa alba semi-plena*; it grows to a greater height than the sport and with half the number of petals a coronet of golden stamens is displayed in the centre of the flower. *R. alba semi-plena* is also known as the "White Rose of York" and in my opinion it is far more strongly scented than *R. alba maxima*.

In English history according to Shakespeare's play King Henry VI part I a quarrel broke out between Richard of York and Somerset of the House of Lancaster in the Temple garden. Richard plucked a white rose and Somerset picked a red rose. Then Warwick gathered a white rose and Suffolk a red rose. Venner, the lawyer, who probably did not want his rose bushes denuded, said, "Stay, lords and gentlemen, and pluck no more Till you conclude that he upon whose side the fewest roses are cropp'd from the tree Shall yield the other in the right opinion". This percipient advice was ignored by Somerset who with myopic stubbornness refused to concede that he had lost the battle of the roses in the Temple garden.

My son, a member of the Middle Temple and Inner Temple, told me that before the building of the Victoria Embankment in the nineteenth century the River Thames at high tide came up to the Middle Temple Hall and tradition has it that red and white roses grew in the rose garden where the fountain now stands. Regrettably, Shakespeare has not been a spur to the Temple to replant these roses. Barristers, it appears, are only influenced by verities.

The War of the Roses, the historical war, went on from 1455 to 1485, through three reigns. After thirty years, the Yorkist Richard III was defeated and the Lancastrians triumphed. Henry Tudor VII married the Plantagenet Princess Elizabeth of York and the White Rose of York and the Red Rose of Lancaster were combined to form the double Tudor Rose.

The newly opened white blooms of 'Mme Le Gras de St Germain' are suffused with a golden glow which subsides as the many-petalled roses mature. The flowers are as fragile as happiness and I know of no other rose so sensitive to bruising; to keep it immaculate it is advisable to put the stem, as soon as the rose is cut, into a damp block of oasis in a basket in order that the flowers do not rub against one another. Unlike the typical Alba roses, 'Mme Le Gras de St Germain' is a lax-growing shrub and virtually thornless. The young stems are a fresh, light green; it is essential to prune the bush and cut out some of the old wood each year after it has flowered. This ensures that the blooms of the following year are a good size and that the new, young, whippy stems are replenished, for the light-green wands add life to a winter garden. The thornless stems of 'Chloris' carry small, two-toned pink roses.

The creamy-pink petals of 'Félicité Parmentier' are of a thicker texture and when the butter-yellow buds fully open the petals curl back into a pompon of rose petals. 'Queen of Denmark' ('Königin von Dänemark'), another rose of quality, was raised in 1826. The bush grows to about five feet, the roses are pink in the centre and pale-pink on the outer, recurving petals. 'Amelia', a rose-bush of about the same height, has semi-double, deep-pink flowers with a golden brush of stamens in the centre.

The eighteenth-century rose 'Céleste' is one of the tall growing Alba roses and should not be confused with the smaller, Damask bush 'Celsiana', as the latter has darker-pink (when they first open) and larger flowers than 'Céleste', also known as 'Celestial'. This Alba rose has outstandingly beautiful pink rose-buds; they open to lovely blooms of sulliable purity, but since the colour combination of grey-green leaves and blush pink roses is so satisfying, the flowers are best left on the bush. One year, before the shrub was in blossom, I picked some of the foliage from the back of the bush. That summer the shrub, as I expected, flowered well but there were no roses from where I had picked the spring foliage. Later in the year a patch of pink roses appeared from the growth of the current year.

'Maiden's Blush' is known in France as 'Cuisse de Nymphe'; 'Great Maiden's Blush' is a similar shrub but with larger, brighter-pink roses and it was logically given the name of 'Cuisse de Nymphe Emue', as the thigh of the nymph was much affected with a brighter blush. 'Le Roiser Blanc Royal' (*Rosa alba regalis*,) illustrated in Volume I of Redouté's 1817 *Les Roses*, is a permutation of the same form, or drawing-room names for identical roses.

'Great Maiden's Blush' was known to gardeners in the sixteenth century; the bush grows to about five feet tall and the flower stems are covered with fine, soft bristles, not normally present in the Alba group and thus an aid in identifying this rose and its forms. The flesh-pink buds open to even paler blooms. In an old garden, Myland Hall, near Colchester, there are vigorous bushes of 'Great Maiden's Blush' flourishing on their own roots and the shrub sends up equally virile suckers and they transplant successfully.

It would be greatly to the advantage of gardeners if all Alba roses were on their own roots, as the scourge of suckers from rose stocks is a grievous and recurring affliction from which we all suffer. There is no reasonable doubt in my mind that in our garden 'Céleste' was budded on to one of William Blake's Monks' briars from his *Songs of Experience*:

> *Monks in black gowns were walking their rounds*
> *And binding with briars my joys and desires.*

The smallest of all Alba roses, and one with fewer thorns than *R. alba maxima*, was introduced in 1876 and the bush grows to the height of four feet and is known by two names, 'Pompon Alba' and 'Pompon Parfait'; when in flower the shrub is floriated with small, blush-white, short stemmed roses like silken rosettes. There are three bushes in the RNRS display gardens at Bone Hill and in the last week of June 1972, the year when summer started late, the bushes carried a light crop of flowers, but roses piled upon roses until in the first week of September the shrubs were conspicuously covered with blossom, accrediting 'Pompon Parfait' with an exceptionally long flowering season.

Alba roses have survived for many centuries in hedgerows; they have flourished in small and great gardens; the flowers have become part of a royal crest and been carved in stone to the glory of ancient chapels and cathedrals. Nevertheless, when each year the scent proclaims the summer flowering of the Alba roses it is hard to realize the weight of years that rests on the older varieties, albeit they are living memorials of antiquity.

> *How fair is the Rose! What a beautiful flower!*
> *The glory of April and May.*
> *But the leaves are beginning to fade in an hour,*
> *And they wither and die in a day.*
>
> *Yet the Rose has one powerful virtue to boast,*
> *Above all the flowers of the field:*
> *When its leaves are all dead, and fine colours are lost,*
> *Still how sweet a perfume it will yield!*
>
> ISAAC WATTS, *The Rose*

# Some Thoughts on Planting

## Dr. A. S. THOMAS, O.B.E., V.M.A., D.H.M.

*(President, National Rose Society of Australia)*

For a great many years some statements have been made, rather dogmatically, about soil conditions for roses and their actual planting. Often there has been little emphasis on provision of adequate drainage which is surely the first prerequisite of all good gardening, except in the case of bog plants. It is commonplace to read or to hear that "roses like clay". It is doubtful if any plants do well if planted in clay or even directly on to clay. A clay subsoil, provided that it is well drained, seems to suit a wide range of plants, especially those that we transplant with bare roots such as roses and most trees. They do best, however, if planted in fairly friable soil and in due time their roots grow down into the deeper and firmer soil. I have, over a good many years, dug out some hundreds of rose bushes and have found it a rarity for the roots to penetrate clay in any marked degree. They will go deeper into heavy loam, but nearly all of the roots run almost horizontally at a depth of no more than about eighteen inches.

As far as I can see, clay has only one virtue—it retains moisture. This helps to steady the temperature of the soil but it is not easy for roots to take up that moisture. Plenty of organic matter incorporated in the soil of the whole bed will steady the temperature more effectively, will give up moisture more readily, and will break down slowly to excellent plant food.

It has been stated more recently that roses need slightly acid soil. In my experience, roses do less well in definitely acid soils than in definitely alkaline soils. Certainly they thrive in neutral soils and they do not resent a slight variation either way, from say pH6·5 to pH7·5. I have seen very poor results at pH5·5 and roses grow wonderfully well in vast areas of Australia where the soil has a pH of 7·5 to 8·5—the latter is very alkaline. In those areas, it is usual to see rose bushes grow to over eight feet in height and six feet in width, with many hundreds of long-stemmed large blooms each year on each plant. Most of those soils are not only rich in calcium carbonate but magnesium carbonate as well. The magnesium may account for some of the health and vigour.

In preparing positions for roses, they should not be in small beds. It is desirable to make fairly big beds if plants of other types are to be grown behind the roses. The bigness of the area makes good drainage easier and the whole area should be dug to a uniform depth of at least two feet. If drainage problems render this depth impossible, the bed should be built so that there is at least two feet of well-dug soil. The digging, the breaking up of all clods and the stirring in of lots of organic matter warrants a great lot of care and time. The organic matter can be well-made compost and old animal manures. Unless roses are not to be planted for many months it seems wrong to bury unrotted vegetable matter. Apparently many English growers use chopped-up turf. Under Australian conditions this would be excellent too, but it would need to be buried long before planting was contemplated.

It has been advocated that the bed should be prepared a year or more before roses are to be planted and that the soil be used for other plants. This can be excellent, but the other plants should not include dahlias, potatoes or tomatoes as these foster harmful fungi in the soil. Best of all is the growing of legumes of some sort and digging them in, not very deeply, just before they come into flower and, of course, a good many months before planting roses. This is not a productive crop but it enriches the soil.

In planting a rose bush in such a bed a wide hole, a little deeper than needed, will give it a very good "home" for its whole life. Even in this type of soil it is desirable to form a mound and to spread the roots downwards and outwards over it. Adjust the mound so that when the rose sits on it the bud union is at the desired level (this varies with climates). Be very careful to clip off any damaged roots and avoid having any of them turning upwards. Undoubtedly suckers emerge from roots which are damaged or turned upwards. Next, a little more than half-fill the whole with good friable soil mixed, if available, with well-made compost. Do not press on it in any way. This is in sharp contrast to frequent advice to firm the soil over the roots thoroughly by tramping on it. In fact, there have been illustrations of grinding the soil down with the heel of a boot! Pressure is apt to bruise the "bark" of the roots. This constitutes enough damage to cause suckering. The roots of some understocks are more prone to produce suckers than others, but they will all do so if damaged or turned upwards.

Fill the hole with water. While doing so hold the plant by its understock (never by its scion) keeping it upright and raising it a little so that the union remains high enough. The water will wash the loose soil in amongst the roots and it will compact it above the roots as well. In fact it will be compacted far better than any tramping can achieve.

The objective of tramping would be firm planting and the obliterating of all pockets of air. The slurry produced by the fine soil and water will do both of these things far better. If necessary for covering the roots, add more soil and more water. Then fill the hole with loose soil. If the union has sunk too low, drag the plant upwards, gripping it by the understock. This will do no harm. It will make the roots point a little more outwards and downwards with possibly some advantage. If this is done, the soil is disturbed a little, so flood it again. Let the water soak away and then fill the hole with loose soil, but there is no urgency about this.

It has been said that no lime or manures should be used when planting. I agree about lime and in regard to soluble chemical manures, but I can see no harm in using a very light sprinkle of blood and bone manure mixed with the soil around the roots. Seedlings of annuals do well with such a sprinkling and roses should be able to tolerate it.

When replacing an established rose with another it has been standard practice to advise the removal of a couple of barrow-loads of soil and its replacement with soil which has not grown roses for some years. The old soil is said to be "crop-sick". Market gardeners and others do not change soil but they rotate crops, alternating root crops (e.g. carrots and parsnips) with leaf crops (e.g. lettuces and cauliflowers) in the same soil. They have found by experience that growing the same crop in the same soil for several years leads to failure, but that alternating crops are successful. This must point to "crop-sickness" not being due to a certain crop seriously depleting some plant food in the soil. Instead, it must point to that crop adding some undesirable product. This would appear to be a product of the decomposition of root fragments in the soil. In recent times I have not discarded any soil. I have dug out a plant and then dug over the soil very carefully, removing every visible root fragment. Unavoidably, some are missed, so I dig out a hole as wide as is compatible with neighbouring plants and I scatter that soil over the surface of the beds. Then I mix compost with soil raked off the surface of other beds for filling the hole. This has no young root fragments and it gives good growth.

Mention has been made of the use of "well-made" compost. All too often the compost heap is made up of only weeds and kitchen refuse and is exposed to the weather. When decomposed, this is a good soil conditioner but it has very little food value. In any case, its constituents are deficient in nitrogen. This can be corrected by the addition of nitrogenous matter such as blood and bone or fresh animal or bird excreta—I prefer poultry manure. Chemical compounds (e.g. sulphate of ammonia, nitrates, etc.) although they hasten decomposition, should be avoided as they keep earthworms away. The heap should be made on earth and should be covered to prevent leaching of valuable plant foods by the rain. An occasional watering is helpful.

# Look to the Rose that ...

## DEREK A. WILSHER
(*Amateur rose grower*)

As the sun declined from its zenith towards its eventual roseate couch in the west, the aged "Son of-a-tentmaker" raised his venerable head from the cushions whereon he had been reclining when taking his ease during the heat of the day. His silver hair proclaimed the dignity of old age—a dignity that was belied by the cynical cast of his features; his keen eyes mirrored the Wisdom of the Ages; his distinguished air marked the mien of a courtier. The cool breeze of evening whipped up the myriad grains of sand in the near-by desert; yet even here, in that small strip of grassy herbage that just divided the desert from the sown was greenery sufficient to satisfy his craving eye, as it sought relief from the fierce harshness of the day.

The flowing stream, close at hand, provided encouragement for the grassy turf; there were low shrub roses, growing wild, profuse with sweetly scented, yellow flowers; the breeze was refreshing; it rendered unnecessary the attentions of the slave-girl who, with a fan of peacocks' feathers, had been protecting his old head from the undue, and unseemly, interest of the insect world. He raised himself on one elbow to survey the scene, illuminated and enriched by the magic gold of the glorious sunset ...

His ancient eyes seized on, and lingered o'er, the shrubs surrounding his rustic couch. Their freshness and colour pleased his aesthetic sense; an habitual philosopher, he pondered what he saw, wondering how these things that *could* be seen could aid him in his life-long search, his quest for those things that could *not* be seen. "Just a shrub?" mused he, "one of the many thousand I've seen since first *I* saw the light of day, in my father's tent! *He* made tents—I've seen them: yet who made that bush?" He paused, an odd thought struck him and with a chuckle he added meditatively, "Made?—or composed? ... I can 'compose' Mathematical Tables (who but *I* devised them?); could I ever, by strict application of the 'Rule of Three', compose such a shrub? ... *I* can reform the Calendar and have done so; *I* can give sage counsel and good advice (when asked!) to the Khalif; I often do so. Could I, with all such wisdom, re-form, could I create, such a shrub? ... Yet, could even the Khalif, with all his might, magnificence, and power do so?" He continued in a reflective reverie.

The sun continued to decline; its latest rays fell on the flowers gleaming amid the verdant foliage; gold gave to gold fresh lustre, as glory reflected glory. "Aha!", quoth the Sage, "such gold have I seen—in the Royal Treasury! Nay, not *such* gold, for never was there gold of such living, vivid, radiance; such living, brilliant hues must stem from Heaven itself." The breeze, the gentle zephyr of evening, soughed among the bushes which shuddered beneath its soft caress. Almost, it seemed to the philosopher that those full-petalled, golden, glistening flowers smiled. . . .

"Yet 'tis but a rose," murmured he, "the ordinary, common, rose—by no means a rare plant here, in our Persian wilderness! The age of this particular specimen few could doubt: it has seen but few earthly years. . . . *I* squared the year to human compass . . . Aie! . . . yet . . . such roses have always been here in Persia! And will ever be? . . . When Sultan Mahmud has long been forgotten, when I am nevermore remembered, such roses will still remember to flower; their flowers will not be forgotten—as my words shall be! All my long life have I known these roses: indeed, in my *Rubaiyat* (will *that* be remembered?) I've made one or two references to them! Yet, could any deny its beauty, its charm? Who could create its equal? Its colour *I* have defined— who could recapture its hues? Is it not unique? A parable, history-lesson, beauty-instruction, all in itself—in one small cluster of soon-to-be-withered silken tassels!"

The last words stirred the poetic chord that lay deep in his sensitive, though philosophic nature. He mused a few moments longer. Suddenly he called for pen and parchment. With these before him Omar Khayyám reflected a while, then wrote swiftly:

> *Look to the Rose that blows about us—'Lo*
> *Laughing,' she says, 'Into the World I blow*
> *At once the silken tassel of my Purse*
> *Tear, and its Treasure on the Garden throw."*

\*   \*   \*

Thus, through the centuries his words ring to us in the translation of a Victorian poet. We need not doubt that *that* rose which inspired this quatrain of Omar Khayyám's *Rubaiyat* was the yellow rose of Persia, *R. foetida persiana*, which today does indeed through "the World . . . blow". It is a rose of great antiquity; from its native Persia it has migrated across many lands and seas, and even in these colder Northern climes it flourishes today.

'GERTRUD SCHWEITZER' (H.T.)
*'Colour Wonder'* × *'Dr A. J. Verhage'*
Raised by W. Kordes & Son, Germany
TRIAL GROUND CERTIFICATE 1973
*See page* 183

Newer Miniature Roses: upper blooms—'Judy Fischer'
lower blooms—'Toy Clown'

# What's New in Miniature Roses

## C. W. GREGORY

(*Rose nurseryman and breeder*)

Miniature roses are not really new, although they have become increasingly popular over the last ten years or so. At one time we thought of a miniature rose as a small bush with petite blooms most suitable for rock gardens or for growing in pots. With the passing years, though, many new colours and shapes have been developed and it is a fact that we no longer tend to look on our miniature roses as truly miniatures in stature, but accept stronger-growing bushes 10 to 18 in. high, with perfectly-formed blooms, tiny thorns and leaves to scale, approaching in vigour and disease resistance their taller cousins, the hybrid teas. This modern story of miniature roses began with the introduction of 'Tom Thumb' in 1933, when this and several other cultivars were bred by Jan de Vink of Holland. Almost without exception the original miniature rose, *R. roulettii*, was used and most of the crossings were with Polyantha roses little grown today.

Our present-day miniature roses have been developed by using as parents many types and cultivars, including species, hybrid teas and floribundas. These crossings have resulted in varieties with a wide range of pleasing colours, and blooms with a diameter of $\frac{1}{2}$ to $1\frac{1}{2}$ in. produced over a long period during the summer. They will stand sun, rain and frost and are easy to grow, both outdoors and indoors. Planted in a sunny border, rockery, stone trough or pots or used as edgings to rose beds or borders they will provide many years of enjoyment.

### What is New?

Although in the past the breeding of miniature roses has been the work of only a few, some of our prominent breeders of today have come forward with some very interesting introductions. McGredy has an eye-catching variety bred from 'Little Flirt' and 'Marlena' named 'Wee Man'. No doubt we shall be seeing much more of this miniature of brilliant scarlet colouring. Also from McGredy, 'Woman's Own' is bushy and compact and smothered with pink blooms. It was bred from 'New Penny' and 'Tip Top'. While these are not truly miniatures, nevertheless they are compact and bushy. Meilland-Universal Rose Selections have made an outstanding contribution with 'Starina'. Almost the perfect miniature with its perfection of form unequalled by many full-sized hybrid tea roses (25 petals), the colour is oriental red with a gold and carmine reverse, which is most attractive. Their other recent introduction, 'Darling Flame', is not quite so double, but its colour is outstanding and best described as mandarin red opening to rich vermilion as seen in the petals of 'Super Star'. 'Rosy Gem' is at the Trial Ground, but not yet available, although it looks promising.

De Ruiter of Holland has started breeding varieties which have stronger growth than other miniatures but are smaller than Polyantha roses and at the same time have miniature blooms. Varieties already raised are 'Scarletta', scarlet; 'Rugal', deep yellow, to be introduced 1974 and 'Estru', pink, which is scheduled for 1975. These have all proved good for forcing and will no doubt be very popular in the Scandinavian countries, where roses are grown mostly in pots.

Undoubtedly the most outstanding breeder of miniature roses over the past 25 years is Ralph Moore of California, who up to date has bred over twenty outstanding varieties of true miniatures and has many more on the way. Some of his varieties which are perhaps not quite so new and are now becoming increasingly popular and are readily available, all being improvements on previous varieties, are 'Beauty Secret', bright red, 'Eleanor', coral pink, 'Easter Morn', ivory white and 'Yellow Doll'.

More recently introduced are 'Gold Coin', buttercup yellow and very nice indeed it is, with a good bushy habit, and 'Lavender Lace', with beautifully formed buds and flowers of soft lavender on bushy, healthy plants (both were illustrated in the 1972 *Rose Annual*). Illustrated in this year's *Rose Annual* are 'Toy Clown', which everyone immediately likes, white with red or pink edges to the petals, a winner at many shows in America, and 'Judy Fischer', selected as the miniature rose of 1970, a lovely shade of rose pink with a soft undertone of gold and very shapely flowers.

Outstanding new varieties from Moore soon to become available in this country are, 'Magic Carrousel', very similar to 'Toy Clown', but the flowers are more double and the plant is more vigorous. Moore says it has superbly beautiful form from bud to fully open flower, with all the flair and excitement of your first visit to a circus. 'Mary Marshall' pleases me because it is orange to orange-coral in colour; it is something different and lively in the garden or even as a cut flower. 'Fire Princess' has brilliant orange-red blooms which, in spite of being very double, look good in all weathers. There are many others yet to prove themselves suitable for our climate and just a few to look out for in the future are 'Fiesta Gold'; 'Top Secret', red; 'Green Ice', pink changing to soft green; 'Janice', pink; 'Nancy Hall', peach-apricot and 'Yellow Jewel'.

Already proved and now very popular, of course, is the miniature rose 'Nozomi' (Hope) from Japan. Introduced two years ago, this is classified by the Society as a climbing miniature, but I like to think of it as a ground-cover rose which bears masses of single, pink blooms which last for six to eight weeks in the summer. The rest of the time it furnishes a green carpet of small, pointed, glossy leaves.

What of the future? Ralph Moore writes: "We have already had the smallest varieties and I do not think I want any which are too small to be practicable, and which only an expert or specialist would be interested in growing. We already have new colours and colour combinations. Perhaps we shall achieve other colour combinations, new lavender shades or even a greeny-yellow shade, but most likely varieties of similar colours on better-growing plants."

Ralph Moore has devoted over twenty years to the task of trying to change the tall, old-fashioned spring flowering Moss rose into an ever-blooming dwarf bush. This has been accomplished to some extent and several seedlings are being tested for later release. Two varieties already released in America are 'Rouge Moss' and 'Gold Moss'; these are not really miniatures, but grow two to three feet high. The first and best miniature Moss up to the present is named 'Kara' (Dear One), the most unusual of all miniatures and it will be available in this country soon. Small, very mossy buds open into bright pink, single flowers and it is repeat blooming all the season. The bushy plants grow ten inches tall. Truly a Moss rose, truly miniature and for me an exciting new development in roses.

Anyone can grow miniature roses. They are easy to cultivate. Treat them as you do your other roses; prune severely if required and they will give years of pleasure. All roses have some fault or other, thank goodness—life would be very uninteresting if all were perfect!

You may be interested to know that the Society is devoting a section of the display gardens at Bone Hill to miniature roses, so you will be able to see all the latest varieties when you next pay a visit.

May I end by quoting Ralph Moore who writes:

*"May your pathway be lined with miniature roses.*
*May their charm and fragrance add to your joy."*

# Summer Fields

**ARBEL M. ALDOUS**

(*Amateur rose grower*)

Summer Fields is a well-known Preparatory School in North Oxford. The Head Master, Mr P. M. B. Savage, and the Head Gardener, Mr Frank Ricketts, are both rose enthusiasts and members of the RNRS. The School stands in about a hundred acres of garden and playing fields extend to the river where it has a swimming reach as well as a pool in the grounds. To a privileged few the name "Summer Fields" may recall "the happiest years of their lives". Did they realize it at the time? Famous names include five generations of Macmillans.

Within the 2,000 yards of perimeter there is a collection of 250 trees and shrubs and over 1,000 roses, including 350 species.

The school takes a special pride in its own 'Summer Fields' Rose, raised in 1970 by John Mattock Ltd, to celebrate its hundredth anniversary. On Open day in July 1973 there was a bed of this rose growing in profusion on the lawn opposite the front door. It can be described as a floribunda or bush of deep crimson, golden at the base of the inner petals and when fully open it reveals a cluster of yellow-pollened stamens.

The school's own catalogue is a brochure expertly compiled by the Head Gardener, in which each rose is given its type with date in most cases and other historical items of sufficient interest.

So we find Albas, Centifolias, Damascenas, Rugosas, Noisettes, Gallicas, Chinas, Bourbons, Mosses, Hybrid Musks, Shrubs, Hybrid Teas, Hybrid Perpetuals, Floribundas, Ramblers, Climbers, and the like.

An especially interesting feature is the Rose Museum, a walled area where species and outstanding items are grown. Here are some of them:

*Rosa alba*, the White Rose of York
*R. gallica officinalis*, the Red Rose of Lancaster
*R. damascena versicolor*, the 'York and Lancaster' Rose
*R. alba maxima*, the Jacobite Rose
*R. farreri persetosa*, the Threepenny-bit Rose
*R. hemispherica*, the Sulphur Rose
*R. chinensis viridiflora*, the Green Rose
Gallica, 'Rose des Maures,' from Sissinghurst Castle
*R. centifolia cristata*, 'Châpeau de Napoléon'.

For some of these and many others the school is indebted to the late Miss Nancy Lindsay, who was persuaded by the Head Gardener to give the results of a life-long series of travels in Persia, China and elsewhere when she decided she could no longer cope with her large garden at Sutton Courtenay. Among them are R. *damascena* 'Omar Khayyám' from the poet's grave and R. *damascena* 'Chateau Galliard' from Richard Coeur de Lion's castle in Normandy. On the wall at the far end of the Museum is a large, semi-double, deep pink climber also brought from Persia and named by Miss Lindsay 'Souvenir of Nora Lindsay', her mother.

Miss Lindsay died in the spring of 1973 and the Summer Fields' Head Gardener is the possessor, donated to him, of the only complete catalogue of Miss Lindsay's 282 roses. Some of her descriptions are little lyrics; she loved her roses.

The perimeter of the actual garden area, which is largely well-kept lawn, is fenced by suitable roses in colour groups, and ramblers and climbers are invited to ramble and climb to their hearts' content, even over the School House itself. Especially flamboyant was a specimen of 'Lawrence Johnston' rising from the other side of a wall like a mass of laburnum.

There is a small corner in which Mr Ricketts takes a special pride. He has a Royal Garden, starting with the Bourbon, 'Prince Charles' (1842) and the Moss, 'Princess Adelaide' (1860) and continuing with 'La Reine Victoria' (1872), 'Princess Marina' (1935), 'Queen Elizabeth' (1954), 'Scarlet Queen Elizabeth' (1963), 'Yellow Queen Elizabeth' (1964), 'Elizabeth of Glamis' (1964), up to 'Princess Margaret of England' and 'Duke of Windsor' (1968). Not yet included in the catalogue is 'The Queen Alexandra Rose' (1918). But with several other forgotten roses I had inherited it in my old garden and I was delighted to hand it over to complete his collection.

A unique feature at Summer Fields is the Genealogy Border; not only are the ramifications of the family tree clearly set out on a framed chart 30 × 18in., (see page 60) but the items are actually growing there in the Rose Museum.

The cultivars mentioned as representative in each case are those that have been selected for the purpose and the work is the result of the united efforts of the Head Master and the Head Gardener.

# THE GENEALOGY OF THE ROSE
## A REPRESENTATIVE GROUP

**ROSA GALLICA [RUBRA]**
Religious emblem of the Medes and Persians 12th Century. Probably the oldest of the garden Roses taken as the badge for the House of Lancaster in 13th Century described as a vivid Red Rose by PLINY was known as the 'Apothecaries' Rose'.
REPRESENTED BY 'GALLICA OFFICINALIS'

**ROSA DAMASCENA.**
Grown in Bulgaria for the famous 'Attar' of Roses
REPRESENTED BY TRIGINTIPETALA 'KAZANLIK'

**DAMASCENA × CANINA**
The wild Dog Rose
Probably as ancient as Gallica. Mentioned by 'HERODOTUS' as growing in the gardens of KING MIDAS of PHRYGIA. Also grown by the Romans at PAESTUM and POESTI

**ROSA ALBA**
Also in cultivation since Roman Times. During the 'Wars of the Roses', it was adopted as the badge of the Yorkists in contra-distinction to the red Rose of Lancaster. Much portrayed by Flemish painters of the 15th Century
REPRESENTED BY 'CELSIANA' *

**BIFERA × ALBA**

**CENTIFOLIA**
PROBABLY GAVE US
It appears that this Rose did not actually arrive until the 16th Century. The Rose of the Dutch painters.
REPRESENTED BY 'RED PROVENCE'

**PARSONS PINK CHINA × DAMASCENA BIFERA**
Parks Yellow China. 1824 was the first source of the Yellow Rose

**DAMASCENA BIFERA × QUATRE SAISONS**
BLANC MOUSSEUX

**BOURBONIANA**
Found growing together with its parents in the French Island of Bourbon 1817
REPRESENTED BY 'LA REINE VICTORIA' 1872

**MOSCHATA × PARSONS P. CHINA**

**NOISETTIANA (1802)**
REPRESENTED BY 'CHAMPNEY'S PINK CLUSTER'

**CHINENSIS × DAMASCENA**

**THE PORTLAND ROSE**

**MULTIFLORA × CHINENSIS**
Wild Rose of China, Japan and Korea

**POLY POMPON**
REPRESENTED BY PAUL CRAMPEL

**TEA SCENTED CHINENSIS × BOURBON**
Hybrid from Gigantea-Chinensis in 1809

**THE TEA ROSE (1830)**

**HYB. PERPETUAL × TEA ROSE**

**WICHURAIANA × MULTIFLORA × HYB. TEA.**

**RAMBLERS**
REPRESENTED BY
FRANÇOIS JURANVILLE

**HYB. TEA.**
REPRESENTED BY LA FRANCE' 1867 'SUPER STAR AND SULTANE' 1942.

REPRESENTED BY BLAZE SUPERIOR' 1932

**GALLICA × MOSCHATA**
(The wild musk Rose)
REPRESENTED BY 'FILIPES'

**DAMASCENA BIFERA**
Referred to in VIRGIL'S 'GEORGICS' 'Biferique Rosaria Pæsti' Frescoes of this Rose were found in the ruins of Pompeii A.D. 79 used in the cult of APHRODITE

**CHINENSIS × GIGANTEA**
The wild Tea Rose of Burma
Introduced from China 1789. The origin of perpetual flowering in Western Roses. Recorded in the 10th Century B.C.

**PARSONS PINK CHINA (1793)**
REPRESENTED BY OLD BLUSH CHINA

**BOURBONIANA × THE PORTLAND ROSE**
Brought from the neighbourhood of PAESTUM Italy early 1800's. Named after the Duchess of Portland

**HYBRID PERPETUALS (1816)**
REPRESENTED BY 'ULRICH BRUNNER'

**FOETIDA LUTEA × HYB. PERPETUAL**
What has sometimes been called the quiet revolutionised the tea rose and gave us all our yellows and bicolours

**HYB. TEA ROSE (TYPE)**
(RÊVE D'OR)

**POLY POMPON × HYBRID TEA**

**HYBRID POLYANTHA (POULSEN 1924)**
or
**FLORIBUNDA**
REPRESENTED BY 'HIGHLIGHT' AND 'QUEEN ELIZABETH'

---

\* 'Celsiana' is a Damask rose and not an Alba. It may be that it was intended that 'Céleste' ('Celestial') should be quoted here. It is noted that the origin of Alba roses given here differs from that mentioned by Tess Allen on page 46. (Ed.)

The late John William Mattock (*see page* 14)

Summer Fields (*see page* 58)

Rooted Air-Layers:

A. *Rosa roxburghii* and 'Arthur Bell' photographed immediately after severing from the parent plants on 27 October, 1973 (*see page 62*)

B. Three air-layers of 'Rose Gaujard' lifted twelve months after planting out in the open, to show root development. Photographed with a potted miniature standard rose (*see page 62*)

# Air Layering Roses—Further Developments

On pages 102–105 of *The Rose Annual,* 1972, two of our members gave details of how they successfully propagate their roses by this method (also known as marcotting), one of its advantages being that the resulting plants are on their own roots and cannot, therefore, produce suckers.

In a footnote to the articles, our Hon. Scientific Adviser, Mr E. F. Allen, included the following two paragraphs:

"As far as rose cultivation in Great Britain is concerned, I have yet to be convinced that marcotting offers any advantage over the rooting of some form of cutting. I myself have been able to root a cutting of the yellow-flowered 'Arthur Bell', although the cultivar is insufficiently vigorous on its own roots for anything but pot cultivation.

"If it proved possible to root a marcot of the double-flowered *Rosa roxburghii,* then I would certainly revise my opinion of the potential useful-ness to the rosarian of this technique."

Mr M. J. E. Wood accepted the Hon. Scientific Adviser's challenge by taking up the cudgels on Mr David Umpleby's behalf, the latter confining himself to the practical aspects of propagation by this method. A summary of Mr Wood's account of the procedure followed by Mr Umpleby is given below:

"Mr Allen included, or rather additionally cited *Rosa roxburghii* with 'Arthur Bell' as being definite criteria to determine whether or not air-layering is commendable as a means of useful plant propagation for the amateur. Consequently, I asked Mr Umpleby if he would conduct the practical aspects of the research were I to obtain the stocks. Fortunately, he was equally concerned to furnish evidence of the air-layering method's credibility and consented.

"Hillier's were able to supply 'Arthur Bell' without trouble, but the double-flowered *R. roxburghii* was not to be secured in the South-East. Hillier's spokesman stated that single or double would prove equally intractable and he echoed Mr Allen's feelings that *R. roxburghii* was out of the question with regard to propagation other than by budding or seed.

"I append, on Mr Umpleby's behalf, details of how the air-layered stems responded to marcotting and request that Mr Allen should have an opportunity to consider this and the photos, although one may consider progress to date as inconclusive pending a final assessment next autumn, when the rooted air-layered stems will have grown independent of all means of support other than their own root system.

Two *Rosa roxburghii* ⎫
Two 'Arthur Bell'  ⎬ shrubs were planted 14.3.73.
Main growths only were marcotted 26.6.73.
Basal shoots (3 only) were marcotted 5.7.73.
Severed (per photo(A)), 27.10.73.

"An air-layered stem of *R. roxburghii* was snapped by accident four weeks after marcotting and, when potted off as an experiment, has survived on the roots which had already formed during those four weeks and made foliage.

"Of the *R. roxburghii* stems that were air-layered, 9 out of 15 have grown roots comparable with those shown on the photograph (A) herewith. The 'Arthur Bell' stems *all* grew roots and all 12 have been potted off or are ready for potting.

"The marcotted stems shown are some 15 in. long. This shows how unsatisfactory the *R. roxburghii* stems were, being no thicker than a pencil, but the roots are there and time will tell. The unnamed variety in the photo (B), with the potted miniature, is I believe 'Rose Gaujard' and indicates the root growth associated with three stems which were air-layered one year, potted off until planted out and grown for the following year in the outdoors, and then dug up to ascertain the precise degree of development at the end of that season. Regarding the photo (A), Mr Umpleby made the point that Mr Allen's expertise will enable him to identify *R. roxburghii* by the foliage.

"The parent stock of *R. roxburghii* and 'Arthur Bell' were grown in black loam, were fed with Phostrogen fortnightly and given the appropriate farmyard manure top-dressing. The loam is well aerated and drained. The treated stems were packed with water-moistened peat moss. After severing from the parent, the stems will over-winter in equal parts of loam, sharp sand and peat moss.

"I am advised by Mr Umpleby, and I would accept all his statements as true, that stems which have grown roots as evidenced in the photos, and subsequently have been potted off prior to planting out, can safely be regarded as being equally successful when they are planted out. He tells me that, other than as a matter of personal choice, *all* shrubs derived as a result of marcotting are grown in the open garden with total success and by their second full year none has failed to achieve proportions equal to or exceeding those of nursery stock budded on to briars: in addition, they are free from the nuisance of suckers and risk of canker. Mr Umpleby estimates that some 200 "free-range" shrubs have grown in his garden from marcots.

"One assumes that Mr Allen will be equally impressed with the 60 per cent and 100 per cent success so far, following as it does many years of unbroken success on Mr Umpleby's part, in view of the boon this method will prove to be in relation to rare, difficult and ultra-expensive types."

Having read Mr Wood's full account of the procedure and having studied the two photographs identified as (A) and (B) respectively, Mr Allen has commented as under:

"I must congratulate Messrs Umpleby and Wood on their skill and enthusiasm. These results are most promising and clearly I must revise my opinion as to the value of marcotting to amateur members in particular. An even greater slice of humble pie has its origin nearer home, since my wife has recently planted and established a magnificent marcot, at least three feet high, of the Dawn Redwood, *Metasequoia glyptostroboides*.

"Incidentally, it appears that 'Arthur Bell' on its own roots has one character of value to the rose breeder. My plant, in a 10-inch plastic pot, this year grew only 2 ft 3 in. tall and ripened 21 large heps, which yielded 210 seeds, all except six being "sinkers". This suggests that the reduced vigour induced by its own root system has led to increased fertility."

*Ah! see, deep-blushing in her green recess,*
*The bashful virgin-rose, that half-revealing,*
*And half, within herself, herself concealing,*
*Is lovelier for her hidden loveliness.*
*Lo! soon her glorious beauty she discovers:*
*Soon droops; and sheds her leaves of faded hue:*
*Can this be she—the flower—erewhile that drew*
*The heart of thousand maids, of thousand longing lovers?*
*So fleeteth in the fleeting of a day,*
*Of mortal life the green leaf and the flower,*
*And not, though Spring return to every bower,*
*Buds forth again soft leaf or blossom gay.*
*Gather the rose! beneath the beauteous morning*
*Of this bright day that soon will over-cast;*
*O gather the sweet rose, that yet doth last!*

TASSO

# The Men behind the New Roses

## NIGEL RABAN
*(Amateur rose grower)*

Over the last three years, the work of 17 international hybridists has been considered in this series, and now a final group of six is added, bringing the total to 23.

I have attempted to make a table showing where their main preoccupations lie. It is a one-horse race. Fourteen rank disease resistance as of outstanding importance. How far their efforts have been crowned with success is open to question. This (1973) has been a season of high disease incidence and the gaps in the Trial Ground beds have shown the weakness of many new varieties. On the other hand, the cleanliness of the RNRS display garden at St. Albans seems to show that sensible and regular attention, using the modern specifics, does give a high degree of protection against Black Spot, Rust and Powdery Mildew. The conclusion reached is that if gardeners will devote that little extra care which they are always prepared to give to other plants, such as tomatoes or chrysanthemums, then there is every chance that their roses will remain clean. Prevention, not cure, is the objective and is achieved by an early and carefully maintained spraying programme.

Of the other desirable qualities mentioned by the hybridists, I was surprised to find that scent comes very low in the list. Only three mentioned it as of outstanding importance, and Mr Swim emphasized that it was not something which he considered made a great difference to the success of a new cultivar. Fifteen or twenty years ago the verdict would probably have placed greater emphasis on fragrance, but nowadays when the majority of the best new roses are not only good to look upon but also delicious to smell, the occasional scentless variety does not attract much adverse comment.

Few of the breeders are looking for sensational new breaks. A number are working back on to the species in the search for hardiness and health. Sam McGredy has already achieved a break with his "hand-painted" strain, of which 'Picasso' is available and several more are to come. Poulsen is looking for plants which will give good ground cover and Delbard–Chabert are striving for flowers with hard petals to give long vase life. Incidentally, this has already come to us through Alec Cocker's 'Anne Cocker', which has quite remarkable staying powers as a cut flower.

There is a general consensus of aim for the low-growing floribunda and the floribunda with hybrid-tea type flowers, though this can hardly be described as a new development, 'Paddy McGredy' having been introduced as long ago as 1962.

Both colour and glasshouse roses have their devotees, mostly from Europe, and presumably it is climatic conditions that produce this trend. Classic form is really the preserve of the British, with Alex Dickson and Jim Sanday as the main supporters. Form can, of course, mean different things to different men and both Lens of Belgium and Swim of America stress its importance, though in their case they are referring to decorative roses of the type of 'Pascali' or 'First Love'. One oddity which was thrown up, was the desire by both Kordes and Delbard-Chabert to produce roses with fewer thorns. Had they just been having a bloody battle with the pruning of a large plant of 'Mermaid' when they wrote that?

It remains only for me to thank all the hybridists who have so kindly given their time in supplying particulars of their work by letter, tape recording or personal interview. Many have been badgered for special bits of information—all have responded with a will—and I would like to record my debt of gratitude for their help and patience.

All of us await their future exploits with eagerness and impatience. We owe them an immense debt for their work in making our rose gardens healthier, more colourful and more fragrant over the years.

## EUGENE BOERNER & Wm. WARRINER

No consideration of the work of Eugene Boerner and William Warriner would be complete without some mention of the firm of Jackson & Perkins Co. with whom the names of both men are closely connected.

The company was founded in 1872 by A. E. Jackson and Charles Perkins in Newark, N.Y. It remained a relatively small but successful company until 1939, when a modest stand was set up at the New York World's Fair, to take mail orders for rose plants. This promotion triggered off a remarkable economic growth in the company's business until today they market between four and five million rose trees annually. In 1952 the company moved to Arizona where it acquired about 360 acres. This was expanded in 1958 to 1,700 acres and then again by 1963 to a total of 5,000 acres. The world's largest rose ranch! In the last decade, the business has been transferred again to California. The rose research facilities are established in Tustin and the nursery is in Wasco, about 20 miles north-west of Bakersfield. All the packing and shipping is done from the company's plant in Medford, Oregon.

It was to this organization that Eugene Boerner came in 1920. He was born in 1893 in Cedarsburg, Wisconsin, and attended the University of Wisconsin during 1911–12, to study engineering. That this was not his bent in life was quickly discovered by the University, who curtly stated that his English was not up to standard and requested him to leave. He then entered the University of Illinois and after a short period as a pilot in the first world war, emerged with a B.Sc. in horticulture.

On joining Jackson & Perkins in 1920, he entered the research department and in 1927 became a part-owner of the company. Ten years later, following the death of the famous Dr J. H. Nicholas—after whom the rose 'The Doctor' was named—Boerner was made Director of Research.

Although he would have denied that he had a special liking for one type of rose over another, it was in the floribundas that he achieved his most remarkable successes and he became known in the U.S. as the "Father of the Floribunda". He particularly liked a strong-growing plant, throwing up a multitude of new shoots which allowed for free and continuous blooming, and he also strove in his crosses to pay especial attention to the quality of form, whether in the heavy, classic hybrid teas or in the much lighter-petalled floribundas.

During his years as a hybridist, he won no fewer than ten All-America Rose Selection Awards for floribunda introductions and a further two AARS awards for hybrid teas. These latter were his 'Katherine T. Marshall' (Unnamed Seedling × 'Chieftain') 1943 and 'Diamond Jubilee' ('Maréchal Niel' × 'Feu Pernet-Ducher') 1948.

As far as Great Britain is concerned, one of his most famous introductions was, 'Masquerade' ('Goldilocks' × 'Holiday') which won a Gold Medal at our Trial Grounds in 1952. It was runner-up for the President's International Trophy to 'Moulin Rouge', which has now disappeared from the catalogues and probably from the great majority of amateurs' gardens, whereas 'Masquerade' is still sold in its thousands and is to be seen everywhere. His other great success here was 'Fashion' ('Pinocchio' × 'Crimson Glory') which received a G.M. in 1948 and which also went on to win gold medals at Portland, Bagatelle and from the American Rose Society. This rose undoubtedly set the pattern for floribunda hybridization for the next ten years, and although in Europe its constitution has been considered suspect and it has also been found to be susceptible to disease under certain conditions, there can be no doubt that it was one of the great introductions of the period, both as regards its colour, which was a soft true salmon, and for its habit.

These two great roses were followed by a further series of successful floribundas in the 1950s which included 'Vogue' ('Pinocchio' × 'Crimson Glory'), 'Ma Perkins' ('Red Radiance' × 'Fashion'), 'Jiminy Cricket' ('Goldilocks' × 'Geranium Red'), 'Spartan' ('Geranium Red' × 'Fashion') and 'Ivory Fashion' ('Sonata' × 'Fashion'). Additionally, his 'Golden Fleece' ('Diamond Jubilee' × 'Yellow Sweetheart') won the gold medal at the Bagatelle in 1955.

Although the 1960s continued to produce for him considerable success in the field of international awards, few of the roses sent out had the impact on British rose gardens of the floribunda series of 1950–58. The one exception was 'Apricot Nectar', which carried off the AARS in 1966 and has proved internationally outstanding. It is the result of crossing an unnamed seedling with 'Spartan'. Mention should also be made of exhibition hybrid tea, 'John F. Kennedy' (Unnamed Seedling × 'White Queen'), introduced in 1965, which in many parts of the world has proved to be the standard white variety for exhibitors.

Mr Boerner remained throughout his life a bachelor, being entirely devoted to his work as a hybridist and to his large garden and farm on the banks of Seneca Lake in western New York State. He died in 1966 and under his will an endowment fund of $120,000 was set up to provide graduate fellowships on rose research at the New York State College of Agriculture, Cornell University. He was recognized during his lifetime as pre-eminent amongst American hybridists and received numerous awards for his work, including the Fuerstenberg Gold Medal, 1951, the Jackson Dawson Medal, 1956 and the Garden Clubs Gold Medal, 1962.

After his death, the directorship of research at Jackson & Perkins was taken over by William Warrriner. Mr Warriner had only started his studies at Michigan State University when the attack on Pearl Harbour brought America into the war and he joined up in the Marines. After the war he returned to Michigan and received his B.Sc. in floriculture in 1946. He moved to California a year later and started work with the Howard & Smith nursery where he began to concentrate on rose breeding under the direction of Fred Howard. In 1956 he went into business on his own account in Patterson, California, and continued with this until 1963 when he was appointed a director of plant research for Jackson & Perkins, assuming the entire responsibility for their research operations on Eugene Boerner's death.

His work in rose hybridization has not been restricted to any particular group, though he feels that his greatest interest lies in working with hybrid teas and floribundas rather than the shrubs and species. Of hybrid teas he prefers the decorative bloom to the large exhibitor's type, because he feels that these are of so much greater value and interest to the average home gardener. Of all the hybridizers who have been questioned for this series on the importance of various qualities in the rose, he is the only man who has given a table of values in a descending order of merit, and it is worth recording this list:

1. Freedom of Flower and Remontancy
2. Vigour
3. Colour
4. Habit of Growth
5. Form
6. Resistance to Disease
7. Resistance to Weather
8. Scent

He makes the qualification that a rose's worth is contingent upon a proper balance of all the elements in its make-up, and he emphasizes that a quality which he might place at the top of the list might prove relatively weak in a certain cultivar, but if other qualities were sufficiently strong, then these factors would more than compensate for the one deficiency.

His aim in hybridizing is to broaden the appeal of roses by producing varieties that are ever easier to grow and of which the flowering characteristics give them continually greater usefulness as garden plants. Brightness of colour is naturally an important part of this appeal and explains why it appears so high on his list of qualities.

The results of his own hybridizations are only now beginning to appear, but already he has won the Silver Medal at Bagatelle in 1972 with the H.T. 'Elation' ('Buccaneer' × Unnamed Seedling) and the American Rose of the Year Award for H.T. 'Golden Gate' ('South Seas' × 'King's Ransom') which also had a certificate at the Bagatelle. His H.T. 'Medallion' ('South Seas' × 'King's Ransom') had the AARS in 1973 with the Rose of the Year Award and the Portland Gold Medal. A number of other seedlings have received awards but have not yet been introduced on the market.

In assessing the work of Mr Boerner and his successor, regard must be had to the economic power and commercial standing of the great Jackson & Perkins Co. The resources thus made available to both men must have helped in the promotion of their extensive breeding programme. But having admitted this fact, it must be remembered that the choice of parents and the scientific elaboration of a long-term breeding plan comes back to a single human brain, and rosarians all over the world have good cause to be grateful for the work initiated and carried through for more than 45 years by Eugene Boerner.

## ALEC COCKER

One autumn evening in 1840 there was an argument between the head gardener at Castle Fraser near Kemnay in Aberdeenshire and the Laird. The difference of opinion was over the picking of fruit on a Sunday. The gardener, James Cocker, told the Laird that he would gather fruit on a Saturday night, no matter how late, but never on a Sunday. The two were unable to resolve their difference and as a result James Cocker left his employment and, coming to Aberdeen, started a nursery business at Sunnypark Nurseries in 1841.

He began by concentrating upon trees, shrubs and herbaceous plants with special attention to the pansy, which was a very popular flower at that time. The business prospered and James Cocker took his son, also James, into partnership with him and opened another nursery extending to 42 acres at Morningfield. This was found to be an excellent location for roses and the Cockers, father and son, won many show bench awards with their blooms.

After the death of the original James Cocker, his son, James, took his own sons, William, James and Alexander, into the business and the firm assumed the title, in 1882, of James Cocker and Sons.

Many years later, after the discovery of Mendel's papers, a series of experiments was carried out with primroses and polyanthuses which resulted in a whole new family of double primroses being raised and becoming known as the "Bonaccord" primroses—Bonaccord being the motto of the city of Aberdeen. For this achievement, the firm was awarded a Certificate of Appreciation by the Scientific Committee of the RHS and some of the primroses are still in existence and have become collectors' pieces.

In the same year, 1902, the new nurseries extending to 62 acres were opened at Springhill on the Lang Stracht. This move was made necessary because of the increasing amount of development at Morningfield, and in 1911 the Sunnypark nurseries had to be given up for the same reason.

In 1915, William Cocker died and the business was carried on by Alexander as sole proprietor until his death in 1920, when his son, Alec, was only 13 years of age. This meant that the business was in the hands of trustees until Alec came of age. On leaving school, he served his apprenticeship in general horticulture with a Scottish firm, but he feels that he probably learnt more running around the nursery with his father than at any time later.

Unfortunately, in 1931 he suffered a very severe setback in a motor-cycle accident in which his right leg was broken in seven places and this meant that he spent fifteen months in hospital and his leg was permanently damaged.

In common with most other horticultural nurseries, a mere nucleus of rose stock was kept during the war and all the emphasis was on growing vegetables. Alec married his wife, Anne, in 1952 and together they built up the business which had been largely in abeyance during the war years and it was at this point that they began total specialization in roses.

Another move had to be made in 1959, again because of building development and the farm of Whitemyres, extending to 70 acres, was purchased and modern offices, with packing shed and stores, erected. Three years later extensive glasshouses covering an area of 105 by 142 feet were put up to enable him to undertake hybridization in a serious way. It should, however, be stressed that this was not a new venture for the Cocker family, as away back in 1890 they had raised a pink Hybrid Perpetual rose called 'Mrs Cocker' which was awarded the NRS Gold Medal and later, in 1913, their 'Mrs Andrew Carnegie' ('Niphetos' × 'Frau Karl Druschki') also won a Gold Medal.

In the last decade the hybridizing work has grown to very large proportions. Alec Cocker now makes more than 12,000 crosses each year, producing anything up to 100,000 seeds for which he expects an 85 per cent germination. Each year some 1,500 seedlings are selected for budding on outside, after which comes the process of ruthless elimination of anything considered at all unworthy. To illustrate how ruthless this culling can be, he says that the 1,500 seedlings of the first year are usually reduced to 50 or 60 in the second.

Recently, much of his interest has been channelled towards the introduction of cut-flower varieties. To produce this type of rose is much more difficult than breeding roses for garden purposes. Equally the reward for a successful variety can be very gratifying.

As far as outdoor roses are concerned, Alec Cocker considers that the main quality for which he seeks is disease resistance, and to this end he is using as parents a number of shrubs and species, all of which have a known resistance to the common forms of fungus disease. A few years ago he had a seedling from 'Parkdirektor Riggers' × 'Piccadilly' which gave wonderfully clean foliage. He has worked a lot with this seedling as a male parent and the later generations, now appearing in many colours, seem to have inherited this healthy strain.

He is also making numerous crosses from a repeat-flowering seedling from 'Cläre Grammerstorf' × 'Frühlingsmorgen' and has many 'Picasso' type seedlings, with some showing more tendencies towards conventional hybrid tea style blooms. The introduction of 'Fragrant Cloud' into this strain has also given a seedling of notable scent which has a mixture of 'Fragrant Cloud' perfume and the lily-of-the-valley type of scent to be found

Eugene Boerner (*see page 65*)

Wm. Warriner (*see page 67*)

Alec Cocker (*see page* 69)

J. L. Harkness (*left*), with his son in the background (*see page* 74)

Douglas Gandy (*see page* 72)

Andries Verschuren (*on right*) with his son, Gerard (*see page* 78)

ROSE GARDEN DESIGN. I. For a long, narrow and enclosed garden (*see page* III)

in the *Spinosissimae*. Experiments are also being carried out with the true *Spinosissima* species—the original plants were dug up on the back road between Birkhall and Balmoral. *R. spinosissima* has about 90 per cent fertile pollen and is a regular tetraploid, which makes it quite adaptable for use with modern roses, but its non-recurrent flowering habit is a dominant feature so that to date successes have been few; but the lure of the hardiness of *R. spinosissima* draws him onwards. He has also been trying to breed a high degree of fragrance into his roses, but it is not an easy problem, especially in the case of the reds, where the majority of seedlings with a stiff flower stalk have no scent. From this he has drawn the conclusion that the genes responsible for the weak flower stalk are closely grouped with those which give the "damask" perfume so much sought after in red roses.

The work of the Cocker breeding establishment has been greatly facilitated by the special relationship with Jack Harkness' nursery far to the south in Hitchin. The two hybridizers exchange notes and information in the first instance and also test out each other's seedlings so that their reaction to varying climatic conditions can be ascertained.

Of the new roses to come from Whitemyres, undoubtedly 'Alec's Red' ('Fragrant Cloud' × 'Dame de Coeur') must take pride of place. It was awarded the Edland Memorial Medal for fragrance in 1969 and the President's International Trophy with Gold Medal in 1970. Another very successful introduction is the floribunda 'Anne Cocker' ('Highlight' × 'Colour Wonder') C. of M. 1969. This upright and vigorous light vermilion rose has remarkable lasting qualities as a cut flower and is one of the first of 'Colour Wonder's' progeny to come on the market. There are clearly many more of this type to follow from the trial beds in Aberdeen.

Alec confesses his own favourite to be 'Rob Roy' ('Evelyn Fison' × 'Wendy Cussons') which received a T.G.C. in 1969. The rose is named after that colourful Scotsman of the seventeenth century and its raiser was amused and delighted to receive a letter from his French agent which read:

"Dear Alec,
    To enable us to take out a trademark for your new rose 'Rob Roy' for France and Italy, we require the written permission of Mr Rob Roy"!

Another unusual floribunda is 'Pineapple Poll' ('Circus' × 'Orange Sensation') introduced in 1970. Although this did not gain an award at the Trial Grounds, it is proving a popular garden variety and is notable for its unusual scent, closely reminiscent of its name and, as far as one is aware, a new break in rose fragrance. 'Glengarry' ('Evelyn Fison' × 'Wendy Cussons'), a vermilion floribunda, received a C. of M. in 1968 and 'Cairngorm' ('Anne Cocker' ×'Arthur Bell') a T.G.C. in 1973. This latter rose is one of the first seedlings to come from 'Anne Cocker' which is now being used extensively in his breeding lines. Some of its progeny appear most suitable for the cut-flower market, with full, hybrid tea type blooms, the same crisp petals as the parent and equally long vase life.

In 1967 Alec Cocker was awarded the Scottish Horticultural Medal and in 1973 the Queen Mary Commemoration Medal by the RNRS for his work as a British hybridist.

He finds that his breeding work becomes ever more exciting as an increasing number of the parents he uses are seedlings of his own raising. Not the least of his pleasure lies in the fact that he is now being helped in crossing and budding by his son, Alexander James, the fifth generation of the family.

## DOUGLAS GANDY

Douglas Gandy of North Kilworth was born in 1908. His father had a large farm in the Kilworth area, but unfortunately tragedy struck the family when Douglas' mother died in 1915 at a time when his father was away serving in the first world war. The boy was sent to various relations with whom he spent his early years, and he recalls with somewhat wry amusement that, due to this fact, he attended no less than six different schools. After the war his father married again and young Douglas returned home to Kilworth, leaving school in 1922. At first he helped his father on the farm and had a personal interest in both cattle and pigs which he raised on his own account. Even at this early age he was determined to break out on his own, and as he had always had an interest in horticulture, he went for nearly four years to the South Kilworth nursery of Harris to learn the business. He actually started in a very small way on his own at the tender age of 17 by acquiring 500 understocks and budding them himself for resale.

In 1938 he procured for himself four acres in North Kilworth, land which is still in his possession though it has now grown to some 82 acres. Hardly before he could become established the second world war broke out, but he managed to keep a nucleus of rose stocks during the war years which proved to be very profitable to him when peace returned. In the 'forties and 'fifties, the nurseries underwent a very considerable expansion and today produce upwards of half a million rose bushes each year, with a large proportion being exported.

Due to this rapid expansion there was no time for Douglas Gandy to interest himself in hybridizing until a fairly late age, when he had sufficiently reliable assistants to help him in the nursery. He first started making crosses in quite a small way about 1964 but it was purely as a sideline and for his own interest. He says himself that he has never wanted his hybridizing programme to become too large or too extensive and he is interested in it only as long as he himself can look after it. Although he has all the professional knowledge and equipment, he speaks of himself, as a hybridist, as working in an amateurish way. The reason for this is quite clear. He is doing it for the love of the work itself, rather than for any commercial success which may attend it. For all this, he has never fallen into the trap which has caught many amateur hybridists—that of just "chucking pollen around", to use Sam McGredy's words. He has always worked with certain definite objectives in view: firstly, he believes that he must use for parents only varieties which have shown a marked resistance to disease, what he refers to as "clean" varieties, because he believes that the eradication of disease in modern roses is, or should be, the ultimate aim of every hybridist. He goes on to say that he feels that everything necessary has already been achieved in colour varieties, and that it is towards greater health that every breeder should direct his energies. Commenting upon the present fashion for low-growing floribundas of hybrid tea type, he considers that this should not be allowed to become preeminent and that it is necessary to maintain a balance of all types of roses. Fragrance, he maintains, is a highly desirable quality in any rose, but thinks that there is little that can be done by the hybridist to achieve it. In his opinion, the creation of strongly perfumed roses is entirely in the lap of nature, although he is experimenting with seedlings from 'Sterling Silver' × 'Wendy Cussons' in the hope of finding some highly fragrant new cultivars.

So far the ultimate prize of a Gold Medal has eluded him, but from the North Kilworth nurseries have come several interesting and attractive new varieties. His first success was with 'Telstar' ('Flash' × 'Masquerade') which received a Certificate of Merit in 1963. This is a typical 'Masquerade' seedling of orange and yellow, flushing scarlet as the blooms age. It was well received on the continent, being awarded a silver medal in Brussels.

Another floribunda which is proving very attractive to many rose growers is his 'Megiddo' ('Coup de Foudre' × 'S'Agaro') and awarded a T.G.C. in 1970. This is a brilliant scarlet, very eye-catching and decorative for bedding purposes. It is named after the ancient fortress town in Palestine where Mr Gandy was taken on a guided tour in the company of the Israeli Minister of Horticulture. Megiddo is also believed to be the site where the last battle will be fought.

In 1972, a TGC went to his new shrub, 'Martian Glow' ('Coup de Foudre'

× 'Joseph's Coat'). This carries semi-double red flowers and has a fine record of remontancy.

Other roses to come from Douglas Gandy's seedlings include the hybrid tea 'Jimmy Greaves' ('Dorothy Peach' × 'Prima Ballerina'), the floribunda 'Saul' ('Super Star' × Seedling) which is a tall, upright grower in magenta pink colour with strong scent, and two hybrid tea seedlings from 'Bettina' named 'Sir William Butlin' and 'Tyrius'.

This year he will be introducing a fine new floribunda which has been called 'Egyptian Treasure' [('Coup de Foudre' × 'S'Agaro') × 'Vagabonde'.] This was particularly well shown by him at the RNRS Autumn Show in 1973. The colour is Mars-orange, shown up by the bronze foliage; the flowers are semi-double and display a boss of golden stamens. It is officially a tall-growing floribunda, but could also be used as a shrub.

Lastly in the 1973 trials at St. Albans, Mr Gandy was awarded a T.G.C. for his yellow floribunda, 'Golden Shot'. This was actually raised by his son-in-law, John Martin, whilst the latter was working in the Gandy nurseries. Mr Martin has now emigrated to New Zealand, so the rose is officially credited to him, although it was bred and raised at North Kilworth. The parentage is Seedling × 'Allgold', but undoubtedly behind the unnamed seedling there is strong evidence of 'Leverkusen', a rose which Mr Gandy has been using extensively in his crosses, in his attempt to produce the main objective of his whole breeding programme, a yellow floribunda of outstandingly clean habit.

## J. L. HARKNESS

The Harkness firm was founded in 1879 in Bedale, Yorks, by two brothers, John and Robert. It started off as a general nursery and continued so for some sixteen years. Then, on the toss of a coin, it was decided that Robert Harkness should move to Hitchin, where he established himself in 1895 and started to specialize in rose growing.

Robert was succeeded in due time by his son William, one of the most famous rosarians of the years between the wars.

William died in 1959 and the firm is now run by his daughter, Isobel, and by the two grandsons of the original John Harkness, Jack and Peter.

During the first world war the firm fell upon difficult times.

Robert, then in charge, died and Willie was away serving his country in the Royal Tank Regiment. In 1918 not much was left and Willie took on the job of publican in Hexton, growing roses by day and pulling pints by night.

Jack, the subject of this article, was born in Shropshire in 1918 where his father was serving in the army.

Shortly afterwards the family moved to Croydon, where he was brought up and went to school which he hated, and with grim determination succeeded in failing every examination which he was made to take. As soon as he could manage to do so, he left school and in 1934 he went to the Slieve Donard nurseries as a result of the personal friendship between his father and Willie Slinger. He pays great tribute to the tuition that he received at Slieve Donard, and emphasizes that it was not a 9 to 5.30 job, but that he was expected to turn his hand to all sorts of work and, consequently, he came away in 1937 with a thoroughly sound knowledge of all the basic skills needed to run a horticultural nursery. He joined the Hitchin establishment, but hardly had time to integrate himself in its activities before the second world war broke out. He recalls that in 1939 he did start to make a few crosses in a lean-to glasshouse which had been built against the packing shed at Hitchin.

He joined the Hertfordshire Regiment and then after receiving a commission was posted to the Sherwood Foresters, but in 1941 went out to India, joining the 2nd Punjab Regiment. He saw service with the 5th Indian Division in North Africa, Iraq and Burma, where he experienced more than one hair-raising exploit, being one of the first officers to land by air on Meiktila airfield whilst it was still being attacked by enemy forces. On another occasion, he had the task of leading a party of walking wounded of which he was one, through the jungle and enemy lines back to a British base more than 20 miles away. He was demobilized in 1946 and immediately returned to the Harkness organization at Hitchin, but it was not until his cousin died that he started seriously to consider the possibilities of setting up a breeding establishment.

In the winter of 1961, a greenhouse was prepared and planted with the varieties upon which he had decided to work and in 1962 the first crosses were made. At this point a most remarkable partnership was born. Hundreds of miles to the north, in Aberdeen, Alec Cocker had also decided to enter the uncertain but exciting world of hybridization and the two men, feeling themselves to be beginners in the task, decided that the work would go forward more smoothly and swiftly if they pooled their knowledge and experience of success and failure alike and learned from these lessons. Jack Harkness says that he owes to Alec Cocker many of his techniques, particularly in the field of germination. Also the fact that seedlings from both houses are interchanged and completely tested upon each other's soils and climatic conditions has been of infinite advantage.

The first crosses made in 1962 were based upon five definite objectives:

the first was health, and to achieve this the seed parents used were such roses as 'Karl Herbst', 'Peace', 'Montezuma', 'La Jolla' and 'Rose Gaujard'. The second aim was to improve the floribundas then available and here the parents chosen were 'Iceberg', 'Orange Sensation' and 'Pink Parfait' amongst others. Thirdly, and perhaps most interesting of all at this date, he decided to go for neat, low-growing types coming from such varieties as 'Baby Faurax' and 'Baby Masquerade'. This was attempted at a time when hybridists had hardly begun to think of this type of rose which now, eleven years later, is becoming more and more popular. Fourthly, he wanted to see some new tall shrub roses for which he used 'Queen Elizabeth' and 'Buccaneer'. Lastly, to use his own words, he wished to 'have a ticket in the blue rose sweepstake' and for this he planted up 'Baby Faurax' and 'Lilac Charm'. In these early days he was fortunate in having as the head man in his greenhouses, Ernest Richards who had as a hobby, for many years, been a keen breeder of rabbits and who was meticulous in the keeping of records. Possibly it is from Mr Richards that the remarkable records maintained at Hitchin are due. Anyone who has the opportunity of seeing the exact notations made of every cross and every seedling, can only be astonished at the care and time devoted to this work. After only a few years, Ernest Richards died and was succeeded by Ted Deards, a different type of man but one who had a deep understanding and love of plants. All too soon ill health caused his retirement and death; but these two splendid men had in different ways taught much to a young man named Berkeley Bathurst, who is now in charge of the breeding houses.

The first crop of seedlings produced a few varieties which were considered good enough to be put into commerce and sent to the RNRS Trial Grounds. These became known as the Round Table group and amongst them 'King Arthur' ('Pink Parfait' × 'Highlight'), won a C. of M. in 1966 and 'Guinevere' ('Red Dandy' × 'Peace') and 'Sir Lancelot' ('Vera Dalton' × 'Woburn Abbey') were awarded T.G.C.s.

In 1967 he won a C. of M. for 'Escapade' ('Pink Parfait' × 'Baby Faurax') which has achieved a most remarkable success since its appearance on the Continent, where it has won Gold Medals in both West and East Germany, the first prize in Denmark, a Certificate in Orléans and the Golden Thorn at Belfast. For some reason it is a rose which has not been widely grown in this country; only those who have put it into their gardens know the remarkable quality of this cultivar in its cleanliness of habit, brightness and continuity of flower. 1967 also saw T.G.C.s to 'Merlin' ('Pink Parfait' × 'Circus') and 'Moonraker' ('Pink Parfait' × 'Highlight').

At this point, Jack Harkness realized that his early programme had produced about ten useful floribundas to every hybrid tea which he considered worth growing-on. Although this was something of a disappointment, he was pleased that it had produced for him strong lines which could be bred back on to the hybrid teas, and in 1969 he won a C. of M. for 'Elizabeth Harkness' ('Red Dandy' × 'Piccadilly') which was the first classic type of hybrid tea to be raised in the Hitchin nurseries. Elizabeth, Jack's daughter, was married last July and the writer had the privilege of seeing the great double line of maiden plants of her rose waiting to be cut to decorate the local church at her wedding. It was an unforgettable sight.

In the same year T.G.C.s were awarded to 'Busy Lizzie' ('Pink Parfait' × 'Masquerade'), 'Devotion' ('Orange Sensation' × 'Peace'), 'Lagoon' ('Lilac Charm' × 'Sterling Silver') and 'Lorna Doone' ('Red Dandy' × 'Lilli Marlene').

At one point a chance cross of 'Orangeade' and 'Lilac Charm', which one might have thought to be a most unlikely marriage, gave four seedlings, one of which was the variety 'Atlantis' which, in 1969, won the Gold Medal for small flowered seedlings in Rome.

The year 1970 saw the first of his low-growing compact floribundas, 'Kim' [('Orange Sensation' × 'Allgold') × 'Elizabeth of Glamis'] which gained a C. of M. T.G.C.s also went to his 'Colour Sergeant' ['Queen Elizabeth' × '(Ann Elizabeth' × 'Circus')], 'Grace Abounding' ('Pink Parfait' × 'Penelope'[1]) and 'Seven Seas' ('Lilac Charm' × 'Sterling Silver'), one of his series of "blue" roses.

The following year (1971), 'Southampton' appeared. This came from [('Ann Elizabeth' × 'Allgold') × 'Yellow Cushion'] and won a T.G.C., which it has followed up with a Silver Medal at Baden-Baden. Finally we come to his new hybrid tea 'Alexander' which is now available, having gained a C. of M. in 1972. The parents are ['Super Star' × ('Ann Elizabeth' × 'Allgold')] and its raiser thinks that it may well be the answer to finding a replacement to 'Super Star', which in so many places seems to have been losing its vigour in the last few years. At the same time he introduced a small floribunda of polyantha type called 'Yesterday', [('Phyllis Bide' × 'Shepherd's Delight') × 'Ballerina'], and he says that it is this cultivar which has given him more pleasure than anything else that he has raised as yet.

In talking to him about his thoughts on hybridizing in general, it immediately becomes clear that disease resistance is something which he regards as of prime importance and he maintains that any hybridist must be

[1] Mr. Harkness confirms that the pollen parent was 'Penelope' and not 'Circus' as shown in the records.

completely ruthless in rooting out any seedlings which do not show a marked resistance to the various fungus diseases. He feels that hybridizing falls into two sections: the business crosses and the pleasure crosses. In the first category he has undoubtedly already raised a number of highly successful cultivars, and those who have the chance of walking through his seedling trials will have realized that there are a number of most interesting crosses, which may in future generations produce something in the form of a new break to delight rosarians of the next decade. Although he realizes that as a hybridist straightforward crosses have to be done for purely commercial progress, his true interest is to break new ground, and he suggests experimenting with varieties like 'Mermaid' or 'Nevada' to achieve graceful plants which will also bear a full succession of beautiful flowers.

Since this article was completed Jack Harkness has been awarded the Queen Mary Commemoration Medal by the RNRS for his work as a British hybridist.

## ANDRIES VERSCHUREN

Like many other successful rose nurseries the Verschuren establishment at Haps in Holland had amateur beginnings. The originator of the firm, H. A. Verschuren, was born in 1846 and spent most of his working life as a school-teacher; but it was his hobby to grow, and experiment with the hybridization of roses and as has happened to many another rose enthusiast, the time spent on his hobby began to outstrip the time which he felt able to devote to his profession and his pupils. At last the Ministry of Education told him that he had to choose between school-mastering and rose-growing. His decision was instantaneous and thus were born the rose nurseries of Messrs Verschuren.

It was only at the end of his life that H. A. Verschuren produced a number of varieties which made a considerable impact upon the rose world. Holland during the first world war was neutral and, therefore, the work of crossing and growing could continue comparatively uninterrupted at Haps and when peace came there were a number of new varieties ready to go out on the market. Undoubtedly the outstanding seedling was his 'Etoile de Hollande' which, for many years, was the premier dark-red variety grown in gardens throughout the world and is still to be met with today in its climbing form. It was a seedling from 'General MacArthur' × 'Hadley' and was, at the time, a variety of quite outstanding merit.

H. A. Verschuren also wrote much on roses in a weekly gardening paper and produced a small book on the cultivation of his favourite flower, which was issued in 1888. He died in 1919 and was succeeded by his son, Andries, born in 1891 and still very active at the age of 82.

Andries started working with his father's roses when he was only 12 years old, after school hours and in the holidays and all his experience was gained in the nursery, as he did not go to university.

Although the Verschuren family have always carried out an active and extensive programme of hybridization, it has been their policy, in the majority of cases, to sell the varieties outright to other rose firms who then introduce them. Some years ago they became extremely interested in the commercial possibilities of hothouse cultivars, realizing that to improve the qualities of these roses carried with it the hope of most glittering prizes and, at the present time, one of the major objectives in their breeding programme is to work on roses for forcing under glass. Mr Verschuren points out that in this type of rose it is the colour, shape, number of petals and scent which are the most important qualities, whereas when he is looking for a garden rose, he gives priority to weather resistance and freedom from disease. He has also been making an extensive series of crosses in an attempt to achieve an improved 'Alain' [('Guinée' × 'Skyrocket') × 'Orange Triumph'] which was originally produced by Meilland in 1948 and which has been for many years an extremely popular crimson floribunda in Europe.

After the second world war, a number of Verschuren roses were introduced in the U.K. of which five are the most noteworthy. The first was 'Charles Gregory' (Parentage unknown) which won a C. of M. in 1947. This was a small decorative rose of outstanding colour, a mixture of velvety red and old gold and possessing very fine form in the young stage. Unfortunately it had a tendency to be slow in producing a second crop and therefore became superseded.

In the following year 'Lady Belper' ('Mev. G. A. van Rossem' × Seedling) was also awarded a C. of M. This was a fine bronzy orange hybrid tea with good scent and became a very popular bedding rose for a number of years. 'Verschuren's Pink' ('Mme Butterfly' × 'Pink Pearl') won an NRS Gold Medal in 1949. A high centred and fragrant salmon pink, it promised well but never gained the popularity that perhaps it deserved. Two other Verschuren introductions must be mentioned here, which were the result of a combined effort with Pechtold. 'Spek's Yellow' ('Golden Rapture' × Seedling) was sent to the Trial Grounds immediately after the war and was given a T.G.C. in 1947. It was very well received by the gardening public and was the outstanding yellow bedding rose of its time, despite its rather untidy upright growth. The flowers, which are small but of excellent form, retained their golden colouring to the end and it was probably used more than any other yellow rose of its time for the artistic classes and for general decorative purposes. The other introduction made in conjunction with Pechtold was also of small size and good form in an orange salmon colour. It was called 'Souvenir de Jacques Verschuren' ('Katharine Pechtold' × 'Orange Delight') and was awarded a C. of M. in 1951. Again, it was a rose which was highly suitable for the artistic classes but, unfortunately, its constitution proved to be suspect in this country and it had a susceptibility to Black Spot. Consequently it disappeared from the nurserymen's lists fairly quickly, but on its day it was a rose of great beauty and charm.

In recent years the Verschuren firm have not sent many of their introductions for trial to St. Albans and thus their varieties have not been as well known in this country as might have been expected; but when one is able to record that during the period 1960 to 1970 they introduced approximately fifty new cultivars, it gives some indication of the activity and extent of their work in the field of hybridizing. Many of their new seedlings were put on to the market in Holland by the firm of van Engelen of Hillegom, and in this country both Gregory's of Chilwell and Blaby's of Leicester have been responsible for bringing over Verschuren seedlings. Andries has now handed over the day-to-day management of the firm to his son Gerard, and it is to be hoped that a new generation of seedlings will find their way into the world's rose gardens and that we shall have the opportunity of trying them out in this country.

# Symposium on the Twelve Best Roses of Hybrid Tea Type for Garden Display

## LEONARD HOLLIS

(*Editor and amateur rose grower*)

In deciding to have a Symposium on this subject the Publications Committee had in mind that it is fourteen years since the previous Symposium appeared in *The Rose Annual* for 1960; in the interim there has been such a flood of new varieties that a consensus of opinions on the best of these should be both interesting and instructive.

A noticeable trend in recent years has been the crossing of the hybrid teas with the floribundas; this has resulted in many roses of intermediate type,

'Fragrant Cloud'

'Pink Favourite'

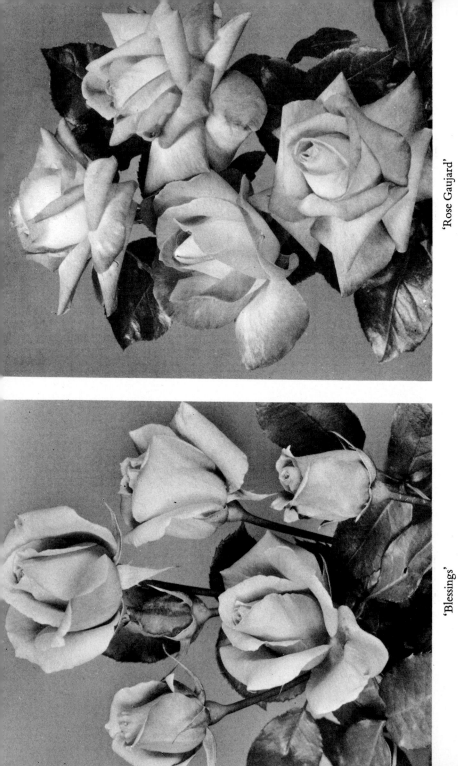

'Rose Gaujard'

'Blessings'

usually having smaller flowers than the hybrid teas but of better form than the floribundas. These have been saddled with the rather unwieldly appellation of floribundas, H.T. type. Some of them (e.g. 'Paddy McGredy') have flowers as large as those of many of the hybrid teas, and in some cases, it has not been possible to state categorically whether or not the variety is a hybrid tea or a floribunda H.T. type. Partly because of this complication and the likelihood that not all of our contributors would be of the same mind about the correct classification, it was made clear to them that floribundas of H.T. type were eligible for inclusion in addition to the more orthodox hybrid teas, if they were considered to be of sufficient merit.

Our contributors were asked to take into account only those qualities affecting garden display, i.e. freedom and continuity of flowering; a clear and well-defined colouring, free from objectionable colour clashes between the young and old flowers; the capacity to open freely during wet weather, and freedom from bleaching and burning in hot sunshine; freedom from disease; a vigorous and branching habit of growth, without a tendency to sprawl; attractive and abundant foliage; a well-poised flower, i.e. held firmly and erect on a strong stem, so that the bloom is displayed to the best advantage. A further important factor in garden display is that the petals are shed cleanly at the end of the effective life span of the flower and that they do not cling to the seed pod as ugly, mummified remains. Unfortunately, not many of the popular varieties shed their petals cleanly in this way.

It was emphasized that a tendency to produce split blooms (e.g. 'Peace' and 'Rose Gaujard') should not prejudice a variety which was otherwise well qualified, as this does not affect garden display as such, although it is frowned upon by the exhibitor of specimen blooms. Indeed, a variety of great freedom of flowering, but with a tendency to produce confused or split centres, will often be much superior for garden display to one of immaculate form, but more sparing with its blooms and perhaps requiring dry weather to open at all.

Fragrance as such, however desirable in itself, is a quality which does not contribute anything directly to garden display; it appeals to the nose rather than the eye and should have been disregarded, except perhaps in the case of two varieties of approximately equal merit for garden display, one of which is fragrant and the other virtually scentless. In such a hypothetical case the scented variety should be preferred, although it must be seldom that one finds the issue so clear cut. Nevertheless, I suspect that some of our contributors have allowed fragrance to influence them more than marginally in making their selections.

All of our twenty contributors are experienced rosarians; ten of them live in the Northern half of the country and ten in the Southern half, the dividing line running from the Wash to the Severn. Grouped accordingly and arranged in alphabetical order within each group they are: *Northern half*: Dr A. Dick, Clarkston, Glasgow; F. A. Gibson, Formby, Lancs; Mrs Maureen Iddon, Hesketh Bank, Nr Preston, Lancs; J. Roscoe, Formby, Lancs; E. Shreeves, Swanland, East Yorks; R. D. Squires, Liverpool; Mrs Doreen Thorn, Craven Arms, Salop; S. G. Thomson, Leeds; Dr J. T. Watts, Conway, N. Wales; R. S. Woolley, Newcastle upon Tyne. *Southern half*: E. F. Allen, Nr Ipswich, Suffolk; L. A. Anstiss, West Wellow, Hants; R. C. Balfour, Nr Chelmsford, Essex; F. M. Bowen, Nr Stroud, Glos.; F. Fairbrother, Taunton, Som.; Miss J. E. Fulford, Bideford, North Devon; S. M. Gault, Barnet, Herts; W. A. James, Salisbury, Wilts; R. L. Pallett, Seaford, Sussex; H. N. Raban, Olveston, Nr Bristol.

Unlike the voting for *The Rose Analysis*, it has not been possible to use a system of scoring which takes into account the position in order of merit as well as points for a mention, as our contributors were not asked to place their selection in order of merit. A point was scored for each time a contributor mentioned a variety in his best dozen. The overall result covering the twenty contributors, is set out below:

| | | | Votes |
|---|---|---|---|
| | 1. | { Ernest H. Morse | 13 |
| | | { Pink Favourite | 13 |
| | 3. | Fragrant Cloud | 12 |
| | | { Peace (incl. Chicago Peace) | 11 |
| Elected | 4. | { Piccadilly | 11 |
| | | { Wendy Cussons | 11 |
| | 7. | Grandpa Dickson | 10 |
| | 8. | Mischief | 8 |
| | 9. | { Prima Ballerina | 7 |
| | | { Rose Gaujard | 7 |
| | | { Alec's Red | 6 |
| | 11. | { Blessings | 6 |
| | | { Duke of Windsor | 6 |
| | | { Diorama | 5 |
| | | { Mullard Jubilee | 5 |
| Not elected | 14. | { Pascali | 5 |
| | | { Super Star | 5 |
| | | { Whisky Mac | 5 |
| | | { National Trust | 4 |
| | | { Peer Gynt | 4 |
| | 19. | { Pink Parfait | 4 |
| | | { Queen Elizabeth | 4 |
| | | { Rob Roy | 4 |

In addition, 'Summer Holiday' scored three votes; eleven varieties scored two votes each and a further forty-nine were mentioned by a single contributor. The thirteen elected varieties scored just over 50 per cent of the total number of points; the remaining 49½ per cent covered the seventy-one other varieties which were mentioned by one or more of our contributors. Seven of the successful varieties were chosen by ten or more contributors.

One of the intentions behind the Symposium was to ascertain the extent to which there was a bias towards certain varieties in the North or the South respectively. With this in mind a breakdown of the overall results between North and South showed the following results:

| North | Votes | South | Votes | Total | Votes |
|---|---|---|---|---|---|
| 1. Pink Favourite | 7 | 1. Fragrant Cloud | 9 | 1. ⎰ Ernest H. Morse | 13 |
| 2. ⎰ Grandpa Dickson | 6 | 2. ⎰ Ernest H. Morse | 8 | ⎱ Pink Favourite | 13 |
| ⎱ Wendy Cussons | 6 | ⎱ Peace (& Chicago Peace) | 8 | 3. Fragrant Cloud | 12 |
| 4. ⎰ Ernest H. Morse | 5 | 4. ⎰ Piccadilly | 6 | 4. ⎰ Peace (& C. Peace) | 11 |
| ⎱ Piccadilly | 5 | ⎱ Pink Favourite | 6 | ⎱ Piccadilly | 11 |
| 6. ⎰ Mischief | 4 | ⎰ Blessings | 5 | ⎱ Wendy Cussons | 11 |
| ⎱ Whisky Mac | 4 | 6. ⎰ Rose Gaujard | 5 | 7. Grandpa Dickson | 10 |
| ⎰ Duke of Windsor | 3 | ⎱ Wendy Cussons | 5 | 8. Mischief | 8 |
| ⎱ Fragrant Cloud | 3 | ⎰ Alec's Red | 4 | 9. ⎰ Prima Ballerina | 7 |
| National Trust | 3 | Diorama | 4 | ⎱ Rose Gaujard | 7 |
| 8. ⎰ Pascali | 3 | 9. ⎰ Grandpa Dickson | 4 | ⎰ Alec's Red | 6 |
| Peace | 3 | Mischief | 4 | 11. ⎰ Blessings | 6 |
| Prima Ballerina | 3 | Mullard Jubilee | 4 | ⎱ Duke of Windsor | 6 |
| Queen Elizabeth | 3 | ⎱ Prima Ballerina | 4 | | |
| ⎱ Rob Roy | 3 | | | | |

One of the most striking differences between North and South is in relation to 'Fragrant Cloud', which secured nine out of ten Southern votes, but only three from the North. On its performance in my own (Surrey) garden—and I have persisted with fresh plants every year without any improvement—I am rather surprised at its inclusion and can only conclude that it does much better elsewhere. I suspect that some of my Southern friends have allowed its undoubtedly glorious fragrance to sway them in its favour and to overlook some of its shortcomings for garden display. 'Ernest H. Morse', 'Peace', 'Blessings', 'Rose Gaujard', 'Diorama' and 'Mullard Jubilee' seem more highly thought of in the South than in the North. On the other hand, 'Whisky Mac', 'National Trust', 'Queen Elizabeth' and 'Rob Roy' are favoured by Northern contributors, whereas they receive little support in the South. In the case of 'Whisky Mac' this is particularly interesting as, in my experience, the wood of this lovely rose is not as hardy as one would like in severe weather and I find one usually has to cut away a lot of dead wood at pruning time.

There are no great surprises in the overall results. If one compares the elected thirteen with the *Rose Analysis* tables for Hybrid Tea Roses for General Garden Cultivation (North and South combined) in the 1973 *Rose Annual* and allows for 'Alec's Red' being in the separate table of newer hybrid teas, the only notable omission is 'Super Star', which occupied fifth place in the *Rose Analysis* tables. It is, though, an unhappy fact that this rose has become increasingly prone to powdery mildew in recent seasons, and the time lag of a further season has served to emphasize the decline of this variety.

Dealing in detail with the elected varieties, the relevant comments of our contributors are also given after a detailed description:

**Ernest H. Morse (13 votes).** Kordes, 1965. Parentage unknown. Gold Medal, 1965. The generally accepted description is rich turkey red, although *Mr Shreeves* calls it bright scarlet and *Mr Roscoe* prefers crimson ("the finest crimson introduced since 'Crimson Glory' "). Several contributors consider it the best red since 'Ena Harkness', but of more upright growth, with a strong pedicel holding the bloom erect. *Mr Fairbrother* finds it a tall, upright grower, with a plentiful supply of rather small, dark green foliage. *Mr Raban* considers it has a splendid habit of growth for a bedder and finds it highly resistant to disease, an experience which I share. All are agreed about its delicious fragrance. In my garden there is a little "blueing" in the later stages and it opens very quickly in warm weather, although it is first class in the rain. Two contributors still prefer 'Ena Harkness', although for garden display the modesty of "Ena" in hanging her head is a fault not found in the newer variety.

**Pink Favourite (13 votes).** Von Abrams, 1956. 'Juno' × ('Georg Arends' × 'New Dawn'). Portland Gold Medal (U.S.A.) 1957. Deep rose pink, often deeper on the reverse of the outside petals. The flowers are large, full and of shapely form, making it a great favourite for exhibition as well as for garden display. There is virtually no fragrance. The flowers are borne freely on strong stems—*Mr Raban* mentions that it must be disbudded to achieve quality. He also calls attention, along with *Mr Gault*, to a rather long gap between first and second crops. *Mr Gault* also points out that it comes into flower slightly later than most. It makes a fine plant with outstanding glossy foliage, with distinctive oval leaflets, and is very disease-resistant, although not immune to Black Spot and powdery mildew. Most of our contributors mention its wonderful foliage. As *Mr Thomson* puts it, "Though a wonderful show cultivar, it is an equally fine bedder, and what rose can boast of better foliage and clarity of colour?" *Dr Watts'* remarks must be echoed by countless growers in pure air districts: "If there were no other reason I must include this variety as it is the only one I have grown which has been free from disease all year, every year. The quality of flower is endorsed by the number of times it has obtained the Best Bloom in Show award." *Mr Allen* refers to it as always reliable if lightly pruned. Both he and *Mr Bowen* bracket it with 'Honey Favourite', which is identical in growth and foliage, but the blooms are a yellowish pink, with a yellow base. This is an excellent sport in a softer shade and one which can be thoroughly recommended. Although given in *Modern Roses 7* as 'Pink Favourite' × unknown, the fact that an occasional petal or part of a petal will revert to 'Pink Favourite' shade of rose pink satisfies me that it is a sport and not a seedling. Not one of our contributors mentions specifically its ability to withstand rain; in my own experience it can look unhappy during prolonged wet spells, although it is able to cope with moderate rain.

**Fragrant Cloud (12 votes).** Tantau, 1964. Seedling × 'Prima Ballerina'. Gold Medal, 1963. President's International Trophy, 1964. Generally described as geranium lake or geranium red, although the colour varies somewhat according to weather conditions. It can look very dull or be a vivid dark vermilion, but it does "blue" badly in the old flowers which may fade to an ugly mauve. *Mr Thomson* describes it as flame-coloured, while *Mr Pallett* approves of its dusky scarlet young blooms. *Mr James* rightly points out that it needs dead-heading more than most to keep the bed looking nice. *Mr Raban* mentions that it needs disbudding to achieve best blooms. I have seen it very rough indeed early in the season, but the later flowers are much better. Growth is vigorous and branching, with plenty of large, glossy, dark green foliage. I have always found it very susceptible to Black Spot in my garden, and perhaps because of the debilitating effects of this disease, I have yet to find a source of plants which will really thrive, although I have had it ever since its introduction. In fact, all the other selected varieties do much better than 'Fragrant Cloud' in my garden. Late in the season it tends to throw up shoots bearing "candelabras" of flowers. The fragrance is, of course, superb, although this is not, strictly speaking, a garden display quality. I cannot help wondering how many of our contributors would have voted for this variety if it had been no more scented than 'Pink Favourite'?

**Peace (11 votes).** Meilland, 1942. 'Joanna Hill', 'Charles P. Kilham', 'Margaret McGredy' and *R. foetida bicolor* appear in its pedigree. Gold Medal, 1947. Its sport, 'Chicago Peace' was introduced in 1962 and is a richer blend of colours than the parent, which is usually pale yellow, edged cerise in the bud, with the yellow becoming suffused with soft pink as the flowers age.

They are very large and full, opening wide with slightly frilled petals, resembling peonies. *Mr Thomson* rightly calls it the Queen of roses, and notes that its growth and trouble-free foliage form a perfect background for the smaller cultivars. The early display is sometimes affected by blind shoots, as several of our contributors point out. Growth is magnificent and wide planting and light pruning are generally advocated to see it at its best. It will then make specimens six feet or more high and broad in proportion, as *Dr Watts* has noted. *Mr James* feels that to get the best from 'Peace' requires young trees. I can only say that I can always rely on a magnificent display from fifteen-year-old specimens, some of which were budded by me on Multiflora and others on seedling briar. *Mr Raban* remarks how good it is at the blown stage, when so many of our roses are distinctly shabby. For health, I would rate it very highly, although it can get Black Spot. *Mr Allen* finds that it never needs spraying. For such a large rose it is quite good in wet weather, although in prolonged rain some of the flowers may ball. There is little fragrance.

**Piccadilly (11 votes).** McGredy, 1959. 'McGredy's Yellow' × 'Karl Herbst'. Certificate of Merit, 1959. The inner face of the petals is scarlet, shading off to buttercup yellow towards the base. The reverse is pale buttercup yellow. In the autumn and under certain conditions the colours may be paler. The flowers are shapely at first, but being of only moderate petalage they open quickly and have only a slight fragrance. Growth is vigorous and upright, rather thorny, with beautiful, glossy, bronze-tinted dark green foliage. It is quick to repeat, opens freely in wet weather and is excellent in the autumn. *Mr Raban* and *Mr James* recommend that it be planted rather closer than usual. *Mr Gault* finds it very free flowering over a long period, while *Mr Balfour* describes it as a bicolour of clear colours, strong and healthy. *Mr Shreeves* feels that it is still the best bicolour, attractive in all its stages, with the foliage and habit of growth leaving nothing to be desired; *Mr Raban* finds that it needs watching for Black Spot and I share his experience. *Mrs Iddon* describes it as a very gay rose, good in all weathers, with lovely bronze foliage turning to dark green. She never disbuds it as she likes to see the large heads of blooms *en masse*. There are several excellent sports from 'Piccadilly', similar to the parent except for the colour. 'Super Sun', a blend of orange and yellow and 'Mellow Yellow', a blend of pink and yellow, both received Trial Ground Certificates. Along with 'Harry Wheatcroft', with blooms striped in scarlet and yellow, they make good companions to the parent.

**Wendy Cussons (11 votes).** Gregory, 1959. 'Independence' × 'Eden rose'. Gold Medal and President's International Trophy, 1959. Cerise, flushed scarlet. The colour varies somewhat on different soils and according to the weather. Some of our contributors describe it as carmine, and it is not an easy colour to fit into a mixed collection. The flowers are large, beautifully formed and exceptionally fragrant, and stand wet weather remarkably well. They are produced with great freedom and, for a rose of this quality, it is quick to repeat. *Mr James* finds it does extraordinarily well on his chalk soil. The habit of growth is strong and branching—*Mr James* describes it as spreading—with numerous stout, thorny stems and dense, dark green glossy foliage, reddish purple in the early stages. *Mr Pallett* notes that it is seldom out of bloom during the season. *Mr Gault* considers it outstanding in growth, producing its large, exhibition-type flowers freely over a long season. *Mr Shreeves* thinks it vigorous, without being too tall and generally a trouble-free rose. *Mr Raban* points out that the later flowers tend to be insignificant in his garden and, along with *Mr Fairbrother* and several others, refers to its susceptibility to Black Spot. In my garden it is nothing like as susceptible to this disease as 'Fragrant Cloud', 'Grandpa Dickson' or 'Piccadilly'.

**Grandpa Dickson (10 votes).** Dickson, 1966. ('Perfecta' × 'Governador Braga da Cruz') × 'Piccadilly'. Gold Medal and President's International Trophy, 1965. Light yellow fading to creamy yellow, edged pink with age. *Mr Woolley*, *Mr Roscoe* and *Mr Fairbrother* describe it as lemon yellow, while *Mr Gault* has pale creamy yellow. The blooms are large and shapely, full-petalled, produced freely early in the season—it is one of the first to come into flower—and resistant to rain. They are carried upright on long, strong stems and there is a fairly quick repeat flowering. Growth is very upright and close planting is necessary on this account, as several of our contributors point out. *Mr Raban* finds it makes only a small bush. The glossy, dark green foliage makes an effective background for the pale blooms, which have little or no fragrance. *Mr Fairbrother* finds that it needs spraying against Black Spot and his experience tallies with mine. *Mr Raban* considers the foliage is poor, but despite this he still feels it is the best yellow rose. *Mrs Thorn*'s plants have flowered continuously from the beginning of July (she lives in a cold, late area) to the time of writing in mid-September. *Mrs Iddon* describes it as a truly wonderful garden rose, very free flowering, first into flower and still repeating well into November until the frosts halt it.

**Mischief (8 votes).** McGredy, 1960. 'Peace' × 'Spartan'. Gold Medal and President's International Trophy, 1961. Coral salmon, paling as the flowers age. The blooms vary somewhat in colouring, with the autumn crop normally really intense. *Mr Shreeves* describes it as a salmon pink, but I hardly think he would quarrel with coral salmon. The flowers are of medium size, normally exquisitely formed and sweetly fragrant. I have known seasons when the earliest flowers have come malformed, possibly because of late frosts. *Mr James'* comment is appropriate: "What a lovely spiral twirl this rose gives to its beautiful coral salmon-petalled blooms—seen *en masse* it is a lovely sight." It is remarkably free flowering and quick to repeat in all weathers, as *Mr Thomson* points out. It is excellent for cutting, too. *Mr Squires* awards it first place in his selection because it has repeatedly fulfilled all of his requirements over a number of years and is still improving with age. *Mr Gault* finds it a good grower, very free flowering over a long season and very resistant to bad weather. The habit of growth is vigorous and branching, clothed to ground level with abundant, light green, semi-glossy foliage. *Mr Raban* considers it has a very good habit and reasonable disease resistance. While it does not suffer much from Black Spot or powdery mildew in my garden, it had a severe attack of Rust some years ago and I had to burn the plants. My new stock of plants has not been attacked since it was planted four or five years ago and does splendidly. I feel that susceptibility to Rust has been inherited from the pollen parent, but it is such a lovely rose that it is worth going to some trouble to protect it from this disease.

**Prima Ballerina** (7 votes). Tantau, 1958. Unknown seedling × 'Peace'. Trial Ground Certificate, 1957. Deep, rich pink. The young flowers have long, elegant, shell-shaped petals, forming a most pleasing high-pointed bloom, opening rather quickly in warm weather. The fragrance is outstandingly rich and penetrating. Growth is very vigorous, tall and upright— perhaps rather too tall and upright to be ideal for bedding, as it makes a specimen over five feet tall in my garden. *Dr Dick* suggests that it is the most reliable pink rose grown today and it is quick to repeat. There is some difference of opinion about its rain-resistant qualities. *Mr Gault* describes it as resistant to rain, whereas *Mr Allen* feels it would have had a higher place had it been more rain resistant. The fact that *Dr Dick* places it among his top three, despite his stated insistence on weather resistance, indicates that he finds it good in wet weather in the West of Scotland, whereas in my own garden I find that some of the flowers will ball in the rain, while others will stain and mottle badly, despite the fact that it is not as full a bloom as some in the list. There is general agreement that the abundant, large, dark foliage is outstanding. *Mr Woolley* refers to it as gorgeously clothed with large, dark green leaves. *Mr Allen* calls attention to its wonderful foliage. *Mr Pallett* describes the foliage as an attractive dark green. *Dr Watts* notes that the reddish purple colour of the young growth seems to persist in the old foliage, though suffused with dark green and I think he is an accurate observer. Certainly there is always a purplish tinge as it grows in my garden. While not prone to Black Spot it will contract the disease, and I have seen plants quite smothered in Rust on a nursery, although it has never been infected in my garden.

**Rose Gaujard (7 votes).** Gaujard, 1958. 'Peace' × 'Opera' seedling. Gold Medal, 1959. The colouring is most difficult to define and seems to vary on different soils and between summer and autumn crops. The official description is white, flushed pale pink, edged and veined carmine, with a silver reverse. *Mr Fairbrother*'s assessment is cherry red with pale pink reverse. *Mr Shreeves* goes for white, heavily marked carmine, while *Dr Watts* only commits himself to white flushed with red, at the same time indicating that the amount of the red and its shade is variable. In my garden, except in the autumn, there is more carmine-red than white in the flowers and *Mr James* finds that the effect in the autumn is much more refined. *Mr Fairbrother* considers the flowers very attractive in the garden when fully open. Several contributors refer to the tendency of many of the flowers to develop with split centres, although this does not affect their merit for garden display. They are large, full and have some fragrance and are carried erect on long, strong stems. I have always found it remarkably free flowering and *Mr Pallett* refers to the blooms as being freely and regularly produced, which *Mr Raban*, *Mr Bowen* and *Mr James* confirm. It is more tolerant to rain than most, although a proportion of the flowers will ball in prolonged wet spells. Growth is exceptionally vigorous, tall and branching, abundantly clothed with large, glossy, dark green, leathery foliage. *Mr James* regards it as the healthiest of them all—vigorous, with magnificent luxuriant foliage. *Mr Bowen* finds it utterly reliable on all counts; *Mr Shreeves* quite frankly describes it as trouble-free and gives this as his main reason for selecting it. *Dr Watts* considers that the dark green foliage on stems holding individual blooms of red and white at medium height gives the variety great charm.

**Alec's Red (6 votes).** Cocker, 1970. 'Fragrant Cloud' × 'Dame de Coeur'. Gold Medal and President's International Trophy, 1970. Henry Edland Memorial Medal, 1969. The official description is cherry red, although this may not convey the exact shade of red to the amateur who has not grown it. *Mr James* describes it as crimson, and I think that light crimson, slightly paler on the reverse, is as near as one is likely to get. It is not a scarlet-crimson and may tend to look somewhat sombre in comparison with, say, 'National Trust'. The flowers are large, full-petalled and globular and are carried both singly and several together. They are sweetly fragrant and produced freely in all weathers over a long period. Growth is strong and bushy, rather upright, of medium height and furnished with abundant matt, green foliage right down to the base. It has given me no trouble at all with disease in the three years that I have had it my garden. *Mr James* describes it as an outstanding bedding rose with a generous offering of nicely spaced, large crimson, globular and fragrant blooms. He further points out that the generous foliage to the very base of the stems gives a ground cover that a good bedder needs. For so full a bloom it stands up to rain very well. It is an outstanding achievement for so recent an introduction to find a place in the best dozen and it should rise even higher as it becomes better known.

**Blessings (6 votes).** Gregory, 1968. 'Queen Elizabeth' × unnamed seedling. Certificate of Merit, 1968. Soft coral pink. At the buttonhole stage it is delightful, with slender buds, opening rather quickly to large-petalled, moderately full flowers which still look attractive when wide open. There is a definite fragrance, although this is not very strong. *Mr Balfour* writes: "For me the outstanding rose in this category, very seldom out of bloom over a long season, beautiful in colour and form and disease-free." Growth is vigorous, bushy and branching with matt, medium green foliage. *Mr Pallett* notes that the flowers are carried well on a healthy upright bush. *Mr Allen* is a little surprised that it is so high in his pointings, but he recognizes that it is splendid for display. *Mr Gault* regards it as a "must" for garden display and approves of its good habit. He mentions that the beds of this variety in Queen Mary's Garden, Regent's Park and at Bone Hill are unsurpassed by any other. *Mr Fairbrother* refers to the high yield per tree of well-formed blooms. The flowers stand up to rain very well in my experience.

**Duke of Windsor (6 votes).** Tantau, 1968. 'Prima Ballerina' × unnamed seedling. Henry Edland Memorial Medal and Certificate of Merit, 1968. Intense orange-vermilion. The flowers are full, of medium size, shapely at first but opening rather quickly. The fragrance is pronounced. *Mr Woolley* finds that it flowers generously. *Mr Squires* considers it the best of the pure vermilion range, while *Mrs Thorn* confirms that it has given an excellent display. *Mr Fairbrother* finds that it bears many blooms, so I must be giving it the wrong treatment, as I find it stingy with its flowers and with a long interval between crops. The blooms suffer from petal damage in wet weather. Growth is short, bushy and compact, with large, dark green, leathery foliage which is somewhat addicted to mildew. *Mr Allen* likes the colour and the dwarf habit and describes the foliage as splendid.

Of the thirteen varieties which were successful the oldest by far is 'Peace' 1942), although it was not until 1947 that it reached this country. The latest is 'Alec's Red' (1970), with 'Peace' in the pedigree of both its parents. The thirteen include eight Gold Medal winners of the RNRS (of which five were awarded the President's International Trophy as the best seedling of its year), three Certificate of Merit winners and one Trial Ground Certificate winner. These also include two holders of the Henry Edland Memorial Medal for fragrance. There is not the slightest doubt that if the President's International Trophy had been offered for the best seedling as long ago as 1947, 'Peace' would have won it. It is the only variety which was also successful in the 1960 Symposium. Of some significance, too, is the fact that, of the twelve other successful varieties in the present exercise, the parentage of 'Ernest H. Morse' is unknown, but nine out of the remaining eleven have 'Peace' in their pedigree. What a tribute to this remarkable rose!

The only successful rose without an award of the RNRS to its credit is 'Pink Favourite' which, however, won the Portland Gold Medal (U.S.A.) in 1957. The raisers of the elected thirteen are Tantau (three), Gregory and McGredy (two each), with Kordes, Von Abrams, Meilland, Dickson, Gaujard and Cocker each contributing one.

# Thoughts and Observations on Black Spot

## C. H. WARNER

(*Amateur rose grower and breeder*)

To most rose growers Mildew is the disease which, on its appearance, causes that sinking sensation, but to those of us living in the south-west, the first sight of Black Spot engenders an even greater sense of foreboding. We know that its appearance means subsequent defoliation, and with defoliation, barren ugly bushes and a considerable span of time before any more flowers appear—if at all.

I have been growing roses and reading about them, avidly, for ten years, and during that time several statements on Black Spot that I have read have stayed with me, namely:

1. The disease is a fungus and it will over-winter on plants already infected.

2. The disease is very prevalent in some parts, particularly the south-west, because of the humid weather conditions.

3. The disease is more severe in wet weather (rose research at Bath University—*Rose Annual* 1968).

4. Herr Kordes has said, I believe, that the disease is spread by rainfall.

5. The disease can be transmitted from one variety to another.

6. When spraying against Black Spot care should be taken to spray from the underside of the leaves, upwards, as the disease spreads from the underside of the leaves.

7. The disease starts at the base of the plant and works its way upwards.

8. Black Spot does not attack young leaves.

9. The fungus needs a temperature of 70° F. for it to become active.

My observations are that certainly the disease must over-winter. Here in the south-west on a few very susceptible varieties it has made its appearance before the end of May—'Heidelberg', 'Fragrant Cloud', 'Gloire de Dijon' and 'Mischief' spring to mind. I have read nothing conclusive on how or where the fungus over-winters, but presumably it adheres to all parts of the rose bush and, as in this part of the country leaves frequently remain on the bush until it is pruned, it is reasonable to assume that considerable quantities of the fungus remain an influence on the following season. I used to be an advocate of very light pruning as I believe that, provided the bush is adequately fed, the bigger the bush the more flowers you get. I still believe this to be true, but I pruned very hard last year in an effort to clear out some of the fungus, and I have noticed a definite improvement in some varieties, with the disease appearing much later than usual. I would add that last year was the first that I have not used either Jeyes Fluid or Bordeaux mixture as a winter spray, as there was no evidence of any benefit.

Black Spot is reputed to be very prevalent in some parts because of humid conditions and more severe in wet weather. Dr Lyle from Texas, addressing the 1968 Rose Conference, said that if Black Spot spores are in water for 24 hours they will germinate and that an atmosphere of less than 90 per cent relative humidity will not cause those spores to germinate. In other words, the wetter, the damper, the milder the conditions, the more active one can expect Black Spot to be. My observations are that exactly the opposite is the case. Of late we have had, by our English standards, a succession of dry summers. This has resulted in long periods of near-drought conditions when roses, unless watered, appear virtually to stop growing. It is in these conditions that Black Spot is rife, and bushes defoliate at an alarming rate. This observation is supported by local rosarians who say that in the last wet summer (1968) there was far less Black Spot than usual. The observation is also supported by articles in the *Rose Annual* by Roy Hay and Peter Beales, who had used overhead watering at frequent intervals on their garden and nursery roses, respectively. Their original intentions were nothing to do with Black

Spot control, but in fact the frequent overhead watering, I believe, kept the disease completely at bay.

It certainly appears that once one variety has become infected, the chances of other varieties in close proximity getting the disease are noticeably increased. But on the other hand, it is clear that in a large bed of mixed varieties the infection spreads not necessarily to the adjacent variety, but isolated outbreaks can occur at various points in the bed. I wonder why?

I would agree that usually Black Spot starts at the base of the plant and works its way upwards. But this is far from being invariably the case. Frequently climbers become infected at varying parts of their growth. This presumably is as a result of spores being located on the object against which the climber is supported. I have also noticed infection beginning on the upper leaves of a bush rose, usually when it has been within reach of a climber. I have only once noticed Black Spot start its appearance on the underside of a leaf. This was after a strong wind, and presumably the leaf had been blown upside down and had got caught on a thorn of its own stem, with the result that the undersurface was facing the sky. I did not notice this occurrence until the unmistakable spots appeared. I would like to repeat that this is the only time that I have seen Black Spot attacking the underside of the leaf first. I think this leads to an assumption of which I should like to say more later.

The fungus is reputed not to attack the leaflets of young foliage. Again, quite definitely this is not so. During very dry conditions, I have seen it not only attack the leaflets of young foliage, but in fact cause defoliation.

Finally, Black Spot is supposed to become active only when a temperature of 70° F is reached. I can only say that this is absolutely untrue. I have observed Black Spot actively spreading during the months of May and October, when the thermometer in the greenhouse read a bare 60° F., with the outside temperature obviously a few degrees below that.

Perhaps at this stage I ought to mention how I attempt to combat the dreaded disease. First of all, after this year's experience I shall continue to prune the bushes fairly hard. In March or April I apply a 3 to 6 in. dressing of cow manure all round the bushes, thus providing a mulch. (I have also added extra Sulphate of Potash during spring and late summer of some years with no noticeable benefit.) I start fungicidal spraying usually during May and continue at three-weekly intervals. I know that I should spray more frequently, but spraying all my roses takes at least two hours and I find it very difficult in a crowded life to find two clear hours. In addition to this, I must admit that spraying is a job I dislike and I tend to put it off as long as possible. I always add a foliar feed to my spray and I have used Maneb and

Benlate as my main agents. Maneb does quite well and, of course, has the added benefit of controlling Rust outbreaks, but as far as Black Spot is concerned in my garden Benlate is more efficient; I think that with more regular spraying than I manage it could almost totally keep the disease at bay. In addition, for what little Mildew I get, Benlate is a marvellous eradicant.

Before attempting any assumptions or conclusions, one must wonder exactly how a Black Spot spore operates. We read that its Latin name is *Diplocarpon rosae*, that it is a colourless fungus and that it is only its action which causes a deterioration in leaf tissue. It is, therefore, only its action which one sees. Also a full-size Black Spot takes at least six weeks to develop, although the incubation period is usually two to four weeks. Research work at Exeter University (1968 *Rose Annual*) claims to show that spores of *Diplocarpon* are mainly dispersed by water splash over short distances. Now if this were the case, surely the disease would be attacking the underside of the leaf, just as much as the upper surface; but of course observation proves that this is not so. My assumption is that in excess of 90 per cent of Black Spot infection is caused by airborne spores. The fact that virtually all Black Spot infection is on the upper surface of the leaf very strongly suggests that the spores are descending on to the leaf surface, and my upturned leaf, mentioned earlier, is a further strong indication that this is the case. I have visions of the dreaded spores floating about in a cloud—perhaps something similar to a soap bubble. I know if it were suddenly to become visible, I for one would be hot in pursuit.

We are told that we get more of the disease down in the south-west principally because of the greater humidity, but surely we also get much milder winters and, therefore, it is reasonable to assume that there is a much higher incidence of over-wintering of the disease, thus leading to a much earlier start of infection.

It may well be that Black Spot spores germinate most readily in conditions of damp, but could not these conditions be created by successive days of early morning dew, and the dryness of the day usually associated with light winds providing the ideal conditions for the spores to spread? If my supposition is correct that the fungus is largely airborne in its influence, this would explain why Mr Beales' and Mr Hay's experiments were so successful. One can visualize the spore attempting to take off and being instantly battered to the ground by a deluge of spray.

I would like to make a further supposition—that the fungus has difficulty making progress or perhaps gaining adhesion on a growing leaf. It does seem to be possible to keep a leaf growing beyond its normal expected size. I have noticed that foliar feeding has the effect of increasing leaf size, sometimes to almost double the norm. My local rose nurseryman tells me of one customer who sprays regularly with only foliar feed and uses no other spray. She is reputed to get no Black Spot at all. Likewise, Mr Bartram's experiments with urea suggest that, apart from any hostile influence urea may have on Black Spot, the high nitrogen content of urea does keep the leaf growing. Again, Mr Hay's and Mr Beales' experiments with water spray, apart from making it difficult for the spores to settle, may well have had the effect of keeping the bush and therefore the leaves growing, and thus made it difficult for the spores to gain adhesion. I believe this may be supported by my observation of Black Spot on young foliage during drought conditions. The drought obviously resulted in the bushes stopping growing, with the consequence that the leaves did likewise, and Black Spot was able, therefore, to spread more or less at will.

Now, what of the disease starting at the base of the plant and working its way upward? Simple logic will tell one that the lower leaves are most likely to reach their full growth first. Thus, having reached their optimum and no longer being a moving leaf, they are more susceptible to attack. Therefore I do not support the theory that the fungus splashes on to the lower leaves from spores lying on or near other surfaces.

One final observation. I have two bushes of the same rose, a seedling climber, growing a few feet apart. One has been virtually defoliated and the other has scarcely lost a leaf. Both have been given the same treatment—a dressing of manure and foliar fungicidal spraying at about three to four week intervals. The infected bush is farther from any other infection than the non-infected bush. However, there is a difference between the two. One is a budded plant growing in what was orginally pasture, with the top inch or two of soil removed. The top layer was of the turf, and this was dumped in a pile and left to rot. The following year, my seedling climber on its own roots was planted in this mixture and this was the one that kept virtually free of Black Spot. Both plants, until the appearance of Black Spot, were almost identical in size, the budded plant fairly rapidly catching up the existing growth of the seedling. This does suggest to me that there is some chemical or combination of chemicals that is particularly helping the seedling on its own roots. It might be extra nitrogen—I feel it is unlikely to be potash.

Where do we go from here? Undoubtedly, good cultivation is essential. Foliar feeding is, as far as I am concerned, an enormous help, and if done regularly can keep the disease away altogether. Likewise, I would say that Mr Bartram has proved the value of urea. But, unfortunately, any spraying needs to be done regularly—anything in excess of a ten-day interval is asking for trouble. What we rose growers really need is a systemic fungicide effective for at least one month—ideally for the whole season. Is it not perhaps also feasible to cover the leaves with some sort of adhesive spray, which would either expand with the leaf or at least allow the leaf to grow out from it, and which would, of course, prevent any infection landing on the leaf? Finally, all breeders please make more efforts to produce very resistant varieties, though I must confess that often though I lament 'Fragrant Cloud' and 'Mischief', I would not be without them, for I love their flowers.

*Note by Hon. Scientific Adviser:*

Local observations such as these are of considerable interest to research workers. Here in Suffolk Black Spot is much less prevalent than in the southwest, but I have had more than usual in 1973 and this I ascribe to my having sprayed much less frequently than usual, largely because I have eradicated Rust with Plantvax.

Where Black Spot does occur here it seems to spread outwards from centres of infection at a relatively slow rate and this agrees with Saunders' findings at Exeter. By contrast Rust can spread very rapidly down wind. However, I also have noticed that relatively isolated wall climbers can become suddenly infected with Black Spot and that the initial infection may occur quite high above ground level. This certainly suggests that wind borne spores spread the disease in some circumstances.

Heavy early morning dews followed by high day temperatures clearly favour the spread of Black Spot and this is why it is so important to spray regularly during August and September, just when so many of us are on holiday. It is easy to achieve a good spray cover on the upper leaf surfaces, but spraying the lower surfaces was advocated because, as Howden and Jacobs have emphasized recently (*Rose Annual* 1973, p. 118), this was essential to control Rust before the advent of Plantvax.

Mr Warner's claim that regular foliar feeding will keep Black Spot away altogether is interesting and I hope that other members who have tried this technique will advise me of their results.

The new systemic fungicide triforine (= Cela W.524) may prove to be a useful aid to Black Spot eradication if my experience with this material is confirmed elsewhere. I hope that it will soon be on the retail market.

I have found it surprisingly easy to breed new roses resistant to all three leaf diseases, but it is quite another matter when it comes to combining that resistance with other desirable characters demanded by rosarians.

E. F. ALLEN

# Steeped in History

## W. A. JAMES

(*Amateur rose grower*)

> *The Roses fearfully on thorns did stand,*
> *One blushing shame, another white despair;*
> *A third, nor red nor white, had stolen of both*
> *And to his robbery had annexed thy breath;*
> *But, for his theft, in pride of all his growth*
> *A vengeful canker eat him up to death.*
>
> (WM. SHAKESPEARE, Sonnet XCIX)

Few, perhaps, except for the most ardent lovers of the old shrub roses, would be really familiar with the striped varieties produced around the middle of the nineteenth century. These were Gallica roses in the main, such as the pale pink and crimson striped carnation-like 'Georges Vibert' (1853), the pale cream-white crimson striped and flecked 'Perle des Panachées' (1845), the semi-double 'Camaieux' (1830) whose crimson striped white petals change to violet and purple and the similar coloured camellia-like 'Tricolor de Flandre' (1846). A notable exception and probably the most striking of all the striped roses of this era is 'Commandant Beaurepaire' (1874), a Bourbon with pink flowers and crimson and purple stripes.

It is, however, a different matter when we mention those two immortals 'Rosa Mundi' and 'York and Lancaster'. 'Rosa Mundi' (*R. gallica versicolor*, *R. gallica variegata*) is perhaps the most popular of all the old roses with its vividly coloured flowers opening flat to give a glorious display of light crimson petals splashed and striped with the palest pink, which are enhanced by its golden stamens. 'Rosa Mundi' has long been accepted as a sport from the light crimson and golden stamened *Rosa gallica officinalis*, the ancient rose of Provins. The other of the two, 'York and Lancaster' (*Rosa damascena versicolor*), is mentioned by John Parkinson in his *Paradisus* (Paradisi in Sole, Paradisus terrestris), published in 1629, in which he tells us he "had to furnish his garden (in London) 30 sorts at least, everyone notably different from the other, and all fit to be there entertained." His description of the 'York and Lancaster' rose is very apt and says "the one half of it sometimes of a pale whitish colour, and the other half of a paler damask colour than the ordinary (Damask); this happeneth so many times and sometimes also the flower has divers stripes and marks on it, as one leafe (petal) white or striped with white, sometimes all striped or spotted over, and at other times no stripes or marks at all as nature listeth to play with varieties in this as other flowers. Yet I have observed that the longer it abideth blowen open in the sun, the paler and fewer stripes marks and spots will be seene in it; the smell thereof is of a weake Damask rose scent." Parkinson does not mention 'Rosa Mundi' in *Paradisus*, nor in his later work *Theater of Plants* which appeared in 1640, although there is a drawing of this rose by Robert which is in the collection of Velins at the Jardin des Plantes in Paris. It would seem probable that 'Rosa Mundi' had not at that time found its way from France to English gardens.

It is said, by way of legend rather than of fact, that 'Rosa Mundi' owes its name to the fair Rosamond who was the mistress of the Plantagenet King Henry II (1133–1189), the great-grandson of William the Conqueror, whose domains eight centuries ago extended over much of France (as we know its boundaries today) and the British Isles. His succeeding sons were Richard I, the great crusader to the Holy Land, and John, who was brought to heel by the Barons at Runnymede and gave us Magna Carta. It is recorded that when Richard's Turkish adversary, the redoubtable Saladin, retook the Mosque Omar from the Christians during the third crusade, he refused to enter until it had been washed and purified with rose water of such quantity that it required 500 camels to transport it from Damascus. Could it be that 'Rosa Mundi' existed in those far off days, in Persia perhaps, and found its way from Asia into Europe around the time of the second crusade in 1147? It does not seem beyond the realm of possibility.

The existence of Rosamond and her association with the unfaithful King at a time when his Queen (Eleanor, the former wife and queen to Louis VII) was conveniently held captive in prison in 1173, can be established beyond doubt. Rosamond was one of six children of Walter de Clifford who was a knight and owned lands in Shropshire. She ended her days as a nun and died at Godstow Nunnery near Oxford in 1176. Her tomb, which has fallen into decay, was said to have contained a brass panel with this epitaph:

> Hic facet in tumba Rosa Mundi non rosa munda;
> Non redolet sed olet quae redolere solet.

My niece, just down from University with a "first" in classics, has kindly given me this literal translation: "Here lies the 'Rose of the World' in her tomb, not (now) a delightful rose, (for) she who is usually (so) fragrant does not (now) smell sweet, but offensive." The poet Robert Southey (1774–1843) wrote this stanza in translation:

*This tomb doth here enclose*
*The World's most beautiful Rose;*
*Rose passing sweet erewhile*
*Now nought but odour vile.*

In Tennyson's play about the power struggle between King Henry II and his Archbishop, Thomas Becket, Rosamond appears as the ward of Becket. He saves her from the murderous intentions of the avenging Queen (Eleanor), to appear, disguised as a monk at his murder in Canterbury Cathedral. Tennyson's play ends with Rosamond kneeling over the martyr's body.

Turning now to happier things; should you be able to visit Bone Hill in high summer, do seek out the bushes of 'Rosa Mundi' growing in the shrub border. The vivid colouring of this rose seen *en masse* is a glorious sight when in full flower in its setting among the lovely old garden roses displayed in the border, which is located beyond and a little to the left of the ornamental pool.

The 'York and Lancaster' rose and the Wars of the Roses are linked for ever with the history and heraldry of these islands. The red and white roses forming the badges of disputants have been conjoined in the heraldic Badge of England, which has been described heraldically as: "A Tudor rose barbed and seeded proper, stalked and leaved vert, ensigned with an Imperial Crown." The Rose in this case has a white inner and a red outer row of petals, and is shown with a part of the stalk and leaves. The centre is seeded gold; it is barbed green and surmounted with an Imperial Crown.[1]

A colourful description of the 'York and Lancaster' rose and the story of its association with the Wars of the Roses appeared in a pre-war *Rose Annual*.[2] It was taken from an American rose catalogue issued nearly fifty years ago and is well worth repeating:

"This historical rose was introduced 378 years ago, and is one of the great romances immortalized by Shakespeare in *Henry VI*, and was connected with a conflict lasting thirty years and known in history as the 'Wars of the Roses'.

Two branches of the Royal Family of England, the House of York and the House of Lancaster, both descended from a common ancestor, Edward III, and claimed the right to the Throne. A bloody war between partisans of the two Houses started in 1455. The House of York had for a rallying sign a White Rose, while the Lancastrians selected a Red Rose. Success

[1] See *The Rose Annual*, 1931: The Rose in Heraldry, p. 41.
[2] 1931 edition, p. 171.

ebbed and flowed until 1485, when Richard III of York was defeated and killed at the battle of Bosworth. But peace was not completely restored for a year, when in 1486 both Houses were united by the marriage of Henry VII of Lancaster with Elizabeth of York.

The legend says that this marriage was brought about by the discovery on the same bush of a rose, partly white and partly red. The war-weary people were quick to attribute the phenomenon to some supernatural interference; the legend was still current in 1551, when a rose collector actually found a bush bearing strangely variegated roses, red and white, no two alike, some striped, some blotched, some half and half, while others were either all red or all white. This curiosity was instantly called 'York and Lancaster', and became in great demand among the descendants of the belligerents; for three centuries it could be found in many gardens of England. However, in the nineteenth century, rose progress was so rapid that this charming rose fell into oblivion. While the name remained a cherished memory, the true stock became very scarce and somewhat mixed. In 1925 we were fortunate to discover in an old English collection a few plants of the genuine strain, from which we propagated the plants we are now offering."

I wonder how they knew they had discovered the genuine strain!

The scars of war have long since been healed and, happily, rivalry between the supporters of the red and white rose respectively is now governed by King Willow. The old enemies, now beflannelled, fight their battles on the fields of Old Trafford, Headingly and Bramall Lane (alas, no more) where, since time immemorial it seems, their skirmishes have been recorded for posterity by that doyen of cricket correspondents, Sir Neville Cardus, their revered historian.

*See where the rose, and Spring to mirth awake.*
*So cheerful looks the rose, 'twere wisdom's part*
*To tear the root of sorrow from the heart.*
*Soft comes the morning wind; the wanton rose*
*Bursts from its cup to kiss the gale that blows;*
*Its silken garment wounds in tender play,*
*And leaves its body naked to the day.*

HAFEZ, by Nott, Ode XIV

'SUNSILK' (floribunda—H.T. type)
*'Pink Parfait'* × *'Redgold' seedling*
Raised by Fryer's Nurseries Ltd.

TRIAL GROUND CERTIFICATE 1972
*See page* 183

'MARTIAN GLOW' (shrub)
'*Joseph's Coat*' × '*Dorothy Wheatcroft*'
Raised by Gandy's (Roses) Ltd.
TRIAL GROUND CERTIFICATE 1970
*See* 1973 *Rose Annual, page* 184

# Fallacies in Rose Growing

## JOHN S. MATTOCK

(*Rose nurseryman*)

John Charles Willoughby Smythe-Smythe is our local village greenfingers—his knowledge of plants is profound—his annual appearance at our local flower show is an EVENT. Nobody can match his leeks and onions, but his roses are a disaster.

Thirty years ago he produced a specimen bloom of 'Leni Neuss' which (human nature being what it is) made the headlines in the National Press, and overnight he became an "expert" in the rose world. Of his more ridiculous observations, some have gone down in the history of rose-growing with very little contradiction: Roses must have clay soil: shiny-leaved varieties do not get disease: pruning at Easter is a must: and his prize morsel of information was the advisability of removing all stems bearing leaves with seven leaflets, because that was when a rose had "reverted".

Such is the way that "do's" and "don'ts" become the gospel truth and fallacies are born. Every community has a John Charles Willoughby Smythe-Smythe in its midst, but how much truth is there in these wild and woolly prognostications?

My Chambers's Dictionary describes a fallacy as an apparently genuine but really illogical argument—a wrong but prevalent notion, and "fallacious" as misleading—not well founded. An illogical argument—roses with seven leaflets and roses reverting. Oh dear, oh dear, the trouble this pearl of wisdom has caused! Smythe-Smythe, of course, could never grow climbers in his garden because every spring they produced new growth that was promptly removed. Most modern floribundas never had a chance to flower, and 'Peer Gynt' was consigned to the bonfire with commendable alacrity, because its leaves were a pale green!

The rose stock used these days (*R.laxa*) has a leaf of a reasonable quality, but fortunately very rarely throws suckers. How can we trace a sucker? For the information of "rose rabbits" the production of rose plants is a fairly straightforward manipulation of a rose stock and a cultivar. The rose stock or briar provides the root of our plant; the cultivar is the fabric of the rose seen above ground level. It follows that the point of contact of these two parts is the significant position we use when tracing the briar (stock) sucker. If the suspect growth emanates at this junction or above it, the growth MUST be the cultivar; if below it, then it is from the rootstock (five, seven or more leaflets and all). The cultivar cannot revert—it will sometimes deteriorate, but never revert! What will sometimes happen is that the rootstock will try to "go it alone", gain an ascendancy over the cultivar, and if not checked, the briar will eventually suppress the cultivar.

**Roses on clay soils.** This story probably originated from the time when all the best roses came from the Essex area, clay soil and all. It is true, of course, that roses appear to produce better blooms on clay, but equally good roses can be grown in lighter soils, although they are probably harder to obtain. The fact is that lighter soils are, generally speaking, hungrier—they require considerably more nutrition to produce the goods, simply because the breakdown of organic material is quicker and the impetus is rapidly absorbed. Again, light soils are generally "warm soils", and growth is generally much earlier because of this. Consequently, the amount of help they require is much greater. It could be argued, in fact, that roses grown on a light soil are more mature, certainly hardier, and inevitably have a better root system.

Smythe-Smythe practised very severe pruning, cutting back to about three eyes in March or April: well, forty years ago this might have been the order of the day, and certainly the bloom size and quality were probably better: but can any of you remember going into an amateur's garden in those days? It was ghastly; rows of trees with two or at the most three shoots reaching for the sky. The whole area covered in bloom shades and half the trees killed through hard pruning.

The modern rose hybrid will not take kindly to this sort of treatment—primarily because so many new seedlings have 'Peace' in their blood. This cultivar has probably had more influence in making us prune lighter than anything else. The fact is that pruning should be done as soon as the weather has broken—normally the end of February—and provided the wood is not in a frozen state, it can be done in quite severe weather. The other important factor is that pruning should be done in such a way as to produce an abundance of bloom commensurate with a reasonable quality. Few gardeners prune very hard these days, and those who do miss the profuseness, generous growth and garden worthiness of our modern roses.

**A mulch of farmyard manure in the autumn keeps roses warm for the winter.** Here we have a confusion of two old rose practices. Many years ago trees had to be strawed up for the winter because of their susceptibility to winter frosts—it had nothing to do with mulching. The proper time to mulch is after Christmas when the beds have been cleared of old leaves—

the ground temperature is then lower, and no harm can come to the plants as there will be no early activity resulting from the application of farmyard manure. Roses these days are rarely killed by frost, unless they have been fed too late in the autumn. If this happens the tree is still in a semi-ripe condition and thus not able to withstand the rigours of an English winter.

**Manure should be dug in three feet deep when planting new rose beds.** I must confess this is a new one to me. Many gardeners do make the cardinal error of putting a layer of manure at the bottom of a trench as the rose bed is being prepared. Those gardeners fortunate enough to obtain this valuable commodity should know that farmyard manure must be integrated into the top spit. There is no value in burying it farther down. Sub-soiling (i.e. the breaking up of the hard pan below the top spit) is an essential part of any good garden husbandry, but be sure to keep that soil well buried.

**Roses should be purchased from a nursery with a soil structure similar to your own garden. Roses should be purchased from a nursery 100 miles farther north.** These two statements show the extremes to which fallacies will take us. The fact that the majority of roses are grown on a few large nurseries obviously explodes that theory. The one about 100 miles north is even more ludicrous. It is essential to purchase roses with a good root system plus hard, stout top growth and well-matured wood. This knowledge can only be gained by personal experience and from the results obtained in your own garden. Buy roses from a "name": the fact that these firms have been in existence for so many years must surely mean that they are "delivering the goods". Cheap roses can prove to be the most expensive in the long run.

The worst fallacy of the lot is to take too much to heart the writings of some of our more glib rose experts. Without being at all personal I can safely say that the outpourings in the Horticultural Press of some so-called experts are very parochial and limited. This is not their fault, but rather the result of assuming that because a Smythe-Smythe can produce twenty good blooms in his own garden, he is necessarily fitted to set himself up as a national garden adviser. Certainly most amateurs have very little knowledge outside their own garden, and cannot by any stretch of imagination prognosticate on varieties to grow three or four counties away.

Fallacies in gardening proliferate as fast as the weeds grow—be careful of the Smythe-Smythes of this world. Common sense is the best rule—do not be led astray!

# The Loveliest Rose in the World

## HANS CHRISTIAN ANDERSEN

*translated by Reginald Spink*

Hans Christian Andersen (1805–75) was a great lover of flowers, and especially of the rose. The following story is typical of Andersen's preoccupation with the flower of flowers. First printed in a magazine in 1851, it was included in his first collection of *stories* (as distinct from the earlier collections of *fairy tales*) which was published a year later. This is a new translation by the author of *Hans Christian Andersen and His World* (Thames & Hudson, 1972), who has previously translated and edited collections of Andersen's fairy tales and stories.

\* \* \*

There was once a mighty queen, in whose garden were the loveliest flowers of every season and from every country of the world. But more than any she loved the roses, and so she had every variety of these, from the wild hedge with the green apple-scented leaves to the most beautiful rose of Provence; and they grew up the palace walls, twining round the pillars and window-sills and into the galleries and along the ceilings of every room; and the roses varied in scent, form and colour.

But grief and sorrow dwelt within; the queen lay on her sickbed, and the doctors had pronounced that she must die.

"Yet there is a cure for her!" said the wisest man among them. "Bring her the loveliest rose in the world; the one that is the manifestation of the highest and the purest love; if that is set before her eyes while they are still unglazed, she will not die."

And young and old came bringing roses from far and near, the loveliest that bloomed in every garden; yet they were not the ones. The bloom had to be obtained from the garden of love; but which among the roses there was the manifestation of the highest and the purest love?

And the minstrels sang of the loveliest rose in the world, each one naming his own. And a message went out across the land to every heart which beat in love; a message to every class and every age.

"No one has yet named the bloom!" said the wise man. "Nobody has indicated the place where it sprang forth in all its splendour. It is not one of the roses from the coffin of Romeo and Juliet, nor from the grave of Walpurgis, though these roses will always remain fragrant in song and legend; neither is it one of the roses which spring from the bloodstained lances of

104

Winkelried, from the blood that gushes hallowed from the hero's breast as he dies for his country, although no death is sweeter, no rose redder than the blood which thus flows. Nor is it that wondrous bloom for whose cultivation a man, in his solitary room, during long sleepless nights, will give the freshness of his life: the magical rose of science."

"I know where it blooms," said a happy mother who came with her baby to the queen's bedside. "I know where the loveliest rose in the world may be found! The rose that is the manifestation of the highest and the purest love. It blooms on the blushing cheeks of my sweet child when, refreshed by sleep, he opens his eyes and laughs up to me in all his love."

"Lovely is that rose, but there is a lovelier one!" the wise man said.

"Yes, far more beautiful!" said one of the women. "I have seen it; a more sublime and holy rose has never bloomed; but it was as pale as the petals of the tea rose. I saw it on the queen's cheeks; she had laid down her royal crown and walked alone in the long sorrowful night with her sick child, weeping over it, kissing it, and saying a prayer to God for it, as a mother prays in the hour of dread."

"Holy and wonderful in its strength is the white rose of sorrow; yet that is not the one."

"No, the loveliest rose in the world I saw before the altar of the Lord," said the saintly old bishop. "I saw it shine forth as if the countenance of an angel appeared. The young girls had gone to communion, renewing the pact of their baptism; and roses blushed and roses paled on their fresh cheeks. A young girl stood there, gazing with the full purity and love of her soul towards her God. That was the manifestation of the purest and the highest love."

"Blessed be it," said the wise man; "but none of you has yet named the loveliest rose in the world."

At that moment a child, the queen's little son, entered the room. There were tears in his eyes and on his cheeks. He was carrying a large, open book; its binding was of velvet and it had big silver clasps.

"Mother," said the little one, "please listen to what I have been reading!" And, sitting by the bedside, the child read from the Book about Him who had sacrificed Himself on the cross for the redemption of men, even of generations yet unborn. " 'Greater love hath no man!' "

And a tinge of roses came into the queen's cheeks, while her eyes grew large and clear; for rising from the Book's pages she saw the loveliest rose in the world, the image of the one which sprang from Christ's blood on the tree of the cross.

"I see it!" she said. "He shall never die who sees that loveliest rose on earth!"

# The Spring Rose Show—Nottingham, 1858-1974

## N. CLARKE

(*Hon. Secretary, The Nottingham Rose Society*)

In common with all show committees, our own is always keenly interested in anything which may arouse the curiosity of those not yet converted to the worship of the Queen of Flowers. Any new idea which stimulates the interest of existing members and may well bring in one or two willing new recruits, is to be fostered.

So in planning our programme for 1974, our historian—every society has one—suggested that we return to the story of the humble beginning of The St Ann's Amateur Floral and Horticultural Society, an account of whose spring show appears in Dean Hole's *A Book about Roses* (Chapter II). This show was held in the late 1860s on an Easter Monday when, as Dean Hole puts it, "As if to heighten our enjoyment of the scene (the rose-laden tables) the day darkened without and the sleet beat against the windows as though enraged by this sudden invasion of flora". As our historian remarked, if those chaps with their limited facilities, their six-by-four greenhouses, their very restricted spare time after a ten- or twelve-hour day in factory, mine or workshop, the almost total absence of specialist nurseries, and their enforced dependence upon teas and noisettes, budded on to Manetti stock, could produce superlative blooms in April, why can't we? After some blank stares, some half-nods of approbation, someone said, "Look at Fred Shaw, a veritable novice and yet he can grow, exhibit and win at the RNRS Spring Show." With this final challenge to our self-esteem, the idea was adopted forthwith and the date fixed as 25 April, 1974. What to do whilst the blooms were being judged? Why not get Fred Shaw to give a talk on "Greenhouse Roses for Beginners"? The Programme Secretary was instructed to write and get Mr Shaw's concurrence and this was received, "provided we helped on a question-and-answer basis". As the programme was already in print, it was as well that Fred agreed!

[1] The St Ann's Society held its first show of pot roses in 1858. Dean Hole first judged at the fifth show held at "The General Cathcart" about 1862. The show was undoubtedly growing and required a "name" as a judge. The reference to 'Maréchal Niel' (1864) and 'Mme Margottin' (1865) in the Dean's book does not refer to his *first* visit but reads: "*and referring to subsequent exhibitions*, I do not hesitate to say that the best 'Maréchal Niel' and the best 'Mme Margottin' (1865) which I have yet seen, have appeared at Nottingham in the ginger-beer bottles." It will be seen that Dean Hole became a regular judge and saw the varieties mentioned some years after his first visit.

It was also decided that the classes should be fairly simple and would be based upon the easier classes in the RNRS Spring Show. That was that, and since then there has been little said about pot roses. This may have been due to the busy summer programme, during which the members of the show and programme committees had necessarily to turn their hands to erecting staging, tents, sign writing, collecting gate money and, if there was time left, exhibiting. They managed this latter with many successes.

I do know, however, that there were enquiries at a local nursery for "two dozen hybrid teas suitable for pot culture", that one enthusiast has erected a ten-by-eight greenhouse exclusively for pot roses, and was last seen promenading on a Nottingham boulevard, the proud bearer of a new greenhouse heater! Others have been overheard asking, "Are whalehide containers any good for growing greenhouse roses?" So the signs for St Mark's Day, 1974, are that, weather permitting, we shall again be invaded by flora. I hope, however, that the Heralds of Spring will not be so affronted by our display of roses as to lash the windows with sleet. For one thing, it keeps the members away and I would not like them to miss the result of the efforts of the more expert among them.

Who is to judge? I have no doubt that we shall manage with the very capable RNRS Judges now available, as we shall be unable on this occasion to invite The Very Revd Samuel Reynolds Hole to make the journey from Caunton Manor, as he did that April day in 1862, to judge the roses at "The General Cathcart" Inn, Hunger Hill, Nottingham. Were this possible, I wonder what mental comparisons the reverend gentleman would make? Would he prefer the globular flowers of the Teas and Noisettes, represented by 'Adam' (T) pale blush; 'Souvenir d'un Ami' (T) pale rose; 'Niphetos' (T) white; 'Devoniensis' (N) creamy white and 'Maréchal Niel' (N) straw yellow, to the present-day varieties? Would he enthuse over 'Royal Highness', 'Tenerife', 'Alec's Red', 'Akebono', 'Red Lion' and 'Grandpa Dickson', as he did over the blooms of 'Mme Margottin' and 'Maréchal Niel'? "The best blooms I have ever seen were shown in ginger-beer bottles at Nottingham."

It is certain that, unlike the blooms of his day, which being so weak or short in stem, required the support of tube or bottle to be displayed properly, he would doubtless comment upon the two-foot stems which proudly bear our modern hybrid teas. As floribundas are difficult to force we should be spared his pronouncements upon the floribunda-H.T. type. Do I even now hear him thundering from some celestial rose show—"H.T. type? They are neither fish, flesh, nor good red herring!"

I prefer to think that the Dean would say that his prophecies have become true, in fact, that the "Rose has gained a staff to lean upon and her crown has become of many hues and brilliancies". And so the giant of rosarians would depart, not to the waiting hansom, the footwarmer and rugs at Nottingham station, but to a waiting car which would bear him swiftly to Caunton in less than the hour.

So with an eye on the past, an eye on the future (our new venture, the Spring Show) we can be glad that although our "stockingers, twist hands and artisans" have given place to retired professional men, agrochemists, civil servants, master builders and those representing almost all human activities, they are all still bound by a common bond—the love of the rose. We can be glad also that we shall not have to take the blankets from the bed to protect the roses, as did those artisan rosarians of long ago. Although, come to think of it, how will the electricity, oil and coal shortages affect us? I must remember to ask the wife to buy two extra blankets tomorrow!

However, come what may, there are sure to be those stalwarts who always produce blooms "on the day". May the best blooms win. We shall all have learned a little, shared a common experience, made new friends, and visited greenhouses we never knew existed.

And finally I hope we can all remember Dean Hole's words:

> Who misses or who wins the prize,
> Go, lose or conquer as you can;
> But if you fail, or if you rise,
> Be each, pray God, a gentleman.

> Thou blushing Rose, within whose virgin leaves
> The wanton wind to sport himself presumes,
> Whilst from their rifled wardrobe he receives
> For his wings purple, for his breath perfumes.
>
> SIR RICHARD FANSHAWE

# Planning for the Rose in the Small Garden

**NORMAN H. J. CLARKE**

(*Landscape Architect*) *with plans and sketches by the author.*

Roses are usually the first flowering plants which spring to mind when plants for a new garden are being considered, and with good reason, for they can be effective when seen in a group, they are not difficult to grow on most soils, they flourish for several years and of course they produce superb individual flowers.

The many books and catalogues, with their attractive illustrations and lists of roses of all sizes, colours and forms, make an instant appeal to owners of gardens, both old and new, and the acres of nurseries devoted to them and the numbers of new varieties sent for trial and introduced on the market are signs of their tremendous popularity.

But in the designing of a garden the contribution that the roses will make to the planting design is often overlooked, because of one's concern with a particular rose or group of roses, the colour of the flowers and the need for blooms for cutting. Indeed, the rose is a difficult subject to include successfully, because the individual bush forms of the hybrid tea, and even the floribunda types, lack the form and foliage density which many shrubs exhibit and which help to furnish a garden throughout a great part of the year; this is aggravated by the need for annual pruning.

To be effective, roses need to be planted in groups, but also their blooms are such that close inspection adds to their enjoyment, and this suggests a more intimate treatment in which they are planted among other plants and close to the observer.

The traditional pattern of the rose garden dates back to the mediaeval garden, in which the enclosed garden was divided into small, regular plots around a central dipping well or fountain, and from which herbs and flowers could be picked from the intervening paths.

In the later Victorian and Edwardian eras the enclosed garden entirely for roses retained this concept of formal beds cut out of the turf around a central feature of pool, sundial or statue and today in many public parks this is still the pattern. Where space permits, of course, this is a suitable method of display for many different varieties but it is dated in design, extravagant in maintenance and not very suitable for the small garden. It also presents an uninteresting appearance for several months of the year.

In today's housing developments, with their small or even medium-sized plots of up to a quarter of an acre, individual rose beds in the manner of the formal gardens of the past would necessarily contain too few plants to make effective colour schemes and some other acceptable method of including roses is required. So why should not roses be treated as the shrubs or herbaceous plants in the mixed border, with three or five bushes in a group in pockets among other plants? This method allows the roses to be set into a background of shrubs or other foliage plants, which enhances their blooms as did the yew hedges in the large rose gardens, for background colour is very important for an appreciation of roses. The matt, dark green of the yew hedge is the perfect foil, but lighter green hedges are not so good, and coloured foliages can clash unless the roses are chosen with great care for a particular effect. Walls of brick or stone or colourwash and timber fencing all need roses of contrasting colour against them for effective results. The different colours of bricks, from dark grey to pale yellow, always require careful thought to select both the colour of foliage and colour of bloom which will show against them to greatest advantage.

If the garden is large enough to accommodate some individual rose beds, then instead of making them similar in size and traditional in layout, a more informal or abstract pattern can often fit better into the site and different-sized beds can lend themselves to a more balanced colour pallette. Thus, a small number of white or intense-coloured varieties can occupy the smaller beds whilst balancing larger beds of the paler and more delicate shades. The choice of varieties is, of course, a personal one, but much more effective colour schemes can be achieved by a closer range of colours than by the use of a wide range of various intense-coloured varieties.

Of all the garden plants the rose probably has the most varied applications, for bedding, for hedging, for screening, for ground cover, and so on. In the small garden these are valuable uses, particularly when their floral assets are also considered, and when climbing and rambler roses are used, these surely represent the most economic use of space for the results obtained.

Some small gardens contain banks which create problems, and for these some of the climbing roses pegged down to the ground will cover large areas for little cost and low maintenance. The ground covering of banks and even level areas by foliages which dispense with the need for grass is becoming more and more in demand and roses can fulfil this need. With the larger-scale requirements of public authorities and others, rose growers might, perhaps, encourage the use of roses for this purpose and the production of a

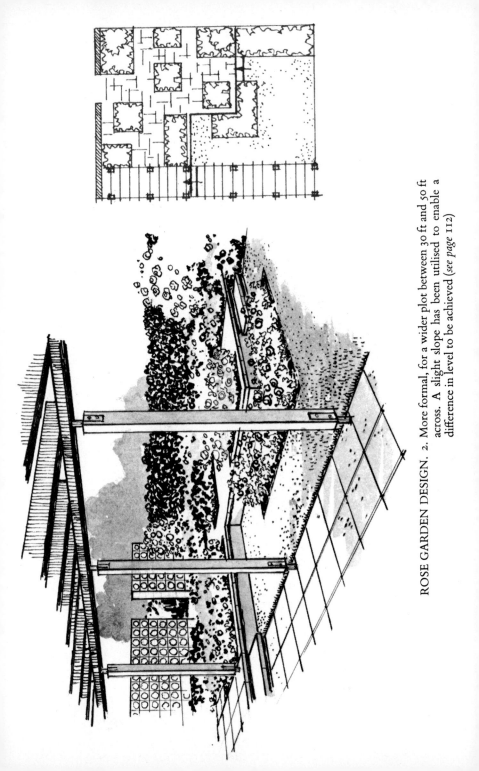

ROSE GARDEN DESIGN. 2. More formal, for a wider plot between 30 ft and 50 ft
across. A slight slope has been utilised to enable a
difference in level to be achieved (*see page* 112)

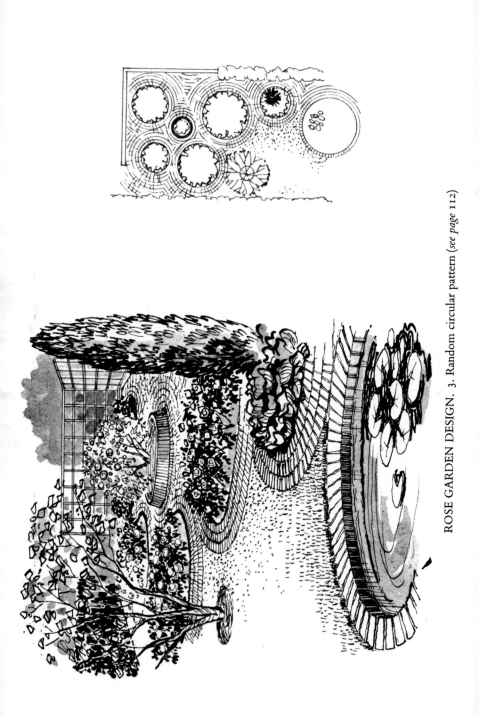

ROSE GARDEN DESIGN. 3: Random circular pattern (*see page* 112)

ROSE GARDEN DESIGN. 4. For a sloping site in which tiered planting areas are retained by stone walls (*see page* 112)

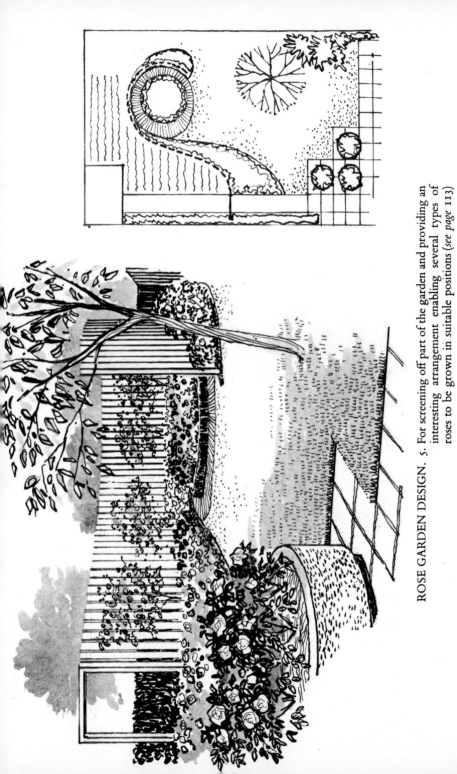

ROSE GARDEN DESIGN. 5. For screening off part of the garden and providing an interesting arrangement enabling several types of roses to be grown in suitable positions (*see page 113*)

low-growing, densely foliaged rose of spreading habit would be of great value.[1]

Rose hedges for boundary definition or internal garden division are also effective and attractive. Some are self-supporting as shrubs, whilst some require only the support of a few strands of wire. Some make low hedges only two feet high and others can form six-feet-high dense and animal-proof boundaries.

The many species of shrub roses are also becoming more and more popular in modern garden design, and even in the small garden a selection of some of these can be suitable, although there are many large-growing species which should be avoided where space is lacking. Their fragrance, varied foliages and habits and the beauty of flowers and heps make them useful as individual shrubs for many effects in the small garden and for adding height to the generally lower growth of the bush roses.

Standard and weeping standard roses, although of interest to the keen grower and of some value in certain situations, are more typical of gardens of the past than those of the present day and are somewhat unnatural in appearance.

Rose gardens, or even a few rose beds in a garden, are usually set out on a level area, for formal-shaped beds laid on a slope look out of place. Such sites need levelling or terracing and the latter can be interesting in producing tiers of foliage interlaced with bands of stone or brick; this can also avoid the show of bare soil which the slope exhibits. The designing of the terracing will depend on the contours of the ground, but often a freer arrangement of walling is more attractive than the rigid formal style.

The accompanying sketches and plans show how some of these suggestions could be used to provide attractive little gardens or perhaps features in larger gardens. The roses are used as elements of the designs, for their massing and foliage colour contrast and not just for their flowers.

The first design is for a long, narrow and enclosed garden, such as can be seen in many housing developments. This calls for a simple solution which would avoid dividing the area in a manner which would increase the feeling of narrowness. Small beds and narrow paths are therefore avoided and a comparatively wide border balances the remaining lawn area. The flowing line of the front of the border gives a sense of movement to the design, but this must not be too sinuous for, although such a line might appear suitable on plan, when transferred to the ground foreshortening can create a too

[1] It will be interesting to see whether the rambler 'Temple Bells', which was awarded a Trial Ground Certificate in 1973, meets this requirement.—*Ed.*

wavy effect. The varied width of the border also allows for diversity in the planting, with shrubs and shrub roses in the wider parts.

Within these shrubs and other foliage plants, some of which would be evergreen or coniferous, could be placed the small groups of floribunda or hybrid tea roses. A hedge behind the border, as on the opposite side of the garden, would be impractical for maintenance reasons, but the curving path of stepping stones, whilst adding a little to the maintenance, would provide a less obtrusive path through the lawn. The placing of the tree is also important in the view of the garden, the design of which could be adapted for any plot between sixteen and twenty-four feet wide and proportionately long.

The second design is for a wider plot between thirty and fifty feet across which would give sufficient space for rose beds to be used. This is a more formal design but in an asymmetric pattern. A slight slope of the ground has been utilized to enable a difference in level to be achieved, for the introduction of a low wall with steps can give added interest.

The rose beds are of different sizes within the paved platform, so that a balanced colour effect could be planned and in the larger gardens even more variety in the sizes of the beds could be introduced. A modern rose pergola in which the timber in the posts is not in direct contact with the ground, thereby prolonging its life for many years, would carry climbing roses on the boundary side.

Contrasting with the formality of this garden is an interesting random circular pattern (No. 3). This type of design could be planned to fit almost any shaped plot, but the beds must be sufficiently close to register as a well-knit design. They should not appear to be haphazardly disconnected.

Circular beds cut out of grass are difficult to edge continuously so that paving is suggested around and between them and for this bricks are chosen, as these can be more easily laid in circular fashion as well as providing an attractive ground texture. The bricks used for paving must be of engineering quality, or similar, if frost is not to disintegrate the surface. To alleviate the flatness of the design, one bed is raised slightly and the bush tree, the conifer and a shrub rose also give vertical contrast to the lower bush roses. The circular rhythm is repeated in the form of the dipping well in the foreground and even in its water-lily pads.

The fourth design is for a sloping site in which tiered planting areas are retained by stone walls. The circular pattern of these walls shows an easy method of terracing with walls of various heights according to the slope of the ground. Such a layout could be increased or adapted to many sloping sites.

An evergreen shrub and some shrub roses build up the background with the beds of bush roses in front, whilst in the foreground of the sketch a bank falling to the lawn is covered with climbing roses pegged down for ground cover.

Lastly, the fifth design is for a feature which could be adapted to many small gardens to screen off a part of the garden and provide an interesting arrangement which would enable several types of roses to be grown in suitable positions, e.g., climbing roses on fencing, rambler rose over the arch, shrub roses against the fencing, hybrid tea and floribunda varieties in bed and border and others in plant containers. The floribunda roses to provide a colourful centrepiece could be enclosed in a dwarf-box edging for a more formal effect, whilst ground-cover plants could be grown in front of the border to hide the soil. The use of ground-cover herbaceous or rock plants may not be approved by the purist, but it can be attractive and also provide some colour and foliage contrast at times when the rose border is an otherwise dull affair.

The screen fencing shown would need to be made to individual requirements and it should be in a natural timber colour which would not require subsequent painting or staining, for ease of maintenance.

None of the plans shown is drawn to a particular scale for, as mentioned, they could all be adapted to gardens of various sizes if in similar proportions. Neither are rose varieties indicated or suggested, for the choice of individual species and varieties depends on many factors, not least being one's personal preferences.

*There's a bower of roses by Bendemeer's stream,*
*And the nightingale sings to it all the day long,*
*In the time of my childhood 'twas like a sweet dream,*
*To sit in the roses, and hear the bird's song.*

*That bower and its music I never forget,*
*But oft when alone, in the bloom of the year,*
*I think, Is the nightingale singing there yet?*
*Are the roses still bright by the calm Bendemeer?*

MOORE, *Veiled Prophet*

# The Beginner's Guide to Exhibiting Roses

**FRANK M. BOWEN**, C.Eng., D.H.M.

*(Amateur rose grower and successful exhibitor)*

Much has been said and written about exhibiting roses and some comments have been critical, or at least have revealed a certain cynicism. Yet the records furnish evidence that before and ever since the Society's first Show was held, this branch of our hobby has had a great attraction for many rosarians the world over. Moreover, one has only to visit shows, large and small, to find proof that today, a sizeable proportion of our membership is still actively interested. If, for old stagers (!) like me, the primary enjoyment tends in the course of time to divert from the actual staging to the reunions with competitors and friends, the many queries and requests for advice from the next generation leave no doubt in my mind that the evolution continues, despite the increasing counter-attractions of the 1970s. Hence, the primary objective of this article is to pass on to beginners and novices some of the practical knowledge I have gained in the past twenty years, during which showing roses has afforded me endless pleasure and relaxation from the daily pressures of business.

My remarks will be confined to operations in the days immediately before and on the Show day itself; I am going to assume that you have perused the Schedule carefully and sent in your entries, having decided the classes which you can enter with reasonable expectation of being able to stage presentable exhibits. This is important because over-optimism is unfair to the Show organizers and bad for an exhibitor's chances of success. Also I trust that you have familiarized yourself with the RNRS *Regulations and Rules for Judging* (a copy may be obtained on application to the Secretary at Bone Hill) which apply to the great majority of shows held in the United Kingdom. Study especially Rule 10 of Rules for Judging, "Definition of Standard", which describes clearly and precisely the standards you should try to achieve; note also Rule 16 and that arrangement and foliage can gain one-third of the total points for each receptacle—the significance of this high proportion is commonly not fully realized.

Now, getting down to business, my routine is based on three main precepts, viz. first, to try always to stage pleasing exhibits, second, to do as much as practicable at home rather than at the Show itself and third, to reduce the work to a reasonable minimum. Starting a few days before a

Show, I find it helpful to memorize or jot down on a slip of paper my total requirements, e.g. 3 specimens, 9 H.T. stems, 5 Floribunda stems; and then to reconnoitre the garden and pinpoint the most likely prospects. If bloom protectors are being used, their final dispositions can be made at the same time but, even if not, this walk round saves much time in selecting and cutting later on. I also make ready the equipment needed at the Show— pruners, wires, a duster, one or two camel-hair paint-brushes, felt pen and name labels, packing for vases, and the vases and bowls themselves, if they are not to be provided by the Show organizers. Finally, I fill up containers for cutting and transporting the blooms to the Show; in so doing, a cut-rose nutrient and lukewarm water have given me best results, especially in transporting over long distances and in avoiding wilting in hot conditions, but opinions vary, so experiment as you wish! Likewise, the containers themselves are a personal choice; last year they appeared to range from beheaded plastic detergent bottles in milk crates, to liver or oil cans in divided boxes, to buckets (small and large, round and rectangular, some probably extracted from the kitchen when the wife was not about) to dustbins (new, clean and obviously bought for the purpose). Having tried most, for roses I now prefer the common rectangular plastic domestic buckets (bought by me, I hasten to add) because they are the easiest to lift about and to pack in the car. Both in buckets and tins, pieces of large-gauge chicken-wire wedged in the bottom prevent the ends of the stems from sliding around.

As to bloom protectors, undoubtedly these are assets for exhibitors who aspire to major competitions but they do involve much extra work so, to encourage rose-lovers with more modest ideas to support their local shows, I emphasize that nice exhibits, especially of floribundas, are still obtainable without using protectors if you are willing to undertake a few simple extra tasks. One is to start cutting earlier than is often advocated. Thus, whenever the weather is unsettled or the sunshine so intense that it may 'burn' the blooms (this actually can happen and did in 1973!), cut some (but not all) blooms two evenings before the Show day, e.g. Thursday evening for a Saturday show. The blooms should be young and in process of unfurling. Some judgment is necessary to know the best stage for different varieties, but this is soon acquired by trial and observation. For the late shows, when day and night temperatures have dropped, one can often start even sooner. Some of these early-cut blooms will pass their peak before the show time but, after a little practice, there will usually be a worth-while residue to stage, which is particularly valuable to people with small gardens or relatively few rose plants. In any case, some varieties, such as 'Ernest H. Morse', will actually mature better in water than on the bush in warm weather and I strongly urge you to put quality and freedom from blemishes before mere size, if only because the resulting exhibits will afford more pleasure and satisfaction to you and the spectators.

Whether or not this early cutting is done, I advise that you finish gathering the roses during the evening before the actual morning of the Show, so that you can sort, prepare and pack them in comfort. I suggest also that from the preliminary reconnoitre to the final packing, it is useful to exercise selective judgment and avoid the temptation of taking every available bloom, remembering that every one cut, prepared and transported means more work and, most important of all, makes the final selection under pressure of time when staging, more difficult. Many awards have been lost by failure to appreciate this simple fact and that, invariably, time really does "fly" in the hour or two before the bell rings to clear the hall. Moreover, why denude the garden unnecessarily? Keep the list of total requirements in mind or in your pocket and, initially, cut only the best you can find; if the resulting crop leaves you short or with an inadequate number of spares, then and only then make up with the best second choices that you can find; and when doing so, do not forget that spares are commonly needed to replace blooms which have matured too quickly, so when in doubt, go for youth and potential quality when possible.

From the time of cutting to the final staging, do handle the roses with loving care and try to avoid any damage, however slight, both to blooms and foliage. I emphasize this because, obvious though it may be in theory, the fact remains that every year I see many potentially splendid exhibits which have clearly been made mediocre by a few moments of carelessness.

As to the actual cutting, in all but really wet conditions I prefer to take out separate containers for hybrid teas and floribundas and to complete each in turn. Immediately after cutting each stem, I split the end and strip the leaves and thorns from a length roughly equal to that which will go into the vase or bowl at the show, before putting it carefully into the container. If there has been rain and no protectors have been used, now comes the next little extra task, viz. hold the stem with both hands, one at the base and the other immediately below the head (this is vital, otherwise you will almost certainly snap some necks) and shake off as much of the moisture as you can by whipping downward movements; if afterwards they are still wet, put the filled container for an hour or so in a warm place, e.g. boiler house, if you can, to help dry off the blooms. If, unfortunately, it is raining when the time comes to cut, you may vent your feelings in a few well-chosen words, but do not despair. Don appropriate apparel, sally forth with a flat box or trug covered by a plastic sheet, cut a few stems at a time putting each under the sheet immediately and rush them under cover. Then when you have finished cutting, do the stripping, etc., in comfort in the dry, taking special pains if you have not had protectors, to shake off all excess moisture. With a little experience, you will soon learn which varieties respond well to, and which do not recover from wetting, but I can assure you that quite a lot of present-day roses do, and it is when conditions are bad, not good, that the exhibitors willing to undertake extra work and care are often duly rewarded at judging time.

When the roses are safely under cover in their containers and enjoying a drink, it is a good time to have one yourself and relax for a while—but remember, if your choice is something stronger than the traditional tea, that you are going to require a steady hand before long.

Next comes the last main task of the evening—the vital preparation. Beginning with the floribundas, I take each stem in turn and first remove *all* old and faded blooms *and* their footstalks. The latter should be cut out completely right at their bases; a pair of nail scissors is a handy tool for this simple task which, if neglected, will leave an untidy appearance and result in loss of points. The stamens of single or semi-double blooms provide an easy guide to age in that, if they have already lost their pristine colour and faded, the bloom will assuredly appear stale in the morning. Moreover, the centre bloom of each cluster almost invariably opens earlier than the rest and will need to be removed; in fact, experienced exhibitors commonly snap off these earlier on the bush, but I must confess that I like to enjoy them in the garden first. All that now remains to be done is to remove any bits of dirt or insects from the blooms with the camel-hair brush, wipe any dirty leaves with a damp piece of cloth and replace the stem upright in the container, placing succeeding ones carefully together so that they will give mutual support in transit. Large floribunda stems may be a bit top-heavy, in which case a string tied round the whole bunch above the top of the container and secured to the handle is a useful precaution. Finally, when all stems are done, check the number against your list of requirements once again.

Hybrid teas ideally are rather less simple, in that they involve the arguable process known as "dressing" and the presentation depends to some extent on what classes you have chosen to enter from the common range of (a) specimen blooms in a box, (b) specimen blooms in a vase and (c) "decorative" (i.e. hybrid tea other than specimen blooms) stems in a vase or bowl.

The Society's Rules 12–15 and 16–17, if read with the care they merit, reveal clearly the radical differences between the judging of specimen and "decorative" classes. Specimens are to be pointed bloom by bloom and in bowls and vases, some points added for foliage and arrangement. On the other hand, with decoratives each complete receptacle is to be judged as a whole according to a points table which is so significant as to merit reproduction here. It applies also to floribundas:

| | |
|---|---|
| Brilliance, purity of colour, refinement and freshness of bloom | 10 points |
| Arrangement | 6 points |
| Decorative beauty and form of blooms | 10 points |
| Foliage | 4 points |

In this 10–6–10–4 ratio lie the reasons for a lot of my recommendations and also, a clearer understanding of the distribution of awards in many well-judged shows. Occasionally, alas, it is not applied accurately by some judges, but it is based on the accumulated experience of eminent rosarians over many years and, to my mind, is hard to fault as the measure for producing exhibits which present roses at their very best. Hence my emphasis throughout these notes on *quality* and my strong belief that any judges who do not recognize the significance of this pointing or are not prepared to apply it *in toto*, should in fairness to the exhibitors stand down from classes to which it is applicable.

If at first all these distinctions appear complicated, do not worry because, in practice, provided you accept my advice always to put quality first, it is only necessary to remember that size, i.e. largeness, is a major factor in specimen blooms. Thus, the procedure I follow and suggest you adopt, at least until you have become really experienced, is to *prepare* all hybrid tea roses in exactly the same way and then simply to select the biggest and best blooms for specimen bloom classes.

The preparation of hybrid tea blooms is commonly linked with three special jobs, viz., "tying", "wiring", and "dressing". The practice of tying a loop of thick wool round all but the outermost petals is still widely practised, but I personally do not use it because it involves much extra work and I do not recommend it to beginners because, also, there is a risk of damage and, most important, few things are more likely to put a novice out of his stride than to have a bloom "blow" when the tie is removed after staging. Nevertheless, this is not a condemnation of "tying"; it certainly must be a valuable aid to transporting safely over long journeys. As to wiring, under the Society's rules, wire may only be used to keep the blooms erect but, if done at home, there is inevitably a secondary advantage in that it provides support and so helps to avoid damage to stems transported in water to the Show. Even so, I have found that a surprisingly high proportion of our modern hybrid tea roses have such strong necks as not really to need wire to keep the blooms erect. Moreover, even with much practice it is still easy to snap off a bloom at the first joint so, leaving others to decide for themselves, I take the easy way and wire only those stems which are of suspect strength and/or not straight in the neck. I do offer two hints to beginners though, viz., use only proper florists' wire which is of just the right size and temper for the job—and practise wiring some expendable stems before tackling those you want to exhibit.

As to dressing, which commonly is taken as meaning manipulation of petals, this is an apparently inexhaustible subject of discussion and argument wherever roses are shown, but the crucial fact in the United Kingdom is that the Society's Regulations and Rules for judging stipulate, in at least three places, that a bloom so overdressed as to alter its character will be treated as a bad bloom, so there is no excuse for either exhibitors or judges disregarding it. Why practise any dressing at all? My friend Lionel Lawrence, Editor of the *Australian Rose Annual*, in answer to a delegate who argued this question earnestly and at considerable length during the New Zealand Convention, simply said, "Would you like your daughter to enter a beauty contest exactly as she got out of bed?" (thereby causing a temporary collapse of both questioner and audience). I see no objection to dressing if it is interpreted as a gentle grooming to help a bloom attain full beauty *without* altering its character in any way and I offer this objective as a general guide.

In the actual process of preparation, again time and effort can be saved later by throughout exercising one's powers of selection so, starting with the apparently biggest and best and finishing with the poorest, I take each stem in turn, wire it if necessary, clean the bloom and leaves (as previously described for floribundas) and finally dress the bloom if needs be. A milk bottle filled with water is a useful adjunct to the last two tasks. On most blooms as cut from the plant, some of the petals in the two or three outermost rings are commonly not symmetrical with the others or need a little aid to open. Dressing boils down to a gentle correction of these deficiencies so as to achieve the desirable even, circular form. It is commonly done either by the fingers or by gentle pressure with the brush or by "pelleting", i.e. inserting small pellets or wedges between petals, which has the effect of opening the outer ones. The pellets are left in overnight and removed during staging at the Show when, generally, the petals will stay in the position desired. Nowadays I like this last method best (though not to the extent used in Australia) and use small wedges of plastic sponge of blue or other colour so distinct from that of the bloom as to reduce the risk of leaving any in it. An ideal tool for removing the pellets or wedges is a pair of stamp tweezers. As each stem is finished, it is put into the container(s), grouping potential "specimens" separately from "decoratives" and also, if the numbers warrant it, segregating obvious reserves from the first choices. Again, all this may sound over-fussy to some readers, but is a well-proved practical way of saving time and worry when the pressure is on at the Show in the morning; moreover, with practice the whole process becomes so natural that half a dozen or more stems can be finished in less time than it has taken me to write this paragraph.

Each container, when finished, needs to be placed in the coolest available place and I say available because if the architect of your house has done his job properly, the pantry floor may well qualify in theory. In an article in the *Rose Annual* some years ago, I suggested that, before encroaching on the said pantry, a man should present the discarded roses to his wife, but I do so no longer because, since then, it has occurred to me that as all exhibitors invariably get their best blooms several days too early or too late for the show, obviously it is much more graceful to present some of those to the boss of the pantry if you wish to use it! Anyway, having disposed the containers, one can then retire to bed to try to get a little well-earned rest before the alarm bell rings, unless the entries include a box of specimen blooms, in which case I prefer to tackle this task at home rather than leave it until the morning.

The preparation of boxes has been so adequately described in publications such as Past-President Fairbrother's and our Editor's well-known books as to need no enlargement by me herein. I only emphasize two things; first, do ensure that damp moss used to carpet the board is really clean and fresh—it is better not to use any than dirty, old stuff—and, secondly, never forget that no foliage other than that growing on the stems is permitted. In other words, never insert any loose leaves in a box, otherwise you will assuredly attract the dreaded "N.A.S." (Not According to Schedule) as did several exhibitors in major shows last year.

Resuming operations on the morning of the Show, I first urge you to allow plenty of time for the transporting and staging. A sound maxim is to add at least half an hour to the period you think will be ample, because you will undoubtedly be glad of it, especially if, like me, you are rather painstaking and slow at staging. For transporting, if as I have assumed so far, you have or can arrange private transport, the containers and equipment will be

'MATANGI' (floribunda)
[('*Little Darling*'×'*Goldilocks*')×['*Evelyn Fison*'×(R. macrophylla coryana×'*Tantau's Triumph*')]]×'*Picasso*'
Raised by Sam McGredy Roses International, New Zealand
TRIAL GROUND CERTIFICATE 1973
*See page* 183

First Prize Vase of six specimen blooms distinct (Class 42, Summer Show)

Both were exhibited by M. L. Watts, Northampton

First Prize Bowl of H.T. roses (Class 43, Summer Show)

ready for loading up and, apart from a last check that nothing has been left out, it only remains to ensure that the containers are so placed and supported as to obviate any serious risk of overturning. Incidentally, a strong breeze will open roses faster than warmth, so think twice before opening wide the car windows! For public transport, a large cardboard box of the type commonly used for distributing carnations to florists is convenient and adequate. Line it with tissue paper and place the roses in rows end to end, with their necks resting on rolls of tissue paper. Carried flat, they will travel safely, especially if tapes are strung over each row and stuck to the sides of the box. I use the same method, without tapes, for carrying roses in the dry by car and have found it perfectly safe, even on long, fast journeys.

Now comes the last act in the production—the staging of the roses. For many participants, this soon becomes and thereafter remains the most fascinating part of exhibiting, embodying as it does an opportunity to exercise one's creative art, spiced with a dash of competitive spirit and, hopefully, the chance of success. Even old hands rarely fail to feel some excitement on arrival at the Show, but this is the moment to proceed calmly and methodically, so do not succumb to the urge to rush in with the roses. Instead, first take your equipment and, unless the Show place is already well known to you, go inside, inspect the arrangements quietly and having located the classes you have entered, find a staging bench conveniently near to them. Collect and fill the receptacles with water, get your cards and then bring in your roses unless, of course, they have been transported dry, in which case the first job is to unpack and put them in water. "Handle with care" should remain your motto now; with everything conveniently to hand, staging can be started and, if there is a specimen box entry, I like to deal with it first by checking all the blooms carefully and replacing any that have blown or appear likely to do so by judging time, removing all pellets or ties and completing any further desirable grooming. The box can then be disposed on the show bench with its lid propped half open (but not removed), leaving one free to concentrate on the vase and/or bowl exhibits. If these include more than one of a kind, e.g. hybrid teas, the principal problem is not the mechanics of staging, but the selection of the particular roses to go in each class. This is largely a matter for personal choice and, whilst some exhibitors like to "split" their strength, I prefer to decide the class I would most like to win and do it first, using the *best* of the material available. The other classes are then done in turn in descending order, leaving the least attractive until the last, so that if time runs out it can be ditched, if unavoidable.

As to the "mechanics" and considering first vases, some packing is needed to keep the roses upright and in place. Cullings of Lonicera are the traditional form but, if used, care should be taken to ensure that only sufficient is employed to keep it down in the vase; overtight packing commonly causes wilting of the roses. Alternatively, sphagnum moss or paper packed between the stems in the neck of the vase will do, but is a rather tricky method and instead blocks of "oasis" or similar material are coming into favour. With all such packing in the top, a chunk of moss or newspaper wedged into the bottom of the vase will be found helpful in maintaining the ends of the stems in the right positions. Whichever method you adopt, I suggest you prepare all the vases and fill them with water before starting on the roses. Bowls provided usually have top and bottom grids, so apart from checking that the grids are firmly fixed in place (if not, change the bowl for a better one if you can!) they only have to be filled up. Do this now because, as with vases, without the weight of the water, containers can easily fall over whilst the roses are being arranged in them. If there are no grids, the ideal alternative is a large pin holder fixed with plasticine to the bottom (another task that can best be done at home if the bowl is your own).

Now at long last we have come to the actual staging of the roses. The blooms in vases and bowls must be arranged according to the staging and this means that where no background is provided and the exhibits can be viewed from all sides, an all-round effect is required. If this is not so and the exhibits can, in practice, be viewed from only one side, then the roses can be and commonly are staged to present a frontal effect. Occasionally no background is provided but two lines of benches are placed back to back with no gangway in between and then, I think, it is only reasonable to expect that a frontal effect is preferable. Thus, always check the staging arrangements before preparing your exhibits.

Whichever effect is appropriate, the objective in disposing the roses in their containers is a well-balanced, symmetrical arrangement, in the case of hybrid tea stems with the blooms spaced nicely and evenly apart (say about 3–4 inches—or if you prefer metric, 75–100 mm.) and whenever possible, in mixed exhibits the colours placed so that the adjacent ones are most complementary to each other. In practice, however, this ideal quite often is circumscribed by the relative lengths of stems available and the best possible effect then rests on the ingenuity and effort of the individual exhibitor.

To achieve a pleasing arrangement, it is helpful to envisage a geometrical pattern or shape and the following are those most commonly favoured for a *frontal* effect.

*Vases*: 3 stems:      a triangle, upright or inverted.
      4 stems:      a square, flat or tilted at 45 degrees.
      5 and 6 stems:  one rose in the centre, the others circled evenly
                   round it.

*Bowls*: A rainbow with the blooms on successive curves radiating upwards
  from the bowl:
  e.g.  9 stems: 3 lines with 4 in lowest 3 in middle and 2 in uppermost.
     10 stems: 3 lines with 3–4–3
     12 stems: 3 lines with 5–4–3 or
                  4 lines with 3–4–3–2, and so on.

These examples are not exhaustive but will, I trust, afford sound guidance until you have developed alternative ideas and preferences of your own.

The same general principles apply to floribundas, excepting that the heads are generally placed closer (but not bunched too closely) together to produce one homogeneous mass of bloom. With all types of roses in bowls I think that to have all the stems leaning forward at an appreciable angle detracts considerably from the overall effect; I try always to keep the back rows upright and fan the middle and bottom ones forward a little. Also, in my opinion, overlong stems are unattractive, though some exhibitors appear to be under the impression that points are gained by sheer length (or possibly imagine the judges will be awed with it)! Both ideas are unsound; the balance and quality of the whole arrangement are the essential criteria, so try for stem lengths which best achieve these criteria and do not hesitate to trim some to fit the overall pattern. As to the blooms themselves, whereas in boxes the largest generally are best put in the back row, in vases and bowls I prefer the opposite, i.e. the largest in the lowest positions. After each container is finished, recheck and make sure that the number of stems and varieties is in accordance with the schedule—it is very easy, especially with floribundas, to make an error.

Time is running out and one or two important jobs still remain to be done, but in any case, there is little more that I can convey in writing about staging that you will not learn more easily by careful observation of the best exhibits in local and national shows. As I have said, staging is an art and to become really good at it, practice and the determination to produce beautiful exhibits are all important.

Going back now to the box class, if you have an entry in it, remove the lid, raise the back a few inches so that the roses will slope pleasingly towards the front, make sure no ties or pellets have been left in the blooms and place name labels and your card in position. It now only remains to do the name labels and place the cards for the vases and bowls before packing up your equipment and departing to wait, as patiently as you can, for the Show to open. Meanwhile, I do ask you please to remember that all roses should be named, and to do this clearly and neatly. If you do not know a variety label it "NAME UNKNOWN". Visitors and even some fellow competitors will certainly be interested in one or more of your blooms if your exhibits are as good as I hope they will be (after reading these notes); and it is most irritating to be left in doubt about the varieties.

Lastly, in fairness to our long-suffering wives, I must mention that a final task awaits the men when they return home—to clear up the débris and put away the equipment tidily. Apart from that, the procedures that I have described will (given reasonably good roses, of course) ensure a fair chance of success in exhibitions at all levels from the small village show to the Society's great National events, but, in conclusion, I would emphasize that whether or not to implement all or only a few of my ideas, or indeed to add further work to them, is entirely a matter of personal choice. After all, exhibiting for amateurs is a hobby and, like all hobbies, is not worth pursuing unless it affords pleasure in one way or another to the participant so, whatever level you choose—good luck!

# On Judging Roses

## NORMAN HARDING

(*Amateur rose grower*)

My love of the rose as an amateur grower and as a member of the RNRS for over fifty years gives me the temerity to write on such a subject. This long association has brought me the privilege and pleasure of judging roses at both national and local levels.

In spite of this long association I am still far from knowing all there is to know about roses; to my mind, this is one of the joys of horticulture—one never finishes learning; the last chapter of the book of knowledge will never be written on a hobby which for me has become a source of real pleasure and fellowship.

What makes a good judge of roses? Firstly, I am sure one must have the love of roses in one's heart—to quote from the opening chapter of that classic *A Book about Roses* written by the first president of the Society, the Very Rev. Dean Hole, and first published in 1869. Secondly, I am sure one must have complete integrity in judgment and the ability to exorcise from one's mind all forms of bias. Bias in favour of an exhibitor is dishonesty; what one more often meets with among judges is bias in favour of a particular variety. I have come across those who, for example, think 'Pink Favourite' or even 'Red Devil' can do no wrong! I am sure they can; for instance bad cultivation by overfeeding can produce coarse blooms which are a travesty of the real beauty of the rose. It is for this reason that I have never been greatly enamoured of the box classes, because I feel they do tend to encourage coarseness. But let me say also that I have seen many truly magnificent blooms in boxes.

The RNRS has now inaugurated an examination for judges, held annually, in two parts, practical and written. Those passing, as far as possible, are given the opportunity of being teamed up with experienced judges at the national shows. This is an excellent innovation, which must make for a more uniform and higher standard of judging throughout the country, if these judges are employed. Their names can be obtained from the secretary.

When I write about national shows please substitute we for I, because at these shows judging is always carried out by teams of a minimum of three, all basically looking for the same things, with the number of classes they are required to judge limited so that they do not have to make hurried decisions. This is something I feel sure local societies might well try to emulate.

Three judges represent the ideal team and although judges are not usually expensive items, I realize this is not always possible at local shows, especially in the case of small societies. Two judges are better than one, especially if a third can be called upon in the event of a difficult decision. Either of these two methods would, I am sure, greatly improve on all counts the standards of judging at local events.

*How do I judge roses?*—I read the Schedule carefully before I go to the show and again at the show in respect of the class I am about to judge. It is the judge's job, not always easy, to interpret the schedule to the best of his ability. It is the show secretary's business, in conjunction with his committee, to word the show schedule, rules and regulations governing the show. Some local show schedules I know only too well are ambiguously worded. There-fore, I would like to suggest to those responsible that they study the National Society's schedule before compiling their own, because much knowledge and long experience have gone into it. Send to the National Secretary for a copy.

The judge's job is made so much easier if the intention is clearly defined which, of course, it should be.

No judge likes marking an exhibitor's card "N.A.S." (Not according to schedule) but he has no alternative, as otherwise he may provoke appeals or even incur the wrath of other competitors. The moral for exhibitors is to read their schedule more than once, because I have seen seasoned national competitors' cards marked "N.A.S." Those exhibits contravening the schedule and regulations are disqualified and although a good judge hates doing this, I have known it to help the offending exhibitor in the long run.

*What do I look for when judging roses?* One learns instinctively to spot good roses, but the RNRS judging rules are the only acceptable procedure and I am sure they should be accepted in this country at least, whether or not a society is affiliated to the National Society. A century of knowledge and experience has gone into them, contributed down the years by the cream of Britain's amateur and professional growers, and where are roses better grown than in this country?

Judges are required to judge exhibits according to their condition at the time of inspection. They must *not* be influenced by what they would have been like earlier or by what immature blooms may develop into later in the day. Having eliminated those exhibits which are "N.A.S." and those not of sufficient merit to warrant more detailed consideration, from those remaining I look for exhibits which come nearest to the definition of standards, Rule 10, which is the fundamental basis of all judging.

The standards required in the case of hybrid teas (Rule 10a) are form, substance, freshness, brilliance and purity of colour—the blooms being of a size fully representative of the variety. Form is accepted as a bloom half to three-quarters open, of circular outline, having a well-formed centre. Both blooms and foliage, where applicable, must be clean, free from disease and damage and showing evidence of good cultivation.

In the specimen classes I disqualify blooms left tied. Blooms with split or confused centres, overdressed or coarse are bad blooms, so I downpoint them, firstly making a mental or maybe a written note. By doing this, one soon gets an overall impression of the worthwhile exhibits. Before making my final decision I again go over all those eliminated, to make sure I have made no mistakes. Here—for the benefit of the uninitiated—I would like to say something about overdressing, because I feel too many overdressed blooms are still getting past some judges. Overdressing means manipulating the petals, usually with a camel-hair brush, so as to alter the character of the variety, thereby producing an unnatural appearance. In bad cases the petals in the two outside rows are forced back so that they reflex as no rose would in the garden. I have even seen the petals broken in the centre from rough handling. Small rubber wedges are now being used to dress blooms, especially in some overseas countries, but little is being done yet with these in this country.

When competition is close Rules 12–15 are applied to specimen blooms in boxes, bowls, and vases. In the specimen boxes individual blooms are pointed, three points being given for a high class bloom, two for a medium and one for others worthy of consideration. Often a three point bloom is selected and referred to in order to maintain an even standard of judging. One or even two extra points may be awarded to an outstanding bloom, the final total then deciding the placings. Specimen blooms in vases and bowls are judged as above where necessary. In addition they are regarded as units and additional points are awarded, up to three per exhibit for quality and condition of foliage and a maximum of three for general and colour arrangement.

Hybrid tea blooms (other than specimen blooms), Floribundas, Floribundas H.T. type and shrub roses (but not climbers or ramblers) are pointed as follows: ten for brilliance and purity of colour, refinement and freshness, six for arrangement, ten for decorative beauty and form of blooms or truss and four for foliage. The definition of standards for these classes is also covered by Rule 10(b). In the case of floribunda and shrub types, I look for those stems with the major proportion of flowers open or partly open and unfaded, with flower heads of a size, brilliance of colour and placement which is characteristic of the variety. Flowers and foliage must be free from disease, major damage and giving evidence of good cultivation. When climbers and ramblers are included in the schedule, as they so often are at local shows, I apply the same basic judging standards. If at national shows all three judges are in agreement, all is well; if one disagrees and is unable to accept the opinions of the other two, then the exhibits are pointed as already discussed; one judge calls the suggested points, whilst the others stand by and stop him when they do not agree, one recording the points. The three are usually ultimately able to agree, sometimes after discussion; if not, it has to be a majority decision, often after consulting an independent judge.

I never award prizes to really inferior exhibits, but I do depress standards somewhat at local shows, depending on my assessment of the quality the exhibitors are capable of, so as not to be too discouraging to worthy efforts. The judge's decision is final as to quality and placing, but exhibitors are usually allowed to appeal where they consider errors have been made in interpreting the schedule and/or regulations.

Judges must never be allowed to adjudicate in classes in which they or their families are exhibiting. Not only must justice be done; it must also be seen to be done. So you see, judges try their level best to make fair decisions. Exhibiting is a great experience and depends upon endeavour; if this it not genuine, then awards are of no value to the right-thinking exhibitor.

So rose lovers and growers, do have a go, and if the judges apply what I have written and you get a first, second or third on your card—what a worth-while thrill!

## SHOW DAY

With water deep and cool in plastic pails
I stand among the roses in the dawn.
The tranquil air still curls with wispy trails,
A perfect July day is newly born.

The stillness has a magic like a spell.
The garden echoes to the call of birds,
Whose busy chatter and the cuckoo's bell
Proclaim their forecast, without need for words.

On such a day of colour and of sun,
May peace of mind and harmony enclose
Both young and old, and rich and poor, at one
United by, and honouring, the Rose.

Today's the day! Today it must be fine!
Today's the day we've waited for since spring,
The culmination of this work of mine,
The savage pruning and the cosseting.

The vigilance for aphids, scourge of weeds,
The spraying against mildew and the rest,
Disbudding, shade adjusting, foliar feeds,
In quest of blooms yet better than the best.

Today's the Show, so now to the selection.
I choose with mixed anxiety and pride.
My beauties stand like spears in their perfection,
The timing's right, and I am satisfied.

For what can match the sheen of velvet petal,
Or tasselled anthers rich with dusted gold?
The sturdy stems, and leaves like polished metal
That servants of 'Pink Favourite' behold.

The perfect rose is exquisite, enchanting.
The duty to present her well is ours.
Cut long, cut carefully, cut clean and slanting
And plunge in water right up to the flowers.

Only the pride is worthy of the Palace.
Only perfection's peak can we engage.
Is 'Grandpa Dickson' worthy of the chalice?
Can 'Canterbury' make the pilgrimage?

The mists have gone. The once green skies of dawning
Are lighting up with radiance, palest blue.
God's surely in His Heaven this great morning,
With lawn and leaf still heavy with the dew.

'Bettina's good, and so is 'Montezuma',
And 'News' with wine-dark mystery is blessed,
Yet 'Papa Meilland'—temperamental bloomer—
Can sweep the board with velvet petal dressed.

Perhaps some 'Peace' and 'Fragrant Cloud' for bankers.
'Anne Watkins' and 'Red Devil' I'll disturb.
'Fred Loads' and 'Evelyn Fison' will be anchors
In their respective classes. They're superb.

All instruments to showman's art essential
Were checked into the postered car last night—
Schedule, containers, wires and cards and pencil,
Soft brushes, secateurs and scissors bright.

And, countrywide, my rivals will be doing
The same as me, with purpose in accord,
And, next to mine, on show-bench will be wooing
The Judges' keen appraisal and award.

*The sun is up! The cargo I've selected*
*Has treasure rich with fragrances and charms.*
*I see still more that should not be rejected,*
*Like 'Margaret' and 'Elizabeth of Glamis'.*

*The car is waiting, and we've far to travel,*
*Though 'Queen Elizabeth' is proud and gay.*
*Is that the theme I'm trying to unravel?*
*Will 'Royal Highness' crown my "Royal" day?*

K. TOWNLEY JOHNSON

# A Breeder's Story

## J. L. HARKNESS

*(Rose nurseryman and breeder)*

It is well known that to attract readers, professional writers have a simple recipe: sex, money and violence. In consequence, roses rarely haunt the headlines. The only time our nursery became front-page news was when the police flushed a wanted man from a hotel in Hitchin. A wild chase ensued. Becoming more wanted every moment, the fugitive escaped in one of the police cars, abandoned it, broke down a front door, took the house-holder's car keys at pistol point, and was run to earth, if that is the right expression, on the roof of our shed. He then threatened to shoot two of our staff, in reply to which the police shot him. He was not, of course, a Hertfordshire man.

The incident at the nursery was over in about fifteen minutes, and the only active part we took was keeping out of harm's way. But this lamentable episode brought the newshawks on the wing, and their flights of fancy brought us more fame than we had earned from many years' industrious toil among our beloved roses.

As a general rule, we cannot give journalists this sort of copy. Citizens of the underworld do not habitually wage their wars on our rose nurseries; lurid excesses of a lustful nature are more commonly brought to light outside the nursery gate, indeed far from it, in sinful sweltering cities. Violence and sex discounted, the journalist who would make news out of roses turns to money.

When I see in print the enormous value of roses, I can hardly credit the statement Barclays Bank regularly sends me. With money flowing on every side of me, I remain like a rock sticking out in the river, dry amidst the wet. For example, *T.V. Times* announced that rose breeding in Britain was a £15 million business (I'm not sure if it wasn't actually £50 million? I discarded the cutting in some distaste). When Grampian Television made a very good film on breeding roses, they had to call it, "There's Money in Roses". The title shot was roses on a background of pound notes, which were probably depreciating faster than the flowers! The lead in this film (but not the title role, although I daresay he tried) was taken by Alec Cocker, who if not an established star of the screen, could well be described as hero of many a staging.

Then *Garden News* chipped in with a bit about an Amateur-raised variety named 'Portrait'. According to them, the raiser was on velvet for the rest of his life; as if the rewards from roses made Littlewood's more generous dividends look like small change. And you, no doubt, are quite used to reading similar tales of treasure trove.

It is not only a shame to mislead people about the value of their seedlings, but also extremely embarrassing to the nurseryman. His cheque for "Share of Royalties—£22" evokes not gratitude, but deep suspicion. Yet such a sum is not unlikely, and at the risk of spoiling the happy dreams, I will now unveil the finances of breeding new roses in all their naked horror.

The total number of roses budded, on which some royalty or commission is payable, is around three million. It is rather a small proportion of the total grown in the country, a fact explained by the reluctance of growers to pay royalties; especially if they grow for stores or garden centres, who just want to sell a red rose or a yellow one, and all at one price.

The commission or royalty usually ranges from 1p to 5p, and if we take 2½p as the average, we are probably putting it on the high side. Multiply 2½p by three million, and you obtain, £75,000.

About 250 protected varieties are on sale, so the share for each is £300. Take away the costs of getting and maintaining protection, of operating the rights, of publicity and other expenses, and £300 shrinks, without even mentioning the cost of breeding in the first place. Allow something for the breeder, something for the distributor, and they are both lucky if their cheque reaches £100.

That is the average. On the bottom of the scale, I and others have actually succeeded in offering varieties for which the receipts (but unfortunately not the expenses) were zero. It is fair to look at the top of the tree also, and I suppose the most successful protected varieties are 'Alec's Red', 'Diorama', 'Grandpa Dickson', 'Arthur Bell', 'Handel', 'Schoolgirl' and 'Whisky Mac'. When you reconsider the three million total spread over 250 varieties, it is obvious at once that any protected rose is fortunate to reach 100,000 budded. The commission on 100,000 at 2p on 'Alec's Red' would yield £2000; that of 1½p on 'Diorama', £1500. It is sums like these that only the outstanding roses have a chance to earn, to pay for the breeding stations which, once in many years, may find such a variety.

When you think that a dozen or more breeding establishments in this country are trying to share the figures I have mentioned, I hope the deceit of riches has been dispelled from your eyes for ever. Any prudent investor would laugh at such a project, and the truth is, I think, that rose breeders are beguiled by sirens other than money.

If an outstanding variety does not turn up, the grower may "promote" an ordinary one. New roses are not exotic treasures found once in a lifetime. They are abundant, raised by an ever-increasing horde of hybridists. Although the great roses are rare, second- and third-rate varieties are common as can be.

I always understood the word "promote" to infer an advancement in rank or status. And I was much puzzled when my friends referred to the task of selling a rose as "promotion". Finally it dawned on me that the trick is to give the variety an advance in rank, say from second rate to first rate, and then sell it. Thus the term "promotion" is a fairly accurate description of an unsavoury business.

But we must be fair and acknowledge the debt we all owe to men of energy and vision who have recognized a first-rate variety and dinned its merits into our ears. That is not "promotion"; it is good salesmanship in the honourable, if little used, sense of that term.

I keep writing the word "variety", and I hope the Editor has let it stand,[1] unlike other Editors who cross it out in favour of "cultivar", thus ruining the rhythm of the sentences. "Variety" is a word to savour on the tongue, soft syllables gracefully arranged, the long "i" holding the word together. But "cultivar" is a graceless word, offensive in almost any context, sounding as it does like a grunt and a belch. But to resume:

Breeders often fail in their work by wrongly appraising their products. For if their duty is to present good roses, they plainly fail every time they sell a bad one. Such mistakes usually happen at the start of one's career, from too much eagerness and haste. But the time of self-deception must soon pass, if one is to gain a reputation for probity and good judgment. As for the man

[1] In the light of this disarming approach, how could I possibly do otherwise?—*Ed.*

who persists in shouting that all his geese are swans, he might just as well beat the drum and announce he is either a fool or a liar, or both.

As money proves a snare and an empty hope to the greedy, so also are those cheated who seek "the bubble reputation". What of the peerless genius, who in those three words laid bare so much of man's folly and his knowledge of it? He has told how fame eats men like rust in iron. The man who wants fame, or having tasted it craves more, blows hard in the pipe, magnifies himself instead of his works, until the bubble breaks and he finds his *raison d'être* has suffered a most unsatisfactory substitution.

It is, of course, agreeable to be well thought of, or even to suppose it. When people take pleasure in his roses, the breeder is a happy man. But let him keep his ego in place. Fame in the rose world it like a splash in a trout stream. Ours is only a little river, with many fish, and the water you or I moved is soon smooth again, until another jumps. The roses we breed have a short life, and the best fame we could earn would be the recognition by men in another century that something we produced had proved the key to their better roses.

Against that is the risk they might curse us as initiators of a line which brought disaster. If we want credit, we must also accept blame; and if we disclaim the blame, then neither is the credit ours to claim.

My own motives for starting as a professional rose breeder may now be confessed. I had played about with a few crosses at home, until I found in 1961 that business and pleasure were both pointing down the same delightful path. Plant Breeders' Rights were obviously coming in; I looked into the future, and saw myself sitting round the table with the Dicksons and McGredys and Meillands, all of them with a big fistful of cards, while poor Jack had none. Thus able to justify the expense to my firm, I had the pleasure of fulfilling a long-felt wish.

We chose what we thought were the best varieties for our breeding in 1962, and I am somewhat ashamed to say that from that year's crosses, we subsequently introduced 24 varieties, some of them ill advisedly. Nevertheless, it was a splendid looking batch of seedlings. Coming at a time when Floribundas were not yet expected to be three-quarters way to Hybrid Teas, my seedlings from 'Pink Parfait', 'Vera Dalton' and 'Ann Elizabeth' were fairly impressive. We brought no scientific knowledge to bear, nor have we learned much since. We had little idea what our parents would do, but about that we are now wiser.

We had enthusiasm, untiring patience, the will to work all hours in any conditions and the drive to shift difficulties out of our way. I am not ascribing these qualities to myself. They were contributed by all of us concerned, in a greater or lesser measure according to the individual. We managed the whole thing on a shoestring to start with.

Our only claim to any special knowledge is what we have gained in observation of the work we have done. Oh, we know a lot about crossing roses now, what this or that variety will do; in proportion, we are like a man carrying a bucket of water out of the sea. But we treasure our bucketful.

The outstanding rose from the 1962 crosses was 'Escapade'. This was 'Pink Parfait' × 'Baby Faurax', rather a strange cross on the face of it. I had thought 'Baby Faurax' an obvious parent if one wanted blue roses; a mistaken thought to date, but I still try; and I mated it with Floribundas of various colours, to observe results. I well remember the seedling plant of 'Escapade'. It was rather lax on the seed bench, but we budded it, and I often wonder whether now it would have been saved. As soon as it flowered in the field next year, it was obvious that here was something quite out of the ordinary. The name occurred to me two years later, when I saw it looking "sweet and saucy in the sun, out on another escapade with the bees". It gave an impression of innocence, of coming from a less naughty world, but ready for such scrapes as young beauty might decently get into. I like the names which my roses suggest to me themselves, better than those which someone else invents for them.

Sam McGredy was very generous in commending 'Escapade', but even his goodwill was unable to turn it into the journalist's dream of a golden money spinner. Its earning power in terms of royalties averages well under £100 a year. To my surprise, it has made more friends on the Continent than at home. It is twice a Gold Medal winner in Germany, came First in the Copenhagen Trials, runner up in Orléans and in 1973 it was chosen as an All German Rose Selection (ADR). The best it did in Britain was the Golden Thorn from Belfast. The Germans are very keen on using it in association with other garden plants, for which purpose some of them claim no rose fits better.

In the following year, 1963, our crosses produced some interesting colours in the lilac to purple range. Most of these are not of general appeal. However, we also found a pale Hybrid Tea, of which I soon became very fond, as you may tell, because I named it 'Elizabeth Harkness', after my very dear daughter. The cross was 'Red Dandy' × 'Piccadilly', the result not what we were looking for! I had noticed 'Red Dandy' gives bicolours easily; hence the mating with 'Piccadilly'.

I firmly believe that "Elizabeth" will make her way in the rose world; an

American catalogue refers to "the haunting beauty" of the flowers, and I find it hard to suppose that anyone can see its shapely and subtly coloured blooms without a tremor of delight. It flowers early, and repeats well. From my nurseryman friends, I have the impression it is a better rose in the south of England than in the north. Like most pale-coloured roses, it looks a bit wet and unhappy in the rain, when the petals tend to close. It needs to open in the sunshine, and when it does so a remarkable feature is the high average standard of the blooms. Most roses flower with some good blooms and some tatty ones. "Elizabeth"'s all seem to be good, as members may have seen in the bed at Bone Hill near the pond.

The year 1964 was a dud year. A few years ago I wrote articles in two *Annuals* to tell the story of our breeding venture. The first was called "Beginner's Luck"; followed by "The Second Step". Had I continued, I should have named the next one "Third Time Unlucky". We had our worst germination ever, and on looking back, I think our choice of parents was bad. We made nearly 1,000 crosses on to mothers from our own seedlings of the 1962 year, which we had not studied with sufficient care to justify so bold (and wasteful) an exercise.

One of those seedlings, however, proved fruitful in 1965. It was from cross number 1 in our seedling book, being alphabetically at the head of the 1962 list. I don't know how many people know 'Ann Elizabeth', a pretty pink Floribunda. When Mr Norman brought it to us, he said he thought it might be a pink 'Frensham'. Well, it was not quite that, being wavy in growth, but it was vigorous and attractive. We had treated 'Ann Elizabeth' with plenty of 'Allgold' pollen, the aim being a stronger 'Allgold'. Now 'Allgold' occasionally presents us with medium-sized, double flowers on its progeny, which I suppose may be due to 'Ellinor Le Grice', one of its parents. I had two such seedlings from 'Ann Elizabeth' × 'Allgold'. One was like a smaller 'Peace', but got mildew, and was destroyed after a year or two. The other was 1H; it had double flowers, well formed, pale yellow. The habit had too much 'Ann Elizabeth' in it, and the seed pods regularly took on a rough, black look. However, with 'Allgold' giving it some yellow, and 'Queen Elizabeth' lurking behind 'Ann Elizabeth', it seemed worth trying.

We put pollen of Armstrong's 'Yellow Cushion' on to 1H; and I have regularly noticed that 'Yellow Cushion' is a surprising little parent. It is not a very strong-growing variety itself, but it is perfectly capable of fathering vigorous children. 'Yellow Cushion' is also, in my experience, as apt to transmit orange colours as yellow. Therefore, I have a favourable opinion of it as a father; as a mother it has not been useful to us, for it does not set seed freely.

The result of this cross was an apricot-orange Floribunda, which in due time, and after some pleasant visits from that city's representatives, we named 'Southampton'. I noticed it doing well in the budded seedlings in the field in 1966, and again in 1967. One of those summers was dry (1966 I think) and the other wet; but 'Southampton' looked very well in both of them.

The Southampton representatives first came in 1967; and we found a very good friend in Alderman Haskell, who in no time at all was Reg to all the family. The Southampton folk had wanted a red or white rose, but knowing what disease is like in the south, I was scared stiff of sending them anything which might easily succumb. So when Reg and his friends arrived for a second look in 1968, I persuaded them, as eventually proved true, that 'Southampton' was the best of the lot. In fact, for a rose in this colour, it has so far proved a most healthy grower, and I notice that we are booking orders for large numbers of it for municipalities even to distant Lancashire. I hope it will continue to thrive, because I don't really like naming roses for other people in case a disappointment might ensue. From the nurseryman's point of view 'Southampton' is a profitable rose, since few varieties give so high a percentage of first grade plants. Unfortunately, like my other varieties, the return on royalties is negligible so far; but that is not the whole story, because my own firm does quite nicely with it.

We had our largest number of seedlings ever in 1966. By now, we had built our own greenhouse, and fully expected that our trials and errors were behind us, and all would be sunshine before us. The seeds germinated like mustard and cress, and selection became a process of exhaustion—mine. But out of all this toil came nothing to shout about.

The next year, 1967, was a vintage one. On the second bench, near the door of the greenhouse partition, a long stem produced a bud of glorious scarlet. As the flower opened, it was obvious that here was something more notable than we were used to seeing in our seedlings. The mother was 'Super Star', and the father was that precious 1 H, which had already given us 'Southampton'. I don't know which of us made the cross, but I am quite sure it was not me, because I would not have thought it a likely one. Anyway, it was logged as F 577 A, and budded.

When the few plants grew in the field next year, F 577 A was so obviously outstanding that I took the shoots for budding as they grew. With the happy result that I got around 200 budded. The scarlet colour, although quite similar to 'Duke of Windsor' when you held the flowers side by side, gave a more luminous effect on the plants. I always thought some of 'Allgold's' yellow must lie within it.

You will have guessed now that F 577 A is 'Alexander'. The name arose in this way: I had for some years been friendly with Major-General Naylor, a most kindly man, to whom I feel much indebted for all his help and encouragement. Now having been a soldier for six years, I retain some fellow feeling for the military, and occasionally Frank Naylor and I would talk of the Army. Not, I hasten to add, on equal terms, because he was a distinguished soldier with a very gallant record, and I was only an amateur. And one day, our conversation turned to Field-Marshal Alexander—known to every soldier as Alex.

I had served in the Battalion of which Alex was Honorary Colonel and had seen him from a respectful distance on several occasions. Like every other soldier, I admired Alex. The man was an example of what a man should be: cool and in command of himself; courteous to one and all, however junior; brave, resourceful and clever; and by no outward hint or sign did it appear that he knew any of these things about himself. He was like a calm animal, that performs the tasks ordered for it in creation, and finds it natural to fulfil them perfectly.

When Frank Naylor told me that Alex was buried in the little Church at Ridge, where Frank was Churchwarden, it was only natural that I should express a wish to visit his grave. And as I stood there, I thought I should like to name a rose for Alex. My Regimental Association joined in sponsoring the idea, and it was duly sanctioned and done. I knew I had a fine, upright, soldierly rose in the right colour for him.

It had been foreseen that the name might not inform everyone who it was intended for. I should have chosen "Alex" myself, but feared confusion in many a packing shed with 'Alec's Red'. Some people assumed I had named it after my best friend, Alec Cocker. I have a story of a lady, with a Scots accent, who was quite sure of it. With a look on her face which suggested she knew the answer, she asked, "Oh, Mr Harkness, and whom did you name Alexander for?" I replied, "After Field-Marshal Alexander." There was a pause—Then, "Oh, do you tell me that? And I never knew Mr Cocker was a Field-Marshal."

So much for 'Alexander'; I seem to have written a lot about it, but I would not mind reading similar details about roses of the past.

I said 1967 was our vintage year, and so it was, because in the same year as 'Alexander', there was born a little treasure of quite a different character.

Back in 1963, I had been working with 'Phyllis Bide', an awkward rose to breed with. I chose it because I knew it from the 1930s, when we tried to include it in every planting scheme which needed climbing roses. Our reason was that 'Phyllis Bide' flowered more freely in September than any other climber of that time. I thought we might use it to breed repeat blooming climbers, and I was trying to get them orange. Therefore I used the pollen of 'Shepherd's Delight'.

The result was a rose of shrubby habit, with orange pink flowers, similar in foliage to 'Phyllis Bide'. This seedling was logged as 1113 A, and obviously was of interest for further breeding. I have been asked if I am sure it was fertilized by 'Shepherd's Delight', or could it have been a self? To which I replied that as the colour was apparently attributable to 'Shepherd's Delight', I had assumed the pollen had worked. But I cannot be perfectly certain on this point.

'Phyllis Bide', I should add for interest, is alleged to be perhaps 'Perle d'Or' × 'Gloire de Dijon'; but as we all know, it is difficult to be sure of these things. If that conjecture be true, I consider 'Phyllis Bide' a variety of extremely attractive ancestry.

Our 1113 A was in due time fertilized with pollen of 'Ballerina'. We had 15 heps from this cross, and I kept only one seedling in my summer selections, discarding the others, except one which had germinated late. This flowered after we had finished budding and we kept the seedling plant over winter, labelled F 263 B.

Next summer, it was still in the greenhouse, and it began to flower with small pink blooms slightly lilac, very dainty, like a firmer, flatter 'Ballerina' flower, but semi-double and much richer in colour. I was busy every day looking at the 1968 seedlings, and as the summer wore on, I never got round to cherishing F 263 B.

One of the pleasures of my life has been the men and women I have worked with, and I had the most splendid man in the greenhouse at the time. His name was Ted Deards (alas, he died last year) and he was one of the two whom the gunman threatened, if you remember him at the beginning of this article? And Ted moved to stand between the gunman and the other person, who was a girl.

Sometime in August I was in the greenhouse, when Ted looked at me, and said, very firmly so that I could not miss the message, "Surely you are going to bud this little fellow?" And if he had not prodded me, I might easily have neglected to do so. This little rose is named 'Yesterday', and I think it has given me more pleasure than anything else I have raised. And I usually think of Ted whenever I look upon it.

I thought of that name in bed one night. I was thinking of F 263 B, instead of going to sleep. Unfortunately, I have never mastered the art of thinking about roses in bed and at the same time letting on to my wife I am asleep. I don't know why my thinking should keep her awake, but she is a very intuitive person, and no sooner am I wandering about the nursery in my mind, when she advises me to stop working and go to sleep.

Anyway, one night I was more cunning than usual, and thought happily about F 263 B. If 'Phyllis Bide' went back to 'Gloire de Dijon' and 'Perle d'Or', it could have been raised in the 1880s instead of the 1920s. If they had got it then, and crossed it with Polyanthas or Chinas, why, this little rose, or its twin, might have been raised in Queen Victoria's time. The material was mostly there. F 263 B could be a rose of yesterday. Yesterday? Is that a silly name for a Rose? 'Yesterday'? I think that suits it very well. I went to sleep then, out of pure gratitude.

It is really too soon to say what (if anything) we have outstanding from 1968 onwards. 'Compassion' (our Edland Medal winner) is from the 1968 crosses, and it certainly looks promising. I think I may have rather a nice Floribunda in orange from the 1969 crosses. The 1970 crosses seem to have been high average without a real high spot. 1971 looked splendid on the seed benches, but less impressive on first view in the field, except for some rather nice short ones. 1972 crosses did not look very good. And those of 1973, when you receive your *Annual*, ought to be germinating.

My own estimate of our varieties is that we can at present say we have raised only five first-class roses out of several hundred thousand seedlings. Yet there are 52 of ours named and (mostly) introduced. Many of these have some feature or other which is of interest. With hindsight, there are probably 20 which I should whistle back into the hutch, if I could call back time. We are much more mature now than when we started, and I no longer care if I have a year without introductions. I would rather wait for the good ones, and issue nothing else.

Running along with the story of our good ones, are dozens of serials, which end each year "to be continued in our next". Some of these may yield fruit in time, and they will arise from the work which has been advancing year by year.

Well, this is where I have got, and these are my thoughts after twelve years at breeding roses. It seems only yesterday we started. I hope that for all rose growers, whether breeders or not, our days among our roses will help to mould us into creatures who perform their ordained tasks in creation more perfectly.

# Lost and Found Roses
# A journey of rediscovery

**L. A. WYATT**
(*Amateur rose grower*)

We have now become highly conservation conscious, although conservationists have been active in the rose world for a number of years. Thanks to their efforts, many of the old garden roses, often referred to as the "old-fashioned" roses were saved from extinction, and through several able publicists, interest in them has revived.

The roses of the title have not been consciously assembled from motives of preservation, but had their origins in a tracing service for commercially obsolete cultivars in *The Rose* journal. The feature was called "Lost and Found", and through the enthusiastic co-operation of the readership in many parts of the world, most of the "lost" roses were brought to light. When the journal ceased publication at the end of 1969, some fourteen or so varieties remained untraced and it fell to me as the last Editor to attempt to find and distribute them.

Although reasons for wanting these old and often obscure sorts were never asked, they were often volunteered and were as varied as the roses themselves. For some it was a wish to renew old acquaintanceships—one had formed a wedding bouquet in the 1920s—others were important missing links in the historical chain of rose development. Sentiment, nostalgia, botanical interest and just plain curiosity all contributed to the quest which has ranged over the five continents. News of the availability of a few surplus plants in *The Rose Bulletin* produced an embarrassing number of additional requests, together with suggestions for the reintroduction of other obsolete cultivars whose owners felt were of sufficient merit for other rosarians to share.

Now that the assembly of the foundlings is as nearly complete as it is likely to be, it might be convenient to make a brief survey of some of the more interesting roses which have come into the net. They cover the period from 1830 to 1930, the most active and productive century in terms of innovations in the whole history of the genus.

The oldest reintroduction, 'Brennus' (Laffay, 1830), is a rare survivor of the once highly popular class of Hybrid Chinas, mostly derived from natural crosses between the Chinas and the once-flowering Gallicas, Centi-

140

'PHILIP HARVEY' (floribunda)
*'Fragrant Cloud'* × *'Circus'*
Raised by R. Harkness & Co. Ltd.
TRIAL GROUND CERTIFICATE 1972
*See* 1973 *Rose Annual, page* 184

'MELODY' (1911).
Lemon yellow, with a pin
haze at the half-open stage
(*see page* 143)

'SOLEIL D'OR' (1900)
Its historical and botanical
significance is of the greate
(*see page* 143)

folias and Damasks. In 1848, William Paul was listing 170 of them; at the beginning of this century, only nine remained, including 'Brennus'. "This very superb rose", wrote Thomas Rivers in 1857, "will form a pillar of beauty but rarely equalled." The latter statement no longer holds good, but it is nevertheless a highly decorative shrub which under correct treatment produces a mass of rich carmine blooms shaded with violet, over a longish, once-flowering period. As with all the older roses, it is wise to follow the cultural advice of those who knew them best and Rivers correctly emphasizes that 'Brennus' requires very little pruning—otherwise it will make wood at the expense of flowers. Historically, its chief interest lies in its contribution to the repeat flowering Hybrid Perpetuals whose advent was near.

The same Jules Laffay was initially responsible for this development, which was to carry through until the end of the Victorian era. His original group sent out between 1837 and 1840 were of little account and quickly disappeared, but his 'Rose de la Reine' (1842) was the real landmark. From it, all modern pink and white Hybrid Teas are descended. 'La Reine', as it is more usually called, had not been available for sixty years. Fortunately, several good colour engravings exist from which a check could be made, as several contenders came in before the authentic variety was found in East Germany. William Paul recalled in 1848 how his excitement at seeing 'La Reine' for the very first time caused a near catastrophe in Laffay's nursery at Auteuil. In his anxiety to get a closer look, he crashed into a bed of young seedlings and thus nearly ended a beautiful friendship (but which, in fact endured for the lifetime of both men). The blooms are large, globular, very full and strongly fragrant in the now fashionable lilac-pink with an intriguing carmine cast to the outer petals. They usually come solitary on long, firm stems on a tall, healthy plant amply furnished with light green foliage, which only falls prey to the leaf-cutter bee. It blooms early and repeats well, a feature noticeable in its seedlings, 'Anna de Diesbach' (1858) and 'François Michelon' (1871). Both are in varying shades of pink. Plant-wise too, they show a close affinity to 'La Reine', but with a deeper cup and a lesser petallage than 'La Reine' which averages 78, they are less inclined to ball in damp conditions. They have inherited the same damask fragrance which they transmitted to their progeny. Only two generations separate them from 'Pink Peace' (1959).

When the then National Rose Society instituted its Gold Medal award in 1883, the first recipient was Henry Bennett's 'Her Majesty'. In a contemporary account, it was reported that "the award was granted by acclamation", judging presumably being regarded as superfluous. The sole consideration could only have been bloom size which by any standard is enormous. For a rose of such historical interest, it is a pity that more cannot be said in its favour. The colour, a medium pink, is not outstanding and the extra-strong thorny growth and foliage are very susceptible to mildew (although this is now easily controlled with benomyl spray). It is quite devoid of scent and very rarely repeats, which is surprising seeing that it is technically a Hybrid Tea and not a Hybrid Perpetual, although it has always been classed as such.

To modern eyes, 'Viscountess Folkestone' which Bennett sent out in 1887 is altogether a much more attractive rose in pale pink with a salmon centre and reflexing petals. The flowering is very free through to late autumn and there is the bonus of a sweet perfume. It is of excellent bushy habit and does well as a standard. As a Hybrid Tea, it was not eligible for consideration for an award as the class was not officially recognized in this country until 1892 when, incidentally, the first Gold Medal to be awarded to a hybrid tea was gained by 'Mrs W. J. Grant'.

The question of whether or not the Hybrid Tea class should be recognized had exercised the Society for thirteen years, ever since Bennett, who had broken the virtual monopoly of the French raisers, had introduced his first "pedigree hybrids of the Tea rose" in 1879. The late Norman Young in *The Complete Rosarian* (1971) doubted whether any of these ten fully authenticated H.T.s were still extant. With commendable assiduity, Mr Derek Herincx has rediscovered two of them, 'Duchess of Westminster', a light cerise, and 'Beauty of Stapleford', a pretty pink with a richer pink centre. It will be returning shortly to the Wiltshire village where it was raised.

The pride of the Hybrid Perpetual class was undoubtedly the crimsons, which trace a common ancestry through 'Général Jacqueminot' (1853), so famous that it did not have to be rediscovered. Although its main descendants which the American, H. B. Ellwanger, described as the "Founding Fathers" have not been commercially available for some years, so many had been cherished by their admirers that tracing them presented few problems. These four mainstays all originated within a period of nine years and remained generally popular, especially among exhibitors, until well into this century because few Hybrid Teas in this colour reached the same level of reliability. 'Sénateur Vaisse' (1859) is the lightest in colour, a brilliant fiery red deepening with age and the lowest in petallage (average 32). This was followed by 'Charles Lefèbvre' (1861), one of the greatest crimson show roses of all time in a rich, velvety crimson with a high centre, a stately bloom which Foster-Melliar called "King of Roses"; 'Alfred Colomb' (1865), a plumper, less shapely flower in a lighter shade than 'Charles Lefèbvre' but probably a little more productive—a case of quality versus quantity—and 'Duke of Edinburgh' (1868), darkest of them all with a hint of maroon and the only one to be raised on this side of the Channel. The same Foster-Melliar considered 'Duke of Wellington' (1864), another French variety despite its name, to be superior to "Edinburgh". It is certainly a good rose, offering the same blackish shading to its large petals. It seems to have been much admired by visitors to Bone Hill.

The description of 'Soleil d'Or' (1900) in George Mount's catalogue for 1904 reads: "Single, deep yellow novelty". The writer was evidently as ill-informed as many later authors about this cultivar which revolutionized the colours in modern roses. It is, in fact, very double with a mass of short petals in butter yellow shot and splashed with red, to give an overall appearance of orange (although this particular shade was developed much later). The blooms come on short stems on a very tall, densely prickled plant furnished with light green, shiny foliage. Contrary to the widely held belief, it is not as prone to Black Spot as many other later introductions, but preventative spraying is nevertheless desirable. The scent is sweet and quite unlike that of any other rose; its remontancy is somewhat erratic, and it is better treated as a shrub rose. Its historical and botanical significance is of the greatest and there are few modern Hybrid Teas whose traceable pedigree does not include it.

Opinions differ as to the rose which brought the ultimate refinement in colour and form to the yellow garden roses. Some authorities give 'Rayon d'Or' (1910) but this had a poor constitution and is probably extinct, as all efforts to trace it have failed. Others suggest 'Mrs Wemyss Quin' (1914). There is, however, another earlier contender to which my attention was drawn by a rosarian who has grown it for many years. It is an American origination, sent out by Robert Scott & Son in 1911, although it is so little known there that it does not have an entry in *Modern Roses 7*, "the rosarians' bible", and another rose of the same name, 'Melody', was permitted to be registered in 1946. Trial plants of the original variety have exceeded all expectations. The colour is exquisite—lemon with a pink haze at the half-open stage of the high centred, scented blooms which usually come solitary on long, erect stems on a healthy plant of bushy habit. This is truly a valued find among the lost roses.

This excursion into the realm of lost and near-forgotten roses has yielded other rewarding finds. The best of the Bourbons, those other mainstays of the Victorian rose garden, have already been collected by Graham Thomas. It was, therefore, pleasing to rediscover the aptly named 'Queen of Bedders' which had been raised by Standish and Noble, the original proprietors of Sunningdale Nurseries in 1871. It is unusual in several respects, being one of the very few English raised Bourbons and falls into the very small group with a dwarf habit. It looks and behaves like a modern Floribunda (and has even been mistaken for one!) with its very deep green foliage setting off its deepest carmine rosettes which, under some conditions, take on a distinct shade of violet seen only in the Old Roses. A most charming little rose whose appeal might be stronger if its name were translated into 'Reine des Massifs', as many collectors expect their roses to be in the French tradition.

Another first-rate Bourbon saddled with a name handicap is 'Kronprinzessin Viktoria'. This sport from 'Souvenir de la Malmaison' arose in Prussia in 1888 and is sometimes recorded as 'Malmaison Jaune'. The yellow is, however, not much in evidence as the predominating colour is white; only the centre has a sulphur tint. In all other respects it resembles its world-famous parent. This sport was rediscovered simultaneously by Graham Thomas and myself in two widely separated localities. To complete this attractive trio, the second sport, often referred to in old literature as 'Malmaison Rouge' but more properly as 'Leweson Gower' has recently been collected. Again, the synonym is inaccurate as the colour is really carmine. It arose in the nursery of Henri Pradel in 1845, only two years after he had sent out its now world-famous parent.

It is a singular coincidence that two other very popular Bourbons, 'Zéphirine Drouhin' (1868) and 'Reine Victoria' (1872) each produced two colour mutations. In both cases, one sport became quite well known, but as far as can be ascertained, the other was never previously introduced commercially in this country. The first known sport of 'Zéphirine Drouhin' occurred in Denmark and was distributed in 1912. Its date of introduction just prior to the First World War probably accounts for its non-arrival here, and in 1919, Alex Dickson & Sons sent out the shell pink sport, 'Kathleen Harrop'. 'Martha' is, however, quite distinct, being a shade of pink intermediate between the other two. Like 'Kathleen Harrop' it does not appear to be quite so vigorous as the parent.

Another decided acquisition has been 'Mlle Alice Marchand', a pale rose pink variant of 'Reine Victoria' which was introduced in 1891. Those who have seen it consider its colour more attractive than that of the earlier sport, 'Mme Pierre Oger' (1878). Personal preferences aside, any addition to this select little group of pure Victoriana is welcome and one can only speculate why it was not introduced here originally and why its existence was not known earlier.

The same does not apply to the colour mutations of that world-beater, 'La France', often claimed on purely conjectural evidence as the first Hybrid Tea, sent out in 1867. 'Mlle Augustine Guinoisseau', also known as 'White La France', is self-explanatory. Originally reported as being less vigorous than 'La France', it now gives every indication of being a stronger grower as the older rose has unfortunately deteriorated. On the other side of the colour scale, Mr Derek Herincx has recently collected the darker pink sport, 'Duchess of Albany', which occurred a year earlier in 1888. Should any reversions occur, they could well be the means of reinvigorating the grand old parent. While on the subject of reinvigoration, it is also pleasing to report that an improved strain of the famous but now much weakened 'Gloire de Dijon' has been brought into the collection. This one is probably the same as that sent out by the firm of Guinoisseau in 1936, when difficulty in propagating really vigorous plants was beginning to be noticed.

Three Edwardian beauties, all Hybrid Teas, 'Mme Mélanie Soupert' (1905), 'Lady Alice Stanley' (1909) and 'Lady Pirrie' (1910) have lost none of their period grace and charm which kept them in the NRS popularity poll for more than two decades, while 'Kaiserin Augusta Viktoria' (1891) still possesses all the qualities looked for, but rarely found, in a white rose. Even the exacting Foster-Melliar could say in 1905 that it was "absolutely reliable". Almost seventy years and countless white Hybrid Teas later the same comment holds good. 'K. A. Viktoria', to which the name was often pruned, has always been popular on the continent where white roses are in greater demand for religious festivals and occasions, but had not been available here for many years. Our stock came from the collection of pre-1914 roses of Baroness de la Roche in Belgium. Shortly after it flowered for the first time, we discovered an ancient standard of it in a garden not half a mile from where this survey is being written. The owner had no idea of its identity.

With the exception of three or four varieties, the Teas which also formed an important part of the Victorian and Edwardian rose scene, have not been in general cultivation in this country for over half a century. It might, therefore, have been supposed that the more important members of the class would have proved extremely hard to find. Enquiries, however, revealed an unexpectedly keen interest and that an encouragingly large number were still being grown by a small band of enthusiasts in various parts of the world, particularly in Bermuda where climatic conditions favour their cultivation. From the original four foundlings, Teas, Dijon Teas and Noisettes have come in from a great many localities stretching from Bermuda to Bexley and from Belgium to Bulgaria, so that the group now numbers nearly

seventy. With the help of experienced growers of the Teas and recent con-
verts to the cult, these valuable acquisitions are now under evaluation. Much
useful information has already been gathered, but in order to do full justice
to this large assembly a separate survey will be necessary. Two popular
misconceptions can, however, be disposed of at once. There are no such
things as "Tea shape" and "Tea fragrance"; these characteristics are as
diverse among the Teas as in any other class.

This journey of rediscovery along the highways and by-ways of rose
history has brought a great deal of personal satisfaction. The elation at
finding the source of a variety previously believed to be extinct and of
seeing it bloom for the first time is something that only rose collectors can
know and understand. As one correspondent has recently written: "It is so
exciting to see 'in the flesh' roses which previously only existed as tantalizing
names in old rose books, even if the end result is sometimes not quite as it was
imagined." None of this would have been possible without the generous
help and co-operation of kindred spirits at home and abroad too numerous
to mention personally. Inevitably in a search of this nature, there have been
a few disappointments and there are still some much sought roses which
exist only as tantalizing names in old rose books. If there are any known
sources of authentic plants of 'Victor Verdier' (not to be confused with
'Madame Victor Verdier'), the polyantha pom-pon, 'Ma Pâquerette' and
'Madame Hoste' (Tea), such information would be greatly appreciated.

# Obituary

## DOUGLAS BUTCHER, D.H.M.

It is with a deep sense of loss which will be shared by many rosarians throughout the
world that I pen these few lines to record the death in 1973 of Douglas Butcher. He
was President of the National Rose Society of New Zealand from 1967 to 1972 and
was an honorary Vice-President of The Royal National Rose Society and holder of
the Dean Hole Medal. Doug, as he was known to all, was a jeweller and watchmaker
by profession and after his apprenticeship progressively established his own businesses
in several townships in the North Island. He was a man of remarkable versatility and
achieved eminence in a wide range of commercial and community affairs. He had the
unique distinction of rising from messenger boy to President of the New Zealand
United Fire Brigades Association and was awarded the Queen's Fire Service medal.

He will long be remembered as the dynamic leader of the large New Zealand contingent which came to London for the 1968 International Rose Conference and for the part he played in bringing about the International Rose Convention in Hamilton, New Zealand in 1971. Our sympathy is with Esme, his widow, who accompanied him on his many overseas tours concerned with their mutual love of the Rose.

W. A. JAMES

## JOHN WILLIAM MATTOCK, D.H.M.

On 16 April 1973 our John Mattock died at the age of seventy-four years: a family lost a fine parent; the rose trade a colleague it respected and of which it was proud—a man does not earn undeservedly the name of "Honest John"—and the Society one of its most outstanding members.

Those of us who were privileged to attend his funeral at St. Aloysius' Church, Oxford could not be other than impressed with our own numbers nor with the solid phalanx of members of his own family on the south side of the nave, and on the other side, that of the employees of John Mattock Ltd, a firm founded by his grandfather nearly a hundred years ago and now to be led by his son, John S. Mattock, who like his father did in 1938, has followed him in becoming a member of the Society's Council.

Measurement of what members contribute to the Society does not necessarily march with its milestones; these pass as they come. John Mattock's devoted services were recognised by his election to a Vice-Presidency in 1964 and the award in 1969 of the Society's highest honour, the Dean Hole Medal, for outstanding services to the Society and to the Rose. These he gave during his membership of the Council, of its Finance and General Purposes Committee, the New Seedling Judging Committee, the Exhibitions Committee and the Gardens Management Committee of which he was Chairman for a number of years.

He was no provider of snap judgements or of ready solutions to problems. Each was carefully thought out, all sides listened to and then came an opinion based on common sense, albeit governed by financial considerations, offered in laconic yet persuasive language. A patriarch, but one in the very best sense of that term. A generous and welcoming host and one who always had the wellbeing of the Society's staff in mind.

A devoted son of the Old Faith: all of us are grateful for having known him, to have enjoyed his friendship, to have appreciated his wisdom and integrity and, above all, to number him among those we recognise as being of the salt of the earth—he never lost its savour.

*(See photograph facing page 60)* G.E.

# Book Reviews

*The Rose in India,* by Dr B. P. Pal, 330 pp. Published by the Indian Council of Agricultural Research, New Delhi. Revised edition, June, 1972. Rs.43.50.

This second edition of Dr Pal's work, enlarged and revised, follows the publication of 1966, reviewed by Mr E. F. Allen in the 1968 *Rose Annual.*

Dr Pal, outstanding in his work for agriculture in India, has a long-standing love of roses. As grower, exhibitor and breeder he has had great success and one can sense his enthusiasm in his written work.

The advanced grower will find much of absorbing material in the book while, for the beginner, the simple language from a man of scientific training is very easily understood. While, naturally, the cultivation of the rose is set out as it applies in the conditions obtaining in India, the chapters on its History and Classification are of universal interest.

The pests with which the rose grower in India has to contend are rather frighteningly set out in the chapter on the subject; the English reader will surely take comfort in being spared the ravages of the Termites or White Ants, which do their deadly work underground, and of the Digger Wasps, which burrow into the pith of rose stems, after they have been pruned, to a depth of $4\frac{1}{2}$ to $6\frac{1}{2}$ in. This allows the entry of the fungus causing the Dieback disease.

Approximately 300 varieties bred in India are listed separately and over 500 are included in the Select List of Rose Varieties. Very many modern roses known and grown in this country are included in this list, but there are some very old favourites now seldom seen in the country of origin. For example, 'Dainty Bess' (1925), 'E. G. Hill' (1929), 'General MacArthur' (1905), 'Hadley' (1914), 'Kaiserin Auguste Viktoria' (1891), 'Lady Hillingdon' (1910), 'La France' (1867), 'McGredy's Ivory' (1929), 'President Herbert Hoover' (1930) and 'Una Wallace' (1921).

There are many coloured plates, some of which are good, but the majority fall well below the standard to which we are accustomed in our own *Rose Annual.* There are many half-tone plates of roses but these, in the opinion of the reviewer, are of very little use to the reader not familiar with the rose. For example, half-tone plates of 'Peace' and 'Virgo' on pages 49 and 84 respectively, of course, give no idea whatever of the colours of the flowers, and they are so much alike that it would not matter if the names were reversed. This criticism applies to all half-tone plates of the majority of roses, not only those in the publication under review.

The printing and the paper are excellent but in the copy which I have there is an unfortunate error in binding, pages 49 to 76 being wrongly placed between pages 98 and 99.

All who love the rose in its immense variety and universal appeal will enjoy the clarity and charm of Dr Pal's book.

R. L. PALLETT

*Roses for Enjoyment,* by Gordon Edwards. Published by David & Charles, October 1973. Price £2.95 net.

This is a revised edition of Gordon Edwards' book of the same name, published in 1962. It discusses how new breeds are developed, how to use roses in the garden, and has chapters on planting and cultivation, feeding, pruning, and details of the main pests and diseases which trouble our roses. It is very readable, and should be of interest to the amateur, particularly those just starting a rose garden, or those with small gardens. There is much good advice based on the author's own long experience growing many roses—as he says, just for pleasure. Sometimes the really important tips to follow are not emphasized enough, and unless the book is read very carefully might easily be missed.

With the vast number of varieties available on the market, though he does choose and recommend some of the best of the modern ones, many of his own favourites are older varieties, some of which might be difficult to obtain from nurserymen today, as they seem to have disappeared from the current rose catalogues.

There are some interesting statistics regarding rose breeders, the numbers of new varieties gaining RNRS awards, the new classification lists, and the expansion of the sale of rose trees in recent years, due to the popularity of roses for the ordinary gardener. The coloured plates, mainly showing roses growing in Mr Edwards' own garden are rather small, and in hardly enough detail for possible purchasers to decide whether they like that variety.

The fly-leaf cover describing the book has two errors. Gordon Edwards was not responsible for the RNRS publications. He was on the Publications Committee and on the New Seedling Judging Committee, but retired from both some two years ago.

A book light, and in many ways entertaining to the rose lover, it has much practical advice to offer, but perhaps is a little expensive at a cost of almost three pounds a copy.

J. H. SHOTTER

*Shrub Roses for Every Garden,* by Michael Gibson, 192 pp. Published by Collins, November, 1973. £2·95.

No doubt protocol lays down that he who writes the foreword should not write the review and the only reason for my doing both, at the urgent request of the Editor, was that there was insufficient time between its publication and our copy date for anyone else to read and review it.

Michael Gibson grows over 200 varieties of roses in his own garden and writes from experience gained there and from observations in many other gardens. He tempers his own enthusiasm for shrub roses with realism, admitting that many have faults and weaknesses, but his aim is to encourage all gardeners to add to the attractions of their gardens, whatever their size or site, by planting at least a few shrub roses.

After a brief look into rose history, he describes many different ways in which shrub roses can be used and gives helpful advice about the choice of varieties and about other plants which associate well with them. He explains how to look after and get the best out of them and uses line drawings to illustrate his advice about planting, pruning and pegging down and about tying in and training.

Most of the book is devoted to detailed descriptions of each of his selections as the best shrub roses, from species roses to some of the modern varieties and including some climbers and ramblers. These descriptions should greatly help the reader to choose suitable roses for his own garden. In this he should also be helped by the quite excellent watercolour paintings by Marjorie Blamey who has also done the line drawings: even the insides of the covers are attractively illustrated.

The book contains an interesting chapter on "Increasing your garden—free" with advice about taking cuttings, budding and hybridising with some clear illustrations which should encourage the inexperienced to experiment. He also lists many of the gardens, including Bone Hill, where shrub roses may be seen.

R. C. BALFOUR

*Roses.* Bibliography of Botanical, Horticultural and Other Works Related to the Genus *Rosa.* By Joanne Werger and Robert E. Burton, 169 pages, £2·50. Published by The Scarecrow Press Inc., Metuchen, N.J., 1972. Agents for the publishers: Bailey Bros. and Swinfen Ltd, Folkestone.

This book is an attempt to gather together particulars of works devoted exclusively (or nearly so) to the genus *Rosa.* This appears not to have been done since Mariano Vergara's *Bibliografia de la Rosa* (1892).

In the bibliography itself, the arrangement is alphabetically by the author (the title in the case of anonymous works) with serial publications in a separate alphabetical list. Works in all Western European, Slavic and Asian languages are included. It is of great interest to note the frequency with which the names of members of our own Society appear in the bibliography and to realize the very considerable part which they have played in promoting knowledge of the rose.

Perhaps the most interesting part of this publication is the 15-page résumé by the joint authors, of the books which, throughout the centuries, have been devoted to the rose. From Homer, the Bible, from Pliny the Elder down to the present decade of the twentieth century the main publications on the rose are discussed and evaluated. Our members will be pleased to read the tribute paid by the authors in this résumé. They say: "Perhaps the single most important source of the rose publications has been The Royal National Rose Society. *The Rose Annual* is an invaluable source of information." This is high praise from the authors, who have so thoroughly investigated the world's literature on the rose.

R. L. PALLETT

*The PBI Garden Book of Europe,* by Dr. D. G. Hessayon and J. P. Hessayon, 160 pp. Published by Elm Tree Books/Hamish Hamilton Ltd, October 1973, £2·25.

This is a very ambitious book and great fun to browse through as it aims to cover the garden scene throughout Europe by means of short but well-researched articles, charts, diagrams and colour illustrations.

Roses are well covered in a concise ten-page section and Britain's "top twenty" are illustrated in colour, the choice of these being based on the Society's Rose Analysis, 1972. In this section also are short biographies of Europe's fifteen leading rose breeders, with a note of their more successful seedlings.

Two items of rose news really were news to me: first the claim that the Imperial Library of China possessed 600 rose books in 500 B.C. (I would like to see a Chinese reference to substantiate this) and, secondly, the aerial photograph (p. 122) of the ultra modern rose garden at Seville, Spain, which was opened in March 1973. This should be worth a visit in a few years time.

Many other sections will interest most gardeners—notably those on early horticultural books, features of the "Grand Garden", lists of Botanic Gardens and short sections on the garden scene in nine European countries. The lists of 132 famous gardens which are open to the public and which summarize their special features (pp. 22, 23 and 26) will be most useful to local societies when arranging outings. I feel sure, also, that the armchair browser will be as intrigued as I was by such gems of information as that recording that the Botanic Garden at Padua is the world's oldest; or that the secret garden of the Villa Capponi was once only accessible through an underground tunnel from the house.

The House Plant section is perhaps the easiest to criticize, but the advice given is clearly aimed at the complete novice and for a majority of species in the various genera. More experienced growers will realize that many species of Aechmea, Columnea, Selaginella and Vriesia, to mention only a sample, can be grown successfully at temperatures well below the recommended 60°–80°F range.

It will perhaps shock East Anglians to find their famous crinkle-crankle walls re-christened "serpentine", but botanists will surely approve of the accurately spelt Latin names. I myself detected only one minor printing error. At a price of £2·25 it is splendid value.

E.F.A.

# Roses are Like People

**NANCY CADE**

(*Amateur rose grower*)

The first roses of my acquaintance lived in my grandmother's garden. One of my favourites, 'Mme Caroline Testout', was not unlike grandmama herself, rosy, round and remarkably hardy; generous with her gifts too, giving us colour and beauty all the summer long with never a grumble about her bed, her food or her companions. I remember Gran saying: "Oh I do love "Caroline", she's so good-tempered," and mama laughing and saying: "Oh darling! You treat roses like *people*."

She did too; she petted and praised them when they were well and dosed and nursed them when they were ill. Her medicine chest contained remedies of all kinds and she had a mother's eye for any symptoms of trouble.

I often think of Gran's garden when I am busy with my own roses—of that delicate gold aristocrat 'Maréchal Niel', palely loitering along one side of the greenhouse, needing much attention, such as sheltering from draughts and careful spraying, and on the other side of the tracks, as it were, there was virile, crimson 'George Dickson', the newcomer from Ireland (this was fifty years ago) and his brother Hugh, two glorious splashes of colour in Gran's rose family. They resided near some tall white lilies. "Just to set them off," said Gran. At the bottom of the garden, romping over a fence, were 'Dorothy Perkins' and 'Crimson Rambler', in a resounding clash of shocking pink and rich red; Gran did like plenty of colour!

When I, too, became a rose person I made a Memory Lane border behind the main rose garden, in which were planted old favourites. I had "George" and "Hugh", of course, and a climbing "Caroline", and 'Ophelia' swooning behind the lavender, and a 'Gloire de Dijon' on the russet-coloured wall, embracing a bold 'American Pillar' who responded with gusto, "That yellow cheek of her's to incarnadine", as my niece (a Fitzgerald fan) remarked.

Old Roses are wonderful for sentiment, but memories do not make a rose grower. Every year the catalogues are peopled with newcomers, with fashions in colours and shapes constantly changing; not so rapidly, not so drastically as our human figures and fashions, but unmistakably changing. We had the craze for many-petalled beauties, but now many of the frills and flounces of the rose garden are relegated to the back row of the chorus or, together with our own old-time frilly fashions, discarded altogether.

The modern rose garden is a symphony of singing colour; flaming orange, burning scarlets, shining golds, with the pinks and creams and whites among them to soothe and cool the scene.

I have all kinds of characters in my garden; most of them, especially the moderns, are sweet-tempered, grateful for attention and extremely resistant to disease.

Lovely, glowing 'Fragrant Cloud' is a favourite with us all and unlike many human Beauty Queens she is not in the least temperamental. She loves sunshine and an outdoor life, but is equally happy indoors, smiling at us all in a big silver bowl, or showing off her charms as a solo turn in a crystal specimen vase backed by a glossy green leaf. She does not care for rain, neither do I, and neither do several other beauties, including one of my favourite pinks, 'Dearest', who simply hates to get wet.

'Super Star', on the other hand, shines and sparkles through rain, wind and anything else our summer can throw at her. That subtle, glowing orange-vermilion colour opened a new phase in rose design. It should traditionally have been too positive a colour to mix with other more modest inhabitants of a rose bed, but now we see 'Super Star' everywhere, mingling happily with whites and yellows and pinks and even with reds and crimsons in big, many-patterned rose gardens, as well as displayed in one-colour glory. 'Super Star' is another fine indoor performer, and as she is a prolific bearer and likes being kept neat and tidy I cut her with long stems and arrange her in a cool, green glass vase.

'Grandpa Dickson' was rather fidgety when I gave him a home on a main corner of a rose bed. As befitting a famous prizewinner I wanted to show him off, so there he was in the place of honour. His first summer was spent there, and he obliged with a few perfect blooms, the cool, pale yellow blending beautifully with his young and lively pink neighbours. Then, for no apparent reason, he rebelled, lost his leaves, started dying back and in spite of much medication lost interest in life. When the appropriate time came we transferred him (we had four bushes) to a sheltered corner of Memory Lane where there was a nice big space vacated by several late lamented "oldies". It had been replenished with new soil, well prepared and deeply dug and settled, and here "Grandpa" lives now, perfectly happy, hobnobbing with our veterans and showing off his fine form and shining yellow face to all who care to admire him.

It is, of course, because the site suits him, but I like to think that he prefers the company. Roses really *are* like people, you know!

# Making a Garden in Derbyshire

## G. A. H. SHELDON

(*Amateur rose grower*)

The old experienced gardeners in the village had advised me that it took five to ten years to create a garden and, as I gazed at the five or six hundred square yards of land on which our garden had to be established, I could well believe it. The builders, like all builders, had thoughts only of producing a house. They had no thoughts of the dilemma which their methods produce when an owner takes possession. I gazed in bewilderment at the heaps of débris they had left in the immediate proximity to the house. There were piles of discarded bricks, broken bricks, tiles, torn fragments of wood, pieces of broken glass, empty paint tins, a lime-pit and quantities of gravel and sand.

The problem was not insurmountable. Even to one who had scarcely handled a spade and was a total ignoramus where gardening was concerned, it was obvious that this rubbish had to be removed first. But as one looked farther down the plot to where the grass, long and dank, and the nettles and bindweed were in complete possession, it produced a feeling of utter despair. Where to begin and how were the problems. Ultimately they were solved as the old sages of the village kindly offered advice as they passed along the public footpath at the back of our plot. The garden which gradually took shape from that miniature jungle was the result of several definite phases, which I can never forget, and as the rose eventually became the subject around which our garden was planned, members of the RNRS might be interested in those phases.

*Phase 1.*—Spade in hand I threaded my way through the long grass and contemplated how I should begin. I stood and stared, utterly nonplussed. I supposed the turf would have to be lifted and stacked and some digging started. Then Old Steve, a worthy villager, stumbled along the pathway, stick in hand and accompanied by his little terrier. His objective was the local, the "Red Cow", to which he was a regular. When he saw my efforts which amounted to little more than a scratching around with the spade he stopped in sheer consternation. Reluctantly and without any desire to hurt my feelings, he spoke. "Beggin' yer pardon mister, tha' wants ter start dern int' corner theer wheer it's lowest part o't garden. Ta't top layer o' turf off an' ta' it back a bit. Ner tha' digs forrard an' ma'es a trench. Put thi turf upside dern int' bottom o't trench, cut it up wi't spade and ner dig thi next bit forrard ont' turf. Tha'll 'a'e a trench ner for thi next lot o' turf." I couldn't really understand these instructions and said so. "A'll cum rernd an' show thi," was the reply. That is how a start was made. But before leaving me he offered me more valuable advice which I followed, and good advice it proved to be. "Dunna do ter much at once, ter ma'e thi sen ill. Do a bit each nate, and ev'ry nate, an' tha'll soon 'a'e it done." Gradually the wilderness became less like a jungle, and more like a ploughed field which, according to the villagers, it had once been.

*Phase 2.*—The area now has two lawns of nice texture. They were seeded and make an ideal setting for the three to four hundred roses that are grown in beds or borders around them.

My interest in rose growing began when a relative with some gardening experience advised me to grow them. "They are very little trouble once established, need a minimum of labour in their maintenance, and are economical in price for they are long lasting." They were the words of advice. At this time a neighbour who was a keen rosarian and a member of the NRS gave me a copy of an *Annual* dated about 1936. I remember the article which impressed me most consisted of a Symposium collected from rose growers in various parts of the country describing the effects which a very late May frost had on their trees. I gathered that the trees in most areas had been almost decimated, the first flower buds and foliage had been destroyed utterly. And yet most of the trees had survived. That was good enough for me. I would grow roses too.

I was introduced to a nurseryman whose rose fields were situated high up in the Gedling area of Nottingham where so many famous roses have been grown. Interest soon developed into zeal and the annual visit to his nursery became one of the important events in my life. It led to a happy friendship with the man who allowed me to wander at will over the glowing, colourful rose fields. One could not move in this delightful scene of brilliant colour, and the fragrance which pervaded the atmosphere, without a feeling of ecstasy and wonderment. One walked slowly along the rows observing the names of varieties on the painted white labels. Discussion with the nurseryman usually followed. Some varieties which had appealed to me met with his approval, whilst he was not reluctant to criticize others. A variety prone to disease or in some way faulty was never recommended. One learned to appreciate the honesty of his judgment. He taught me to be selective, to admire vigour and freedom of growth, and discard the types addicted to Mildew and Black Spot. I was very much indebted to him. Alas, he passed away a few years ago, as did his nursery, once his influence had gone.

Present-day buyers of rose trees might be interested to learn that my first purchases from him were at the rate of 70/- per 100 trees. That works out at 8½d. each.

*Phase* 3.—The lawns were made, the rose beds had been well prepared with a fair amount of farmyard manure incorporated in the bottom spit and the trees bought and planted. They gave us great pleasure, beginning to flower in June and continuing some years until December. On rare occasions a vase of roses formed a table decoration for the Christmas dinner. We continued to read any information about the rose which became available. We were now members of the NRS and *The Rose Annual* was eagerly anticipated each spring. We felt something was needed to relieve the flatness of the garden. A number of climbers were tried, but though there is ample scope for them in a big garden, in our small garden they served no real purpose. Now we have three which cover the wall of a sixteen-foot garage, 'Schoolgirl', 'Copenhagen' and 'Casino' and a small screen is covered with 'Danse du Feu' and the clematis 'Kathleen Wheeler'. On the front of the house we have clematis —'Jackmanii'—and the rose 'Mermaid', trained on a trellis.

*Phase* 4.—Still keen to break the monotony of flatness we considered the use of standard rose trees. I watched the budding of briars by professional growers and decided after the demonstration that standards budded by myself would be the answer to our last problem and phase. My wife and I were keen hikers, and we now spotted on our country walks seedling briars which would not be too difficult to lift in the autumn. We found in a country lane leading to a Derbyshire beauty spot overlooking the beautiful River Wye, dozens of suitable seedlings on each side of the cart track. We noted the position of the track and early in November, accompanied by my married son who had also become interested in budding *Rosa canina*, we set out in the car with spade, secateurs, rope and sacking, hoping to dig up sufficient for our needs. We were very excited as we approached the track and could hardly get there fast enough. The car was parked, and the implements, rope and sacking were carried to the spot. Alas, imagine our thoughts and chagrin when we discovered that every briar had been cut down to the ground by the workers of the County Council. It was a bitter disappointment and a blow to enthusiasts.

But rose enthusiasts are not easily deterred and an alternative source was found in a disused railway track where the metals have disappeared, whilst rose briar seedlings have thrived. It has proved a veritable treasure ground. We had no difficulty finding as many briars as we required. They were planted in every bed and border and were budded in pairs: 'Fragrant Cloud',

'Piccadilly', 'Iceberg', 'Super Star', 'Chicago Peace', 'Wendy Cussons', 'Pink Parfait', 'Peace', 'Stella' and 'Elsa Arnot'. Some of these standards now have heads three feet wide and three feet high, and serve our purpose ideally. They are supported on angle-iron posts and securely tied. Their creation has been the final phase in the making of our rose garden. The five to ten years forecast by the village gardeners, and quoted in our opening paragraph for making a garden, have proved to be more like thirty years, but what a great pleasure our roses have been to us during that time!

# Tale of a Certain Bronze Medal

## ROBERT J. KOPECKY, OMAHA, NEBRASKA, U.S.A.

A few years ago that eminent ambassador of rosedom, Harry Wheatcroft, visited Omaha, Nebraska, to address a national convention of the American Rose Society. At that time I requested and received a copy of his catalogue. Enclosed in the catalogue was a membership application form of The Royal National Rose Society. I was intrigued by the possibility of joining what is, perhaps, the oldest and largest horticultural society in the world. Within a short time I became the first person belonging to The Omaha Rose Society also to become a member of The Royal National Rose Society. Since then I have continually encouraged others to enrol, with the result that several rose growers in the Omaha area now comprise a nucleus of the Royal National/ Omaha Rose Society. Though small in numbers we take great pride in our affiliation. In fact, the ORS is now listed on the rolls of the RNRS as an affiliate society.

We were delighted to learn that the ORS would be able to secure a Bronze Medal from the RNRS. The Medal was to be awarded at our annual show, the class to be selected by the Show Chairman, within the guidelines set forth by The Royal National Rose Society. Everyone in the Omaha Society connected with the Royal National felt that in this way we were actually taking part in the activities of the RNRS.

As Show Chairman, apart from being the prime mover in promoting The Royal National in Omaha, I wrote to the Secretary, requesting our Medal and certificate. In their usual competent manner the staff at Bone Hill made certain we had our Medal in sufficient time for our show during the early part of June.

It had been decided that the Medal would be awarded to the person exhibiting the best English Box of six hybrid tea blooms. Furthermore, everyone agreed that the Medal would be awarded outright, as all of our trophies are of the perpetual challenge type, awarded to the winners on a yearly basis, to be returned prior to next year's show.

When the Medal arrived it was mounted on a background of dark green velvet and framed by a bronze oval frame to further enhance its appearance. Appropriately, the certificate was lettered in Old English script. The English Box classes of hybrid teas and also miniature rose blooms have become among the most interesting features of our show since their introduction. These classes draw considerable attention from the viewing public, while attracting more exhibitors each year.

It takes skill and ingenuity on the part of the rose growers in the Omaha area to have blooms ready for the show. We are continually beset by all manner of pitfalls and problems, for our local and climatic conditions are really not the best for growing roses. Late frosts, high winds to damage foliage and blooms, hail storms and excessive heat (temperatures in the upper 90's) at the wrong times, make the exhibitor's lot a trying one. Just as we solve one problem another will invariably come along to try our patience. I know all rosarians the world over have similar problems, but the tendency is to feel that you are being singled out for special treatment!

In showing English Boxes we feel the blooms should be of one variety, with each bloom at exactly the same stage of development. For my entry I had selected the variety 'Oldtimer', a lovely, large bronzy-coloured rose, but temperamental. Since timing is perhaps the most important factor, it seemed as if hourly checking would be needed for me to cut the blooms at their most perfect phase of natural beauty.

Prior to leaving for work one morning I checked the bushes, noting that some of the blooms were just about ready to be taken, but in my judgment they needed a wee bit more time on the bush to be at the very peak of perfection. Within an hour or so of my departure a strong south-westerly wind sprang up, accompanied by increasing temperatures and high humidity—a dreaded combination, as I have previously noted. These combined factors were to play havoc with my well-planned scheme to win the Medal. My wife, noticing the changing conditions that make rose growers in this part of the United States gnash their teeth and pull their hair, tried to contact me, but to no avail. She chose not to cut the blooms, knowing that I had checked them a short time before; she thought I would surely arrive in time to cut them myself. Needless to say, by the time I arrived home for lunch the blooms were far beyond their peak of perfection. Try as I might, I could not within the remaining time find blooms of the same excellent quality that the specimens of 'Oldtimer' would have possessed. However, I did enter a box, composed of two each of the varieties, 'Century Two', 'Pink Favourite' and 'Tiffany'. I realized that my chances of the Judges awarding me the coveted Medal were mighty slim indeed. With the added inducement of the Medal, everyone would be trying to win the English Box class. We knew the competition would be fierce with the quality of blooms second to none.

The recipient of the Medal proved to be Mrs Arley (Marian) Goodenkauf, one of the premier exhibitors in our Omaha society. In fact, Mrs Goodenkauf is one of the very best exhibitors in The American Rose Society. From a garden considered small by most standards, she continually produces magnificent blooms which time and again win "Queen of the Show". As usual, she displayed outstanding blooms of the rose 'First Prize'. Surprisingly, my entry was second to Mrs Goodenkauf's. I am hopeful that next year the gods will smile on my garden, allowing me to attempt to equal what I consider to be one of the very finest English Boxes that has been exhibited in any show I've attended or judged during the past few years.

The members of The Omaha/Royal National Rose Society are most grateful to have had the Medal to stimulate the growing and showing of the best possible blooms for our show. It gave us something just a little bit different to foster friendly competition.

Over the years all our members feel that we have gained much from our association with The Royal National Rose Society. The Medal was the frosting on the cake. Several others like myself are already planning ahead to next year.

This, then, is what it is all about—all rose growers, no matter where they reside, trying to raise that perfect rose or group of blooms.

Lastly, with the approaching centenary of The Royal National Rose Society, some members of the Omaha affiliate will perhaps find it possible to attend the convention. If they put forth the effort to attain this goal as they did in the pursuit of the Bronze Medal, I know that somehow, some way they will retrace the journey of that certain Bronze Medal of '73.

# The Decorative Classes

**JULIA CLEMENTS**

*International judge, lecturer and author on Floral Art*

Few can deny the attraction of the Royal National Rose Society's shows, and when they are favoured by a hot summer's day, as they were in 1973, they are even more appealing. I am always fascinated to see exhibitors rush into the Hall after judging to see the results and in the decorative section one can nearly always guarantee that Mrs Wells and Mrs Ward, both from Kent, will be among the prizewinners.

This year Mrs Judy Ward won three first prizes, one second and one fourth and the Queen Alexandra Memorial Trophy for the best decorated dinner table. This table was a dream. She used pink lace over a white cloth edged with silver, and on a pink velvet centre stand there rose a white figurine which she surrounded low down with pink and white roses. The four corner pieces were made in white-painted sardine tins and held pink and white roses with silver bows of ribbon. The staging was impeccable.

In complete contrast, Mrs K. Wells used a lemon-coloured cloth with coral napkins, the table being crossed lengthwise with narrow velvet ribbon in flame, coral red and green. The centrepiece was in flame, yellow and red roses flanked with tall coral candles standing on black bases. Very well executed, it came second. Mrs Pitman of London came third with a beautiful pink and cerise table decoration introducing purple grapes around the silver candelabra. Silver goblets were accessories.

This and other classes are restricted to those who grow their own roses and when I asked Mrs Ward how many roses she grew, she told me that she and her husband grow 250 rose bushes comprising Hybrid Teas, Floribundas, Shrub and Old Fashioned and that she brought eight buckets of roses to London for the show. She and her husband pick for two hours the day before the show; she then sorts them, strips them of lower leaves and thorns and leaves them in deep water, setting out the next day for the drive to London. She started staging about midnight and worked through without a break until 9.45 a.m. just before the judges arrival. And then we have the nerve to analyse and judge their exhibits! I think the exhibitors deserve a medal, each one of them.

There was a newcomer this year in the name of Mrs J. E. Tunmore and although it was her first try at the Society's summer show, she came away with three first prizes and one second out of five entries. Of course, she was

Class 97 at the Summer Show. "Reflections". An arrangement of roses, with rose foliage only. First Prize: Mrs E. M. Woodcock, Westcliff-on-Sea

Class 51 at the Autumn Show. "Sunset". An arrangement in a basket.
First Prize: Mrs K. Wells, Dover.

allowed to go into the Novices class as she had not shown before, but obviously she will not be a novice any longer. Her work was interesting and technique very good.

In the 'Riotous Red' class Mrs Ward took a first, using a black wrought-iron tripod standing on a back drape of red crystal nylon chiffon over orange taffeta, her roses being scarlet, crimson, cerise and flame red made in a tall triangular shape.

Almost all the exhibits in the "Victoriana" and "The Good Old Days" class were excellent. Mrs K. Wells took first here with a tiered pink glass epergne filled with old-fashioned roses and asparagus fern staged against plush velvet.

I often prefer some exhibits which have not won prizes. It may be that some technicality in the schedule has prevented them winning; for instance, in the class entitled "In the year 2000" I liked very much Mrs Wells' design using two metal rings placed crosswise one on top of the other, into which she inserted three roses and three twisted allium buds, in a forward movement. It was an eye-catcher, but perhaps the judges did not think it was *avant garde* enough for the year 2000. I liked also a tall styrofoam skyscraper-like effect, out of which protruded roses; I think this was by Mrs Ward. However, in this class Mrs Tunmore took first prize with an arrangement of lichen-covered branches in a modern pottery container standing on slate, with 'Handel' roses adding a second placement of roses and grey Onopordon thistle leaves. She said she meant it to represent from now to then. Of course, the schedule did not say from *now* to 2000, it said "In the year 2000", just that, so Mrs Tunmore was lucky, for her modern pottery container would probably be out of date in the year 2000!

The Colchester Rose Society's exhibit in the Affiliated Society class was one of the best I have seen. It represented "Holidays" and the roses used were allowed to come from any source. They used white 'Iceberg' roses bursting from a huge greeny-white plaster wave, the accessories being sunglasses, bikini and of course driftwood. It won first prize deservedly, my own analysis being that I felt a greeny-white/grey light and frothy type base material would have been better than the green and gold satin used. A minor point, but in top-class show work, it might be the one point which would lift the exhibit above another.

### The Autumn Show

After a superb summer—in such contrast to last year—the sun shone warm and brilliantly on the opening day of the Autumn Show on 14 September.

As usual the floral-arrangement classes proved very popular with the public who, with concern and admiration, added their own judgment to that of the official judges who were faced with classes such as "Trio", "Carnival", "Guy Fawkes Party", "The Jewel Box", "Caprice", "Sunset", etc.

Mrs K. Pitman entered in six classes and won a first and several seconds and thirds. She is a good exhibitor, yet she says she enters only three shows a year, that of the Summer and Autumn RNRS shows and one for her Club, adding she has so many other interests. She took first prize in the "Carnival" class, showing a grouping of yellow, red and flame roses, intertwined with paper streamers and yellow and blue masks against a red background. I liked her second-prize basket arrangement also.

In this "Carnival" class I loved the exhibit of Mrs J. Ward—in fact, I had picked it for first prize. She made and used a pink-covered oval base standing on four white tins, making it appear as a Carnival float. On the base was fixed a white arch topped with a gold crown and roses, and under the arch was an exquisite arrangement of pink and white roses joined by streamers to a prancing white horse, as though he was pulling the chariot. At the side "romped" the figure of a clown. It was a beautiful set-piece and Mrs Ward is an artist who certainly takes extreme trouble in the creation of her bases and accessories. She only came third in this class and the judges felt that pink was not a gay enough colour for "Carnival". I see their point, but others felt it represented a feminine Carnival Queen's float. So you never can tell!

However, Mrs Ward was rewarded with The RNRS Challenge Trophy for the best exhibit with her entry in the "Guy Fawkes Party" class. Five-foot width was allowed but with this width, I did not think enough height was given to obtain good balance for a set-piece. Nevertheless, she created a red, flame arrangement of roses at the right interspersed with dry dock and drift-wood, adding a left-hand grouping of fireworks, rockets, sparklers, matches, etc. This all stood against a black background covered with a shorter night blue skyline cut-out in felt, on which were pinned two huge dry *Allium giganteum* seed heads stuck with sequins to represent bursting fireworks.

Mrs K. Wells came second in this class with a central arrangement of orange and red roses with blacked bulrushes on a barrel, flanked on one side with a bottle out of which rockets and bulrushes appeared; the other side showed a grouping of fruit by a figure in a black felt cloak and hat.

Third prize went to Mrs D. Scanlon, who expertly grouped a mass of flame and red roses and croton leaves around a large barrel (gunpowder?). It was well done, though perhaps more accessories were needed.

An interesting entry in this class was made by Miss E. Champion, a visitor from the Cape Province of South Africa. She made a most original, almost vertical design of pink roses and maroon Dracaena leaves in a tall, pink glass goblet, placed on a pink/gold lurex cloth base and finished with pink/purple plums low down. It did not seem to interpret our idea of a Guy Fawkes Party, but then perhaps English history is not so well studied in South Africa! Nevertheless I liked her original style in this and other classes.

In the "Trio" class, using three roses only, Mrs K Wells took first prize, her additional foliage being most attractive, placed on top of a bronze figurine; she also won the "Sunset" basket class. Mrs D. Scanlon won the "Summer's End" (Rose foliage and heps) class and Mrs J. E. Tunmore took first prize in the "Caprice" class which was for roses incorporating a fan. This she did expertly, placing pink and white roses in front of and at the back of the white lace fan, giving the whole a three-dimensional effect.

Mrs K. Wells took first prize again in "The Jewel Box" class, which was for an arrangement of roses and rose foliage only. I felt accessories should have been allowed in this class, for it is difficult to portray an interpretation of jewels without the addition of some colourful beads, pearls or jewellery.

The schedule was certainly very interesting and must have presented a challenge to the exhibitors. I am always humbled when I see their imaginative work, but delighted that they come each year to give such pleasure to so many who admire their artistry.

## TO A ROSE

*What sight more full of beauty*
*Than the opening of a rose,*
*Its soft pink petals lustrous*
*With a silken sheen, enclose*
*A golden heart that's yearning*
*To be free to catch the sun,*
*Fragrant in the morning air,*
*Hiding when the day is done.*
*Does a subtle mystery*
*Dwell within a rose so fair?*
*Locked inside that golden heart*
*Is it love that blossoms there?*

DOROTHY HONOR THOMAS

# A Difficult Year

**VERA F. P. DAY,** N.D.H.

A comparatively mild winter in East Kent was followed by an unpleasantly cold spring, with exceptionally heavy rainstorms at intervals; and this was the pattern of the year—long dry spells with occasional torrential rain.

Roses were a little late in starting in our garden and I did not think there could be anything to say about my few bushes, but the unusual weather conditions produced a few unlooked-for happenings.

At the end of June I had a short holiday in Hereford, where there were marvellous roses all over the city. The earlier heavy spells of rain seemed to be concentrated mainly in south-east England; and I arrived home to find my bushes heavily plastered with brown rotting flowers—which I cleared off as soon as I was out of the taxi! There had been no wind to shake them off.

Then came mildew with the next bad weather: it is not troublesome as a rule, but like the mildew that attacks Michaelmas daisies it can be rampant in hot, dry weather. The old-fashioned moss roses were the worst affected. Strangely, it was the plants facing south-west that were badly attacked; some facing east and partly sheltered by a myrtle were very little affected, while others facing north-west—strong growers—were completely free.

In despair, I did nothing about the badly affected plants, and it cleared right off when cooler weather set in. There was very little Black Spot, and it did not appear until late September, when 'Magenta', 'Fashion' and 'Super Star' were badly attacked, the first two losing all their leaves.

Throughout the year my roses were remarkably free from insect pests. Leaf rolling sawfly caterpillars are usually very troublesome—but they could have been counted on the fingers of one hand! While blackfly is a nightmare on herbaceous plants, greenfly is never very troublesome at the seaside, and there was hardly any on the roses, and what there was the tree sparrows—more prevalent in this area than house sparrows—set to work and cleared—I didn't have to!

Owing to the very heavy first crop and subsequent lack of rain, secondary growth was very slow; in fact, there could hardly be said to be a second blooming. I wonder if this was the case in other areas?

# The Summer Show

**PETER WOOD, N.D.H.**

Having become used to the spaciousness of Alexandra Palace, conditions for the Summer Show were rather cramped in the halls of the Royal Horticultural Society in Vincent Square, London, on 29 and 30 June. The show opened on a gorgeous sunny day, bringing in the crowds which packed both halls, as well as Mr Edward Heath, the Prime Minister, who was interested in 'Alec's Red' and enquired whether it was named after "our Alec", referring to Sir Alec Douglas-Home. He was also introduced to 'Eurorose' on Dickson's exhibit.

Once again R. Harkness & Co. won the Championship Trophy for the best exhibit, as well as the Coronation Trophy for the best exhibit over 450 sq. ft, and a Large Gold Medal. I do not think that anyone would quarrel with the decision of the judges as it was a magnificent exhibit of roses, filling a large area of wall beneath the clock in the New Hall. Rush matting was used as background material and for the base on which the blooms of excellent quality were displayed. I was interested in their new small-flowered 'Yesterday', classed as floribunda-polyantha type. The blooms, paler in the centre, deepen at the edges to pinkish-purple. Some of the best blooms of 'Curiosity' I have seen were displayed here as well as 'Gay Gordons', 'Alexander', 'Rob Roy', 'Seven Seas' and 'Fairy Dancers', to mention only a few of the excellent range of varieties.

Bees Ltd took the Queen Mary Cup for the best exhibit over 300 sq. ft but under 450 sq. ft, and a Large Gold Medal. It was certainly a magnificent spectacle and most of the blooms appeared in excellent condition. They had a dark-coloured base to their island display on which low white tables, white trellis and pillars were used to display large bowls of blooms. Particularly good were the tall pillars of the red 'Cassandra' and 'Beauté'. Other popular varieties which were prominent included 'Arthur Bell', 'Milord', 'Iceberg', 'Duke of Windsor', 'Fragrant Cloud' and 'Josephine Bruce'.

Warley Rose Gardens made a real effort in their staging and were rewarded with the China Trophy for the best exhibit over 150 sq. ft and under 300 sq. ft and a Large Gold Medal. There was a grey base to their island exhibit with the sides edged in pale blue, and white stands were used for large bowls of blooms. Among their varieties were 'Miss Harp', 'Charleston', 'Fragrant Cloud', 'Golden Treasure', a bright yellow, clustered-flowered floribunda and a fine pink and silver hybrid tea called 'Admiral Rodney'.

'Whisky Mac' was looking good here as well as 'Piccadilly' and 'Princess Margaret of England'.

Once again E. B. LeGrice (Roses) Ltd won the Norman Rogers Cup for the best exhibit of 150 sq. ft or less as well as a Gold Medal. They used grey cloth for the base of the exhibit and their roses were arranged in silver bowls. A hybrid tea of promise here was 'Worthwhile', although the blooms were rather weather damaged. I also admired 'Dainty Maid', 'Shepherd's Delight', 'Maturity', a pink hybrid tea, 'Ripples', a lavender-blue floribunda, 'News', 'Just Joey', 'Dusky Maiden' looking in fine form and 'Fervid', bright scarlet.

A Large Gold Medal went to Cants of Colchester, who staged a large island exhibit in the centre of the New Hall. A beige-coloured material covered the base and at either end were two large platforms covered in the same material. Silver bowls at varying heights were used to display the roses and I admired their 1973 introduction 'Avignon', a floribunda with golden yellow blooms with a pink tinge. They also had a big display of 'Just Joey' as well as many other popular varieties, including 'Alec's Red', 'Red Planet', 'Prima Ballerina' and 'Arthur Bell'.

C. Gregory & Son received a Large Gold Medal for a good display of blooms. They concentrated their new varieties at one end, showing them in large urns on a polished wood base. They had a big group of 'Just Joey' and their new floribunda 'Fleur Cowles' was well displayed. It has pale cream, flushed pink blooms. 'Living Fire' was also living up to its name and 'Vanda Beauty', chrome yellow, was also good. The rest of the exhibit had a black base with white pillars for displaying the roses in black bowls.

The remaining Large Gold Medal was awarded to John Mattock Ltd. Not as ambitious as in the past, they made use of split bamboo screening to surround their pedestals for large vases of roses. The base was green and prominent varieties were 'Just Joey', 'Peer Gynt', 'Iced Ginger', 'Arthur Bell' and 'Franklin Engelmann'. Some of their old fashioned roses were 'Charles de Mills', 'Pink Grootendorst', and 'William Lobb'.

As they have done before, Peter Beales Ltd made a successful attempt to have an exhibit entirely different from everyone else. They deserved their Gold Medal and following their pattern of last year they divided their exhibit into colour groups, separated by walls of wattle hurdles. The red group consisted of varieties such as 'Europeana', 'Frensham', 'Evelyn Fison' and 'Lilli Marlene' on a white base. A blue base was chosen for 'Orangeade', 'Battle of Britain', 'Piccadilly' and 'Alison Wheatcroft'. Among their yellow and orange roses were 'King's Ransom', 'Allgold', 'Peace' and 'Vienna Charm'. White roses included 'Iceberg', 'Message' and 'Virgo' and these were displayed on a pink base. They were certainly interesting colour combinations.

Sunningdale Nurseries displayed their usual exhibit consisting of golden urns stood on large black and white tiles. They were awarded a Gold Medal. In the centre they had a stand of gold-painted wrought iron, and among their best roses were 'Gay Gordons' and 'Duke of Windsor'. 'Kathleen Joyce' in very pale pink was an interesting floribunda.

Harry Wheatcroft and Sons had another Gold Medal exhibit. Displaying against a wall of the hall may present problems, but here and in other exhibits the use of brass drawing-pins to hold up black cloth for a background is ugly. Harry's own rose 'Harry Wheatcroft' was well displayed with 'Oxfam', a pink hybrid tea, 'Fountain', 'Battle of Britain' and 'Whisky Mac'.

John Sanday (Roses) Ltd made a serious attempt to brighten their wall exhibit by using white and green drapes on a black base. The roses on white stands were well arranged and included 'City of Bath', the new 'Kenmore' and 'Emma Jane', as well as 'City of Gloucester', 'Bristol Post', 'Chatterbox' and 'Bob Woolley'. This exhibit was awarded a Silver Gilt Medal.

Once again Mark Court Nurseries won the William E. Harkness Memorial Trophy with a bowl of 'Alec's Red' roses. They also won the John Hart Memorial Cup for a box of 48 blooms and the A. C. Turner Challenge Cup for 15 distinct vases. Geo. Longley and Sons won the Kilbee Stuart Memorial Cup for a box of 24 distinct blooms.

### Amateurs

There were some excellent roses to be seen in the Old Hall where all the amateur exhibits were displayed, and none better than the 12 blooms which won the Edward Mawley Challenge Cup for F. E. Owen. His box consisted of 'Royal Highness', a very good 'Grandpa Dickson', 'Gavotte', 'Memoriam', 'Peter Frankenfeld', 'Red Devil', 'Akebono', 'Red Lion', 'Amatsu Otome', 'Isabel de Ortiz', 'Embassy' and 'Pink Favourite'. They were all beautiful blooms with hardly a fault. Mr Owen also took the Lindsell Cup for a box of 24 blooms. These were magnificent and included 'Grandpa Dickson', 'Brilliant', 'Lively', 'Christian Dior', 'Silver Lining', 'Alec's Red', 'Anne Letts', 'Embassy', 'Norman Hartnell', 'Royal Highness', 'Peaceful', 'Memoriam', 'City of Gloucester', 'Klaus Störtebeker', 'Northern Lights', 'Akebono', 'Red Lion', 'Gavotte', 'Sam McGredy', 'Peter Frankenfeld', 'Red Devil', 'McGredy's Ivory', 'Princess' and 'Bob Woolley'. Mr Owen also retained The Courtney Page Memorial Cup for the most successful exhibitor in classes 16 to 29 inclusive or 26 to 39 inclusive.

'Embassy' appeared to be a variety in good form for the show, as it appeared in many of the successful exhibits. It was also the Best Bloom in the Show shown by E. Plumpton in class 17. He also took the S. W. Burgess Memorial Cup for six vases of hybrid teas. These were some of the best I saw and included 'Royal Highness', 'Pink Favourite', 'Red Devil', 'Grandpa Dickson', 'Fred Gibson' and 'Isabel de Ortiz'. 'Red Devil' was particularly good.

Another highly successful exhibitor is Captain C. A. E. Stanfield, R.N. He won the Frank Naylor Memorial Class for a vase of five stems of climbing roses. 'Handel' and 'Swan Lake' were the varieties he used and they were in nice condition. Captain Stanfield also took the Brayfort Challenge Cup in class 31 for a box of six specimen blooms, which included 'Gay Crusader', 'Silver Lining', 'Gavotte', 'Akebono' and 'Red Devil'. I also liked his bowl of hybrid teas which took the Alfred Hewlett Memorial Class and included 'Red Devil', 'City of Bath', 'Grandpa Dickson', 'Summer Holiday', 'Peter Frankenfeld', 'Ernest H. Morse' and 'Silver Lining'. All the blooms were good, although one or two showed signs of weather damage.

R. L. Dillon showed good vases of floribunda roses and won a RNRS Trophy in class 23 with 'Happy Red', 'Kassel' and 'Iceberg'.

This year L. Poole from Cardiff won the H. R. Darlington Memorial Cup in class 36. He had six good vases of 'Gavotte', 'Red Devil', both marked a little, 'Royal Highness', 'Red Lion', 'Peter Frankenfeld' and 'Grandpa Dickson'.

Repeating his success of last year, L. E. J. Wood took the Nicholson Challenge Trophy in class 30 for a box of 12 blooms, all distinct varieties, with 'Fragrant Cloud', 'Pink Favourite', 'Grandpa Dickson', 'Charles Warren', 'Femina', 'City of Gloucester', 'Memoriam', 'Embassy', 'Red Devil', 'Gold Crown', 'Royal Highness' and 'Red Lion'.

Division C is devoted to amateur rosarians with not more than 500 rose trees. Class 40 for the Sam McGredy Challenge Cup is the stiffest test of all and it was won by M. L. Watts with an excellent box of 12 specimen blooms. Those he used included a lovely bloom of 'Embassy', 'Red Devil' (2) 'Isabel de Ortiz', 'Royal Highness', 'Gavotte', 'Grandpa Dickson', 'Jimmy Greaves' (2), 'Red Lion', 'Akebono' and 'Perfecta'.

In the same division he went on to win The Edward J. Holland Memorial Cup in class 45 for three distinct vases of hybrid tea roses. The blooms of 'Red Devil' were a little marked, but 'Royal Highness' and 'Isabel de Ortiz' were good. It was not surprising that he won the Edward Mawley Memorial Medal for the highest aggregate number of points in classes 40 to 48 inclusive.

The Gilbert Burch Memorial Class is the most important box class in Division D for amateurs with no more than 250 rose trees. This trophy was won by K. E. Poole with a box of six 'Red Devil', all very well matched. In the same division The Slaughter Memorial Cup is for three distinct vases of hybrid teas. J. K. Stevens was successful here with three excellent vases of 'Pink Favourite', 'Royal Highness' and 'Gavotte'. They were all evenly matched blooms and thoroughly deserved to win.

For amateurs with no more than 150 rose trees the most important box class is for the Charles Rigg Cup. It was won by R. West with 'Red Devil', a little marked, 'Fred Gibson', very good, two well-matched blooms of 'Gavotte', 'Pink Favourite' and 'Royal Highness'. They were smallish blooms but all the same very pleasing.

The Cocker Cup in class 58 is for a vase of six specimen blooms. F. E. Rixon was successful with 'Red Devil', 'Grandpa Dickson', 'Fragrant Cloud' and 'Pink Favourite'. 'Red Devil' was marked and one bloom of 'Pink Favourite' was not up to scratch, but all the same it was a reasonably good vase.

The Kathleen Louise Mahaffy Class is for amateurs with no more than 100 rose trees. This year it was won by M. Thompson for a box of rather small blooms which included 'Red Lion' (2) 'Piccadilly', 'Wendy Cussons' and 'Memoriam' (2).

The winner of class 72 for The Albert E. Griffith Memorial Class for amateurs with no more than 50 rose trees was E. W. A. Perry. In his vase he used 'Rose Gaujard', 'Shannon', 'Perfecta', 'Isabel de Ortiz' and 'Wendy Cussons'.

Once again Worcester Park Horticultural Society were the winners of the Hereford Centenary Cup in the Affiliated Societies section. Their exhibit was very similar to those of previous years. They made use of black and green drapes to display their large bowls of hybrid tea and floribunda roses. I have seen this society producing better roses, although there was no doubt that they were the winners of the class.

The East Kent Horticultural Society also repeated their success of the previous year by winning the Franklin Dennison Memorial Cup with two very good bowls of hybrid teas and floribundas respectively.

The Gardeners Company Challenge Cup for the most successful exhibitor in classes 75 to 89 inclusive was awarded to J. H. Anthony, and the Rev. H. Honywood D'Ombrain Memorial Cup for the best bowl of floribunda roses in classes 25, 39 or 46 went to M. E. Bullen.

# The Northern Rose Show, 1973

## R. D. SQUIRES

As Honorary Secretary of the North Western Group of members perhaps I could be excused for being biased toward the Lakeland Rose Show, who were our hosts for the 1973 Northern Show at "stately home" Holker Hall, Grange-over-Sands. However, I am an exiled Hampshire Hog and also a lover of the Leeds Flower Show and Roundhay Park; consequently I was able to view the Lakeland venture with an (almost) unjaundiced eye.

Unbounded enthusiasm, an army of volunteer workers, efficient organization and hospitality of the highest calibre are always evident at the Lakeland Show, but like our Yorkshire hosts of previous years, they were not able to control the pre-show weather, or the wholesale cancellations which inevitably followed and almost made it the "non-event rose show". To rose exhibitors and thespians alike, the battle cry of "The Show Must Go On" means just that. Everyone rallied round and the show did go on.

### Trade Section

A huge marquee, half empty, is a sad sight at any flower show and the sadness deepens when we know that the empty spaces should have been roses. The nurserymen who did stage deserved the highest praise. Fryer's Nurseries Ltd took the show's premier award, the "Barrow News & Mail Series" Perpetual Challenge Trophy and a Large Gold Medal for an island display which featured the new fragrant pink and silver bi-colour hybrid tea, 'Bobby Charlton'. The variety which caught the eye, however, was the vermilion-orange hybrid tea, 'Cheshire Life'; the several bowls of this variety all showed a lot of weatherproof potential. 'Aquarelle', a multi-coloured floribunda of orange, yellow and crimson also looked good, even if the colours are a little harsh. I particularly enjoyed the display of John Mattock Ltd, of Oxford, who made the long journey with some very interesting varieties and were awarded a Large Gold Medal. The display included species, old favourites, climbers and latest introductions, including 'Eurorose' and 'Bonfire Night'. An excellent bowl of the shrub rose 'Fountain' was as good as anything in the whole show. There were bowls of hybrid perpetuals, 'Baron Girod de L'Ain', 'Paul Neyron' and 'Souv. du Docteur Jamain', and a fine display of their new deep golden climber 'Dreaming Spires'. Robert Wright Ltd, of Formby received a Silver Gilt Medal, and their compact stand featured many established varieties with 'Megiddo' and 'Evelyn Fison' in excellent condition. C. Gregory & Son Ltd., of Stapleford were almost forced to cancel, but finally staged a display of their popular miniature roses, backed up by just two bowls of the orange and flame-red 'Living Fire', which won them a Silver Medal. Waterhouse Nurseries of Radway Green, near Crewe and F. W. Shaw and Son Ltd, of Gainsborough, also received Silver Medal awards for small but praiseworthy displays. Just two bowls of seedlings were submitted by the Trade in Class 202 and most interest was shown in that displayed by Robert Wright Ltd, a 'Spartan' × 'Orangeade' pink and gold floribunda with a distinct, fruity fragrance.

## Amateur Section

The benches in the amateurs' marquee also had a lot of vacant spaces and it was a great pity that the judges were forced to disqualify some of those that were staged! The tables were littered with cards bearing the dreaded "N.A.S.", mainly for the use of incorrect-sized vases and also for the use of too many stems. No one likes to see this—the exhibitor, the judge or more important, the visitor to the show—so exhibitors, please be a little more observant in future. Fred Owen of Tamworth gained three trophies, the Jubilee Trophy as most successful exhibitor in Divisions A or B, the Harry Wilding Trophy for a box of twelve in Class 204 which included fine specimens of 'Goliath', 'Akebono' and the old reliable 'Sam McGredy' and the Grange U.D.C. Silver Rose Bowl for three vases of hybrid teas in Class 209. Mr Owen's outstanding exhibit was a box of six which won Class 205 with two blooms each of 'Fred Gibson', 'Red Devil' and 'Grandpa Dickson'. Members from Scotland took full advantage of the new venue and staged a "mini-invasion" ably led by Lawrence Marcantonio of Ayr, who staged in Divisions A and B and gained four firsts, a second and a third. The three specimen blooms of 'Wendy Cussons', 'Royal Highness' and 'Red Devil' with which he won Class 207 were exceptionally clean and fresh and belied the pre-show weather. Also making his presence felt was kilted Jock Stewart from Stranraer, who took the Society's Silver Gilt Medal for Best Bloom with a fine specimen of 'Red Lion'. Jock, who was well known in rose circles in the Colchester area several years ago, proved that the move back north has not diminished his prowess at all, although he did say that the credit for the bloom should go to "those wonderful Ayrshire and Galloway cattle"! Some cattle!!! A reproduction French Carriage Clock, presented by a Barrow businessman, was won by the show's general secretary, Mike O'Loughlin, who staged the best vase of six hybrid teas in the show. Maureen Iddon of Hesketh Bank was awarded the Mabel Askew Trophy with a bowl of twelve hybrid teas in Class 221.

It was also good to see exhibitors who had travelled from Yorkshire supporting the show and undoubtedly their finest exhibit was a bowl of floribundas in Class 210, staged by J. I. M. Naylor of Leeds, which gained the Club Union Trophy for the best floribunda exhibit. R. Hall of Cullercoats, Northumberland, gained three trophies and was the most successful entrant in the 500 trees Division (C) and also in the classes for roses introduced prior to 1910. George Armer of Kendal had outstanding wins in Classes 236 and 228, relying in both cases on blooms of 'Red Devil', 'Gavotte' and 'Norman Hartnell'. The trophy for the most successful exhibitor in Division D was won by R. Venables of Sutton Coldfield, whose blooms stood out for their sparkling freshness. In the lower divisions it was notable to see many winning exhibits from members in the Bolton area, and none was better than the vase of 'Red Devil', 'Fragrant Cloud' and 'Ernest H. Morse' staged by H. Thomas in Class 250. 'Peace', 'Red Devil' and 'Fragrant Cloud' stood out in Class 245, which was won by D. J. O'Kane.

Undoubtedly the finest exhibits in the whole show and the most keenly contested were the classes for Affiliated Societies, where Congleton Horticultural Society once again proved themselves masters, winning both classes from the Yorkshire Rosarians Group. Congleton's three vases of floribundas were 'Lilli Marlene', 'Queen Elizabeth' and 'Megiddo' and in their bowls were good sprays of 'Satchmo', 'Korona', 'Europeana' and 'Fred Loads'. The Affiliated Societies Section is excluded from the award for Best Bloom; had this not been so several blooms in this section would have come in for consideration by the judges.

### Floral Art

The Society's classes formed only a small part of the Decorative Tent where the Lakeland Show's own floral arrangement classes were staged. However, the displays which were restricted to roses caused a great deal of interest and satisfaction. Winner of the Balfour Cup for best exhibit was senior citizen Mrs Hilda Smith of Orrell, Wigan with a pedestal arrangement of roses and assorted foliage entitled "Summer Profusion".

*          *          *

It made a wonderful setting for a flower show and one to which I feel sure many of us will look forward for return visits. Meantime, it is back to Roundhay Park, Leeds in 1974. Our grateful thanks are extended to Mr and Mrs Hugh Cavendish and their very helpful staff at Holker Hall, the President, Officers, Committee and workers of Lakeland Rose Show.

# The Autumn Rose Show

## ROY HAY

The Autumn Show at Westmininster was, I am sure, a delight for all those who visited it. I have been growing roses and reporting rose shows for getting on for forty years, and I did not see what the real rose specialist saw— that owing to the dry weather petals were shorter and flowers less full petalled than they ought to be. As far as I was concerned the blooms, undamaged by rain and, to my eye, very true to colour, were really lovely.

I might add that no matter what specialists' show I visit to report upon, whether it be irises, sweet peas, delphiniums, dahlias or chrysanthemums, there are always plenty of people who take a ghoulish delight in telling me quietly, "Of course, the quality is not here this year." Or, "The young 'uns don't have the knack of finishing their blooms properly." Or some other sour comment.

Of course, over the years one becomes accustomed to these sour comments, and we know that, to the ordinary member of the Society or of the public, the rose shows are as attractive as ever.

If I have a critical comment at all it is that I feel the number of varieties shown diminishes as the years go by. This is, of course, reflecting the general trend in the trade—growers are drastically reducing the number of varieties they stock. Probably this is no bad thing, provided they throw out those most prone to disease. It was noticeable that 'Super Star' was conspicuous by its absence. I saw it only once, and that was in an amateur class.

At this show R. Harkness & Co. Ltd won the Autumn Rose Challenge Cup for the best trade exhibit, also the Lewis Levy Memorial Cup for an exhibit of over 450 sq. ft, and, of course, a Large Gold Medal. John Mattock Ltd, who have been consistent winners of the big trophies, had to be content with second place—the D'Escofet Cup and a Large Gold Medal. But I confess I would not have liked to be a judge who had to decide between the exhibits of these two firms.

Harkness had lovely blooms of 'Allgold', 'Dandy Dick' and 'Busy Lizzie' (pink), and the climbers 'Pink Perpêtue' and 'Schoolgirl'. Among their hybrid teas 'Troika', a lovely coppery orange, 'King Arthur', salmon pink and the creamy white 'Mr Standfast' took the eye.

Mattock's showed fine blooms of the climber 'Handel', the single crimson 'Altissimo' and the shrub roses 'Fountain' and 'Frau Dagmar Hastrup'.

The RNRS Challenge Cup for a group from 151 to 300 sq. ft was won by

Wm Lowe & Son (Nurseries) Ltd who had fine blooms of 'Pascali', 'Vienna Charm', 'Alexander' and 'Piccadilly'.

The Jubilee trophy for a group of 150 sq. ft or less was won by Peter Beales Ltd, and I humbly apologize to the firm because I did not make any notes about the varieties they were showing. I think that, as so often happens at shows, some old friend came up and started a conversation and I was put off-course.

C. Gregory & Son Ltd won a Large Gold Medal with a very nice group in which they showed 'Living Fire', 'Elizabeth of Glamis', 'Fleur Cowles' and 'Lively Lady' among their floribundas, and 'Leslie Johns' and 'Duke of Windsor' among their hybrid teas.

Gandy's (Roses) Ltd won a Gold Medal, and in their group I thought 'Summer Sunshine', 'Queenie' and 'King's Ransom' looked very good.

E. B. Le Grice (Roses) Ltd, in their Gold Medal exhibit, had good blooms of 'News', 'Scarlet Queen Elizabeth', 'Wendy Cussons', 'Arthur Bell' and 'Pink Parfait'.

Cants of Colchester, who also won a Gold Medal, showed among many others, fine blooms of 'John Waterer', 'Wendy Cussons', 'Typhoon', 'Pascali' and 'Red Devil'.

Warley Rose Gardens included a display of 'Admiral Rodney', their new two-tone pink hybrid tea, in their Gold Medal exhibit and also showed 'Princess Margaret of England', 'Red Devil' and 'Whisky Mac'.

Silver Gilt Medals were awarded to A. Dickson & Sons Ltd, Hillier & Sons Ltd, John Sanday (Roses) Ltd and Harry Wheatcroft & Sons Ltd.

Silver Medals went to Garnette Holding, C. Newberry & Son and Northfield's Roses.

## The Amateur Classes

It is becoming almost monotonous to record that F. E. Owen, Tamworth, won the Dean Hole cup and was the amateur champion. However, he did not win the Cant Trophy which went this time to L. E. J. Wood, Waddesdon —this, of course, goes to the exhibitor who gains the highest aggregate of points in classes 8–17 inclusive. The Lillian Gertrude Brooks Memorial Cup for the highest aggregate of points in classes 18–25 inclusive was won by J. H. Anthony, Pelsall, and the Franklin Dennison bowl for the highest aggregate of points in classes 42–49, the novices classes, went to F. Birch, High Offley.

The best exhibit in the floral arrangement classes which won the RNRS Challenge Trophy was entered by Mrs J. Ward, Herne Bay. The award for the best bloom in the amateurs' classes went to A. J. Goodgame, Winslow, for his bloom of 'Red Devil'. One day, perhaps, somebody will tell me how the judges finally pick on one bloom out of thousands as the best bloom in the show.

Now let us look at some of the varieties that won the prizes. In class 8, for a box of twelve specimen blooms, W. D. Parker, Morpeth, showed 'Red Lion', 'Red Queen', 'Perfecta Superior', 'Mr Standfast', 'Stella', 'City of Bath', 'Embassy', 'Northern Lights', 'Isabel de Ortiz', 'Perfecta', 'Red Devil' and 'Norman Hartnell'. In class 9, a box of six specimen blooms, three varieties, won by L. E. J. Wood, I liked very much 'Gavotte' and 'Red Lion'. In class 10, six blooms, four or more varieties, H. A. Thompson, Lincoln, showed fine blooms of 'Red Devil', 'Super Star' (the only blooms of this variety I saw in the show), 'Perfecta Superior', 'Grandpa Dickson' and 'Fragrant Cloud'. This little lot, I thought, with the possible exception of 'Super Star', was a good basis for anybody's rose bed.

In Division B, restricted to amateurs with not more than 500 rose trees, I found some really lovely blooms. In class 19, for a vase of three specimen blooms, M. L. Watts, Northampton, showed 'Peace', 'Pink Favourite' and 'Fragrant Cloud'. Looking back, I can remember when 'Peace' and 'Pink Favourite' were shown in dozens of exhibits, but not so nowadays, although they are still jolly good roses. In class 23, for three vases of not more than six stems of three varieties, the RNRS Challenge Cup went to B. S. Pearce, Sutton Coldfield, who showed 'Red Devil', 'Royal Highness' and 'Grandpa Dickson'. In class 29, in the division for amateurs with not more than 250 rose trees, R. N. Venables, Sutton Coldfield, put up some lovely blooms of 'Gavotte', 'Red Devil' and 'City of Gloucester'.

Moving down the schedule—that is, into the classes for growers with fewer and fewer rose trees, we had G. J. Busby, Solihull, winning the class for six specimen blooms in Division D—amateurs with not more than 150 rose trees—with 'Gavotte', 'Fred Gibson', 'Grandpa Dickson' and 'Norman Hartnell'.

In the "novices" division—the classes for amateurs who have never won a first prize at any exhibition of the Society, F. Birch, High Offley, really cleaned up the prizes, winning first prize in seven out of eight classes and, of course, the Franklin Dennison bowl. He won all these prizes with a small range of varieties, but the blooms were really good. He showed 'Grandpa Dickson', 'Akebono', 'Northern Lights', 'Fred Gibson' and 'City of Gloucester'.

In the class for new seedlings raised by Amateurs, G. W. T. Langdale received a commendation for a pink unnamed hybrid tea variety.

# The Provincial Display Gardens

## S. MILLAR GAULT

Most of us with an interest in gardens look upon Easter as something of a Spring Festival, with the daffodils dancing, and enhancing the scene. It is also a time, often belated, to get on with many of the jobs which are crying out to be done. Not so in 1973 in this area, where the weather at Easter was more miserable than usual.

Ever unpredictable, we had a complete somersault on 25 April so that it was in a spirit of elation I travelled by the A1 to Yorkshire and the Harrogate Spring Show. My elation was short lived, however, as duties completed I took a walk round the well-known Valley Gardens in Harrogate, the site of the Show. Coming to the roses, deflation set in, particularly when I saw a hedge of 'Evelyn Fison' which had been lightly pruned for some years. Here it was quite evident that a severe frost had caused so much "dieback" that severe dehorning would be necessary to reach live wood.

In consequence, I had some qualms about what I might see at Harlow Car, a much more exposed garden. In the event, when I walked round with the Superintendent, Mr Geoffrey Smith, my fears subsided to some extent, although climbers had suffered severely, the only exception being 'Maigold' which was unscathed.

The week following I accompanied Mr Turner to Norwich where we met the Director of Parks, Mr Anderson. Visits were made to various parks and a site chosen for a Display Garden. This has now been confirmed by Council, so that our members in East Anglia will soon be able to see varieties which have in recent years received awards at our Trials at St. Albans.

We had a wonderful display of roses at our Headquarters in June, so that I was not surprised when Mr Fairbrother impressed upon me that an early visit to Taunton was imperative. Not being unduly superstitious, even the fact that this visit was made on Friday, 13 July, could not detract from my enjoyment. Calling first at Mr and Mrs Fairbrother's new home, the prelude of freshly picked raspberries was a delight. After lunch we proceeded to Vivary Park; fortunately, with his intimate knowledge of the area, Mr Fairbrother ensured that the problem of parking would not hamper my visit. We met Mr Verrier and Mr Reynolds and inspected the roses. This was easily the best display I have seen at Taunton and I was most impressed. 'Fred Loads' has always excelled here and was doing so again and I am sure Jack Harkness would have felt proud of 'Southampton' on this showing.

As usual I combined a judging engagement at Leeds Show with a visit to Harlow Car. There is little need to remind readers of the weather at this time; suffice it to say that 17 July left Easter well behind. Even Mr Smith, generally so cheerful, was disappointed at the damage the torrential rain had caused to the blooms. In such conditions assessments are somewhat difficult, but at least the incidence of dieback was no longer evident, illustrating the recuperative power of roses to the full. We visited the newly designed and newly planted rose garden, with three varieties in each bed. It will be most interesting to see these combinations in better weather conditions. Two varieties which seemed oblivious to the rain were 'Kerryman' and 'Yesterday'.

With the arrival of August, weather conditions improved so that my journey to Redcar, although accompanied by a strong, blustering wind, was at least dry. At Redcar Mr Dodds was preoccupied by some of the changes taking place administratively in the Department, so I met his henchmen, Mr Hitchin, who is due to retire shortly, and Mr Gibson. The District Superintendent, Mr Ralph and Mr Phillips, who is in direct charge of the roses, were also present. Situated so near the east coast, roses do remarkably well in the Borough Park and 'Nozomi' was still in full bloom at the time of my visit. 'National Trust', a variety which has proved itself at all the display gardens, was outstanding here and it seems evident it is a very reliable garden rose. I was informed that this garden had proved a source of great interest to rose lovers in the area and further improvements are contemplated. These consist of car-parking facilities and fencing, both assets which will be appreciated, the former by visitors, the latter by the roses, which will appreciate a little shelter.

Continuing my journey northwards, my next port of call was Edinburgh, where Mr MacBean, Director of Parks, was on holiday. I did, however, meet Mr Horsfall, the Deputy Director, when I went to Saughton Park where the roses are now in the care of Mr Lownie. A young man, he has a great interest in roses, acquired in the first place when he trained with Messrs Dobbie & Co. in their rose department, an interest he is now able to put to good use, as he gave me a list of most useful notes regarding the behaviour of the new roses. In the rose garden at Saughton Park, 'Colour Wonder' was quite impressive and in a sheltered position 'Elizabeth of Glamis' was most attractive. 'Dearest' has always done well here in front of the glasshouses and on this occasion 'Manx Queen' was trying hard to do so also. 'Shot Silk' is still grown in this garden and still attracts, although not perhaps as vigorous as forty years ago.

There is little inducement for lingering on the road from Edinburgh to

Glasgow as far as scenic splendour is concerned. Mr Oldham, the well-known director of Parks, had to attend a hastily convened meeting so I saw him for only a few minutes and Dr Dick's visit was curtailed by the urgency of his medical duties. At Pollok Park we adjourned to the Rose Garden accompanied by Mr Gilmour, Horticultural Officer, Mr Mullard, the Area Superintendent and Mr Hastie who looks after the roses. Now that the roses have become established in this new garden the display has become much more effective. However, the influence of the Clean Air Act, without doubt of great benefit to the citizens of Glasgow, has proved of doubtful value so far as roses are concerned. Previously only known by name, Black Spot has made its presence quite obvious and I was shattered by its effect on last year's President's International Trophy winner, 'Topsi'. 'Typhoon', 'Troika', 'Korp' and 'Just Joey' have done well, with 'Southampton' excelling. 'Alexander' has attained the proportions of a shrub but with very serrated petals. I was mystified by a bed of 'City of Glasgow' roses; we have a number of cities represented by roses, some very well, but this particular variety doesn't seem likely to do much to project the image of Scotland's largest city.

My next visit was combined with judging at Southport Flower Show when, duties completed, I accompanied Mr Turner and Mr Fred Gibson to the Botanic Gardens. Mr Boocock, the Director of Parks, was as usual very much occupied by his duties at the Show, but continues his interest in the new roses and ensures they are well looked after. This is self-evident on inspection and makes me wish the area was somewhat larger, so that wider spacing could be used, particularly in years when there are a goodly number of awards. 'Red Planet' does better here and continues to justify its high award in 1969.

My tour this year was completed when I went to Wales early in September, mainly by the M4. Reaching Cardiff, a new road avoiding the confusion of the city takes one quite close to Roath Park and its Rose Garden. Unfortunately, a meeting arranged with Mr Nelmes, Parks Director, did not materialize—an office mix-up—but I have seen him since. Black Spot is always more prevalent late in the season, and it is hardly necessary for me to comment that 1973 was a bad year for this disease. The roses at Roath Park were no exception in this respect, as will be seen from my summarized report. I was attracted by 'Grace Abounding' in this garden and 'Typhoon', 'Just Joey' and 'Nan Anderson' showed great promise for another year. I must thank all who helped me; many have been mentioned and I hope they consider this a worthy exercise on behalf of the rose and our Society.

## THE PROVINCIAL DISPLAY GARDENS

| AWARDS | Cardiff | Edinburgh | Glasgow | Harlow Car | Redcar | Southport | Taunton |
|---|---|---|---|---|---|---|---|
| **1970** | | | | | | | |
| **Gold Medal** | | | | | | | |
| 'Alec's Red' | 1 (SBS) | 2 | 1 (SBS) | 2 | 2 | 2 | 1 |
| 'News' | 1 | 2* | 1 (BS) | 3 | 2 | 1 (very good) | 1 |
| **Certificate of Merit** | | | | | | | |
| 'Chorus Girl' | 1 (BS) | 1 (good) | | 1 | 1 | | 1 (SBS) |
| 'Golden Chersonese' | 1 | 1 (good) | | 2 | 2 | 1 (good) | 1 |
| 'Kim' | 1 (BS) | 1 (good) | 1 (SBS tall) | | | 1 | |
| 'Picasso' | | | | 1 (good) | 1 (very good) | 1 | 1 (very good) |
| 'Sunday Times' | | | | | | | |
| **Trial Ground Certificate** | | | | | | | |
| 'Charles Dickens' | 2 (BS) | 1 (very good) | 1 (good) | 1 | 1 (very good) | 1 (very good) | 1 (SM) |
| 'City of Gloucester' | 1 | 1 | 2 (BS) | 3 (BS) | 1 (very good) | 2 | 1 |
| 'Colour Sergeant' | 1 (BS & M) | 1 | 1 (tall) | 1 | 1 (very good) | 2 | 1 (tall) |
| 'Dorril' | 1 (SBS) | 1 | 1 (tall) | 1 | 1 (very good) | | 1 |
| 'Esther Ofarim' | 3 | 3 (1st year) | 3 (BS) | 3 | 2 | 2 (BS) | 1 |
| 'Gold Coin' | 2 | 1 | 2 (SM) | 1 | 1 (M) | 2 | 3 |
| 'Golden Times' | 1 | 1 | | 1 | 2 | 1 (good) | 1 |
| 'Grace Abounding' | 1 (very good) | 1 (very good) | 1 (tall) | 1 (good) | 1 (very good) | 1 | 1 |
| 'Gypsy Moth' | 1 (M) | 1 | 1 (very good) | 2 | 1 (good) | | |
| 'Lavender Lace' | 2 (BS) | 1 | 2 | 1 (very good) | 1 (very good) | 1 (SBS) | 2 (BS) |
| 'Megiddo' | 1 (BS) | 1 (BS) | 2 (BS) | 1 | 1 (very good) | 1 (very good) | 1 (SBS) |
| 'National Trust' | 2 | 1 (very good) | 1 (very good) | 1 (very good) | 1 (very good) | 1 | 1 (very good) |
| 'Nozomi' | 1 (SBS) | 2 | 1 | 2 | 1 (very good) | 1 (good) | 1 (good) |
| 'Roaming' | 1 | 1 | 1 (BS) | 1 | 1 | | 1 |
| 'Rosy Mantle' | 1 (very good) | 1 (very good) | 1 (M) | 2 | 3 (1st year) | 2 (M) | |
| 'Seven Seas' | 1 | 1 (very good) | 1 (very good) | 2 | 1 (SM) | 1 (very good) | 2 (1st year) |
| 'Snowline' | 1 | 1 (very late) | 3 (M) | 1 (very late) | 1 | 1 (good) | 1 (very good) |
| 'Stephen Langdon' | 1 | 1 (very late) | | | 3 | | |
| 'Taora' | 1 | 1 (very good) | 1 (very good) | 2 | 1 (very good) | 1 | 1 (very good) |
| 'Poppy Flash' | 1 | 1 (late) | 1 (very good) | 1 | | 1 | 1 (SBS) |

1 Very good (addition of very good or good means even better)  2 Good  3 Fair
BS Black Spot   SBS Slight Black Spot   M Mildew
SM Slight Mildew   1st year = planted 1972-73   *Damaged by rabbits

# The Trial Ground and Display Garden, 1973

**L. G. TURNER**
(*Secretary*)

When the Council took the unprecedented step of moving the headquarters from London to St Albans, one of the main ambitions was to create a rose display garden where members could enjoy the beauty of our favourite flower in all its different forms. In 1973, after many years of re-development, which so often entailed the removal of well established trees, the gardens were at last beginning to look established and presenting that picture of maturity that comes only with age. Now the trees planted around the perimeter are truly forming the back-cloth against which the many different shades of the roses are shown to great advantage. The climbers on the pergola are covering the connecting beams, and the beds of bush roses and borders of shrub roses are well filled and producing a riot of colour throughout the season. It is, however, disappointing, not only to the Council but also to the staff who are responsible for the maintenance of the garden, that during the season less than 10 per cent of our members found time to pay a visit.

The new beds of 'Marlena', 'Topsi', 'Living Fire', 'Typhoon', 'Southampton' and 'Poppy Flash' and also 'Fountain', 'Goldbonnet', 'Sunblest' and 'Alexander' have grown well and certainly enhance the eastern side of the main lawn. Work is now in progress in re-planning the western side of the lawn and preparing large beds in front of the pergola. A garden for miniatures and the less hardy varieties is being constructed, and the lawn outside the Visitors' Lounge is also being replanted.

The replacing of the drink vending machine by a staffed cafeteria was appreciated by many visitors and we look forward to making further improvements in this direction during the coming season.

Members who came in 1973 will recall the unusually high incidence of disease in the trial ground (perhaps it gladdened their hearts to realise that the roses in their own gardens were not the only ones that were suffering) and there is no denying the fact that this has given the Management Committee some concern. Nevertheless, it is evident from a comparison with the roses in the display garden, where there was little evidence of disease, that some responsibility must rest with those of our senders who are not testing their new seedlings thoroughly before submitting them for trial. The growing conditions at St Albans are severe—the soil is not first class and the aspect is bleak—but they are no worse than the conditions the roses will meet generally when they no longer have the protection of their native soil.

In recent years it has often been said that too many new roses of doubtful quality have been introduced, and undoubtedly our trade members, who have the problem of deciding which of the new varieties to stock, will agree. Possibly the newly formed British Association of Rose Breeders may help to overcome the problem by backing a limited number of novelties. Let us also hope, however, that the novelties that are backed pass their health test with flying colours. The presence of a little Mildew in late autumn may be acceptable, but any sign of disease earlier in the season should debar a variety from introduction, irrespective of all its other virtues.

During the last year no fewer than 170 varieties were removed from the trials and of the original 319 varieties that completed the three year trial this summer, only 100 remained. This may be considered a serious indictment, but one must applaud the Committee for facing up to the problem and taking such drastic steps. Those varieties that withstood the onslaught, whether they received an award or not, certainly had a clean bill of health.

The presence of so much disease may have accounted for the fact that no Gold Medal and no President's International Trophy were awarded. The most successful variety was the climber 'Compassion', raised by R. Harkness & Co., which received the Henry Edland Memorial Medal for fragrance, the first climber to do so, having won a Trial Ground Certificate in 1972. I am sure it will be a welcome addition to many small gardens, where an attractive, fragrant climber is particularly pleasing. 'Living Fire', from C. Gregory & Son, 'Troika', from Niels Poulsen of Denmark and 'Kortor', from Reimer Kordes of Germany, are welcome additions to the list of bedding varieties. Particularly outstanding was the rambler 'Temple Bells', raised by D. Morey of U.S.A. For ground cover and impenetrable screening it will be ideal, and although during the first two years of trial the number of flowers was disappointing, in its third year it was a mass of delicate, white, single blooms which lasted for several weeks in late July.

We are not yet seeing any of Sam McGredy's New Zealand-produced seedlings, but there still appear to be plenty in the pipeline as a result of his work in Portadown. Of the twelve varieties that received a Trial Ground Certificate, including those awarded subject to naming, McGredy raised over half—an outstanding achievement by any standard. It is for his success in Northern Ireland that the firm was awarded the Queen Mary Commemoration Medal for the second time. E. B. LeGrice (Hybridisers) Ltd. of North

Walsham and A. Dickson & Sons of Hawlmark also won this award for the second time. Continuous success for over fifteen years is a notable achievement, and one that I am sure James Cocker & Sons, R. Harkness & Co. and John Sanday (Roses) Ltd, who received the award for the first time, will strive to emulate.

# The Awards to New Roses in 1973

*Denotes varieties for which it is understood protection is being sought under the Plant Varieties and Seeds Act, 1964.

*The Henry Edland Memorial Medal, awarded to the most fragrant rose on trial, irrespective of country of origin, was awarded to:*

*COMPASSION (Clr.). *Raiser:* R. Harkness & Co. Ltd, Hitchin. Trial Ground No. C184. 'White Cockade' × 'Prima Ballerina'. Bloom: pale salmon-orange, lighter reverse, full (39 petals), very fragrant, borne several together and in trusses. Growth: very vigorous, upright, 7 to 8 ft. Foliage: glossy, dark green. (*See illustration in 1973 Annual, facing p. 185.*)

*Certificates of Merit were awarded to:*

KORTOR (Flori.). *Raiser:* W. Kordes & Son, Germany. *Distributor:* A. Dickson & Sons Ltd, N. Ireland. Trial Ground No. 2616. 'Europeana' × 'Marlena'. Bloom: bright scarlet, moderately full (18 petals), slightly fragrant, borne several together. Growth: moderately vigorous, bushy and compact. Foliage: semi-glossy, dark green. (*See illustration facing p. 17.*)

*LIVING FIRE (Flori.). *Raiser:* C. Gregory & Son Ltd, Nottingham. Trial Ground No. 2293. 'Super Star' × unknown. Bloom: orange shading to scarlet with golden yellow base, full (34 petals), slightly fragrant, borne several together. Growth: vigorous, upright. Foliage: glossy, dark green. (*See illustration in 1973 Annual, facing p. 184.*)

*TROIKA (H.T.). *Raiser:* N. Poulsen, Denmark. Trial Ground No. 2423. Parentage unknown. Bloom: light apricot to orange, edged and veined scarlet, full (29 petals), fragrant, borne singly and several together. Growth: vigorous, upright. Foliage: glossy, medium green, large. (*See illustration in 1973 Annual, facing p. 16.*)

WEE MAN (min.). *Raiser:* S. McGredy & Son Ltd, N. Ireland. Trial Ground No. 2260. 'Little Flirt' × 'Marlena'. Bloom: signal red, semi-double (14 petals), fragrant, borne in trusses. Growth: vigorous, dwarf, bushy and compact. Foliage: semi-glossy, light green, small. (1972 award).

## Trial Ground Certificates were awarded to:

GERTRUD SCHWEITZER (H.T.) *Raiser:* W. Kordes & Son, Germany. *Distributor:* A Dickson & Sons Ltd, N. Ireland. Trial Ground No. 2301. 'Colour Wonder' × 'Dr. A. J. Verhage'. Bloom: orange-salmon to light apricot, moderately full (25 petals), free flowering, borne singly. Growth: vigorous, upright. Foliage: semi-glossy, medium green, bronze tinted in early stages. (*See illustration facing p. 54.*)

GOLDEN SHOT (Flori.). *Raiser:* J. Martin, New Zealand. *Distributor:* Gandy's (Roses) Ltd, North Kilworth. Trial Ground No. 2498. Seedling × 'Allgold'. Bloom: golden yellow, moderately full (18 petals), exceptionally free flowering, quick to repeat, borne in trusses. Growth: very vigorous, tall, bushy. Foliage: semi-glossy, medium green, small. (*See illustration facing p. 184.*)

MATANGI (Flori.). *Raiser:* Sam McGredy Roses International, New Zealand. *Distributor:* Sam McGredy Roses, N. Ireland. Trial Ground No. 2577. [('Little Darling' × 'Goldilocks') × ['Evelyn Fison' × (*R. macrophylla coryana* × 'Tantau's Triumph')]] × 'Picasso'. Bloom: orange vermilion, silver eye and reverse, moderately full (23 petals), slightly fragrant, borne singly and several together. Growth: vigorous, upright. Foliage: glossy, dark green, tinted copper when young. (*See illustration facing p. 120.*)

*MEIPUMA (Flori.). *Raiser:* Mrs M. L. Paolino, France. *Distributor:* Universal Rose Selection (U.K.) Ltd, Waltham Cross. Trial Ground No. 2737. ['Tamango' × ['Sarabande' × ('Goldilocks' × 'Fashion')]]. Bloom: vermilion with silver reverse, full (36 petals), fragrant, free flowering, borne several together. Growth: vigorous, spreading, bushy. Foliage: semi-glossy, medium green.

OLD MASTER (Flori.). *Raiser:* Sam McGredy Roses International, New Zealand. *Distributor:* Sam McGredy Roses, N. Ireland. Trial Ground No. 2266. [('Evelyn Fison' × ('Tantau's Triumph' × *R.macrophylla coryana*)) × ('Hamburger Phoenix' × 'Danse du Feu')] × ['Evelyn Fison' × ('Orange Sweetheart' × 'Frühlingsmorgen')]. Bloom: carmine with silver eye and reverse, moderately full (18 petals), slightly fragrant, borne several together. Growth: vigorous, bushy. Foliage: semi-glossy, medium green, bronze when young.

SUNSILK (Flori. H.T. type). *Raiser:* Fryer's Nurseries Ltd, Knutsford. Trial Ground No. 2340. 'Pink Parfait' × 'Redgold' seedling. Bloom: pure lemon yellow, full (30–35 petals), slightly fragrant, borne singly. Growth: vigorous, upright. Foliage: semi-glossy, medium green. (1972 award.) (*See illustration facing p. 100.*)

*TEMPLE BELLS (Ramb.). *Raiser:* D. Morey, U.S.A. *Distributor:* Sam McGredy Roses, N. Ireland. Trial Ground No. C209. Parentage unknown. Bloom: white with pronounced yellow stamens, single (6 small petals), fragrant, free summer flowering, borne in trusses. Growth: very vigorous, spreading. Foliage: glossy, light green, small.

# International Awards 1973

## ROME

LARGE FLOWERS
| | | |
|---|---|---|
| Gold Medal | 'Grand Nord' | M. Delbard, France |
| Certificate | 'Mabella' | W. Kordes Söhne, Germany |

SMALL FLOWERS
| | | |
|---|---|---|
| First Certificate | 'Foc de Tabara' | Statuinea Experimentala Hotivinicola, Romania |
| Certificate | 'Sunshine Girl' | C. Gregory & Son Ltd., England |

The other awards went to unnamed seedlings.

## MONZA

ROSE OF THE YEAR (H.T.)
| | | |
|---|---|---|
| First Certificate | 'Lancome' | G. Delbard, France |
| Second Certificate | 'Carinella' | L. Meilland, France |

ROSE OF THE YEAR (FLORI.)
| | | |
|---|---|---|
| First Certificate | 'Scherzo' | L. Meilland, France |

The other awards went to unnamed seedlings.

## MADRID

| | | |
|---|---|---|
| Gold Medal and Prize of the City of Madrid | 'The Sun' (flori.) | Sam McGredy Roses International, New Zealand |
| First Certificate | 'Lancome' (H.T.) | G. Delbard, France |
| Second Certificate | 'Grand Nord' (H.T.) | M. Delbard, France |
| PERFUME CUP | 'Typhoo Tea' | Sam McGredy Roses International, New Zealand |

The other awards went to unnamed seedlings.

## GENEVA

LARGE FLOWERS
| | | |
|---|---|---|
| Silver Medal | 'Mabella' | W. Kordes Söhne, Germany |
| Certificates | 'Carinella' | L. Meilland, France |
| | 'Mme Louis Armand' | Mme J. Croix, France |

SMALL FLOWERS
| | | |
|---|---|---|
| Silver Medal | 'Scherzo' | L. Meilland, France |
| Certificate | 'The Sun' | Sam McGredy Roses International, New Zealand |

CLIMBER
| | | |
|---|---|---|
| Silver Medal and Prize | 'Sensass Delbard' | G. Delbard, France |

The other awards went to unnamed seedlings.

## COURTRAI

| | | |
|---|---|---|
| Golden Rose 1973 | 'Typhoo Tea' (H.T.) | Sam McGredy Roses International, New Zealand |
| Silver Medals | 'Mevr. M. J. Gillon' (H.T.) | R. V. S. Melle, Belgium |
| | 'Fragrant Hour' (H.T.) | Sam McGredy Roses International, New Zealand |

'GOLDEN SHOT' (floribunda)
*Seedling* × *'Allgold'*
Raised by J. Martin, New Zealand
TRIAL GROUND CERTIFICATE 1973
*See page* 183

'ADOLF HORSTMANN' (H.T.)
'Dr A. J. Verhage' × 'Colour Wonder'
Raised by W. Kordes & Son, Germany
TRIAL GROUND CERTIFICATE 1972
See 1973 Rose Annual, page 183

The immaculate specimen of 'Embassy' which won the medal for the Best
Bloom at the 1973 Summer Show for E. Plumpton

'The Sun' (flori.)                Sam McGredy Roses International,
                                  New Zealand
'Parure d'Or' (Clg.)              Arboflora
'Lily de Gerlache' (H.T.)         R. V. S. Melle, Belgium
'Kon-Tiki' (flori.)               R. V. S. Melle, Belgium

The other awards went to unnamed seedlings.

## THE HAGUE

**HYBRID TEA**
*First Certificate*          'Lancome'                Delbard-Chabert, France

**FLORIBUNDA**
*Gold Medal*                 'Directeur Rijnveld'     Darthuizer Boomkwekijen, Holland

The other awards went to unnamed seedlings.
In the beds of roses planted out in the Westbroekpark the International Jury awarded the *Golden Rose of The Hague* to 'Scarlet Queen Elizabeth', raised by Alex. Dickson & Sons, N. Ireland; *First Class Certificate* to 'Esperanza' (flori.), raised by S. Delforge, Belgium; *Second Class Certificate* to 'Criterion' (H.T.), raised by G. de Ruiter, Holland; *Silver Medal* to 'Petite Folie' (Min.) raised by Meilland, France; *Silver Medal for Fragrance* to 'Criterion' (H.T.) raised by G. de Ruiter, Holland.

## BADEN-BADEN

*Silver Medals*          'Lolita' (H.T.)             W. Kordes Söhne, Germany
                         'Happy Wanderer' (flori.)   Sam McGredy Roses International,
                                                     New Zealand
                         'Coventry Cathedral' (flori.) Sam McGredy Roses International,
                                                     New Zealand
                         'Arnaud Delbard' (flori.)   G. Delbard, France
                         'Princess Chichibu' (flori.) J. L. Harkness, England
                         'Southampton' (flori.)      J. L. Harkness, England
*Bronze Medals*          'Alec's Red' (H.T.)         A. Cocker, Scotland
                         'Anne Cocker' (flori.)      A. Cocker, Scotland
*Most Fragrant Rose*     'Alec's Red' (H.T.)         A. Cocker, Scotland
Other awards went to unnamed seedlings.

## NEW ZEALAND

*'Gold Star of the South Pacific' and Certificate of Merit*   'Landora' (H.T.)   Tantau, Germany

*'Gold Star of the South Pacific' and Certificate of Merit*   'Picasso' (flori.)   Sam McGredy Roses International,
                                                                                   New Zealand

*'Most Fragrant Rose' and Certificate of Merit*

*Certificates of Merit*   'Westerland' (Clg.)        Kordes, Germany
                          'Iskra' (Clg.)             Meilland, France
                          'Adolf Horstmann' (H.T.)   Kordes, Germany
                          'Kerryman' (flori.)        Sam McGredy Roses International,
                                                     New Zealand
                          'Liverpool Echo' (flori.)  Sam McGredy Roses International,
                                                     New Zealand
                          'Apollo' (H.T.)            Armstrong, U.S.A.
                          'Minnie Watson' (flori.)   Watson, Tasmania
                          'Green Ice' (min.)         Moore, U.S.A.

## COPENHAGEN

| | | |
|---|---|---|
| *First Certificate* | 'Helma' (flori.) | G. de Ruiter, Holland |
| *Second Certificate* | 'Scarletta' (min.) | G. de Ruiter, Holland |
| *Third Certificate* | 'Havam' (flori.) | H. A. Verschuren & Sons, Holland |
| *Climber* | Unnamed | Georges Delbard, France |

## BELFAST

**HYBRID TEA**

| | | |
|---|---|---|
| *Gold Medal and Prize*<br>"*Uladh*" *Award for* | 'Mala Rubinstein' | Alex Dickson & Sons Ltd, N. Ireland |
| *fragrance* | 'Mala Rubinstein' | Alex Dickson & Sons Ltd, N. Ireland |
| *Certificates* | 'Kalahari' | Sam McGredy Roses International,<br>New Zealand |
| | 'Adolf Horstmann' | W. Kordes, Germany |

**FLORIBUNDA**

| | | |
|---|---|---|
| *The* "*Golden Thorn*"<br>*Award* | 'Picasso' | Sam McGredy Roses International,<br>New Zealand |
| *Certificates* | 'Grub an Bayern' | W. Kordes, Germany |
| | 'Kerryman' | Sam McGredy Roses International,<br>New Zealand |
| | 'Sunday Times' | Sam McGredy Roses International,<br>New Zealand |

## ORLÉANS

**FLORIBUNDA**

| | | |
|---|---|---|
| *First Certificate and*<br>*Special Prize* | 'Sweet Home' | Louisette Meilland, France |
| *Certificates* | 'Florian' | Louisette Meilland, France |
| | 'Alouette' | Delforge, Belgium |
| | 'Prominent' ('Korp') | W. Kordes Söhne, Germany |
| | 'Sable Chaud' | Delbard-Chabert, France |
| | 'Rubella' | G. de Ruiter, Holland |

**"GRANDIFLORAS"**

| | | |
|---|---|---|
| *First Certificate* | 'Devotion' | R. Harkness & Co Ltd, England |
| *Certificates* | 'Hertfordshire Glory' | R. Harkness & Co Ltd, England |
| | 'Toro de Fuego' | Delbard-Chabert, France |

## JAPAN

**HYBRID TEA**    All awards went to unnamed seedlings

**OTHER THAN H.T.**

| | | |
|---|---|---|
| *Certificates of Merit* | 'Migniardise' | H. Delforge, Belgium |
| | 'The Sun' | Sam McGredy Roses International,<br>New Zealand |
| | 'Sunshine Girl' | C. Gregory & Son Ltd., England |

The other awards went to unnamed seedlings.

# On Staging Inter-Society Exhibits

**H. P. PORTER**

(*Amateur rose grower*)

Over the years Worcester Park Horticultural Society has been very successful in Affiliated Societies competitions at the National Rose Shows and I have often been asked why this is so. This short article will, I hope, induce more Societies to compete.

Some years ago I started an index of names and addresses of members of our Society who grow roses, many of whom are not exhibitors, but who grow this wonderful flower for the pleasure only a true rosarian can understand. Our members are circularized by hand (by Committee men and volunteers) with a Newsletter and they are asked to keep a lookout for any potential addition to my index. At our Shows, too, any new exhibitors are noted and approached as to whether they would be willing to donate blooms to the Society's exhibit.

When The Royal National Rose Society's Show Schedule arrives it is studied carefully. When, some years ago, a new class was started for an exhibit of roses 5 ft long, 7 ft 6 in. high and 4 ft wide, for a new cup kindly donated by the Hereford Society, I approached two ladies to ascertain whether they would stage this exhibit; I have been fortunate in that they have done so for each of the last five years and make an ideal team.

In the lounge of the home of one of these ladies we set up the bowls, stands, baskets and drapes, to the dimensions in the Schedule, to enable us to work out roughly how many roses will be needed to fill them, also to work out the best position, this being a new venture. On arrival at the show we found that this planning in advance paid dividends.

The weekend before the show I distribute a list of names and addresses to six or more members with cars and make sure they have sufficient buckets filled with water (because the blooms are placed in them as soon as cut) and one helper is allocated to each car.

The night before the show a central collecting point is set up—generally my garage—where buckets are placed filled with water to receive blooms as the cars return.

The sorting then commences, both hybrid teas and floribundas being sorted according to colour. The stems of blooms which are selected for taking to the show *are all dethorned* (I think this is most important, as it is very easy to spoil a bloom if a thorn comes in contact with a petal). The best as selected are then placed in containers ready for the journey.

I prepare a list of necessities, such as secateurs, brushes, scissors, spray and Schedule, and tick off each item to make sure we have everything we need. The ladies look after refreshments for the stagers, in the form of a flask of coffee and snacks to keep the inner man happy.

If we are fortunate to be able to borrow a van, this is then loaded and packed carefully to see that the blooms do not touch; canes are wedged across the containers to hold the stems in place. I finally check to see that we have enough blooms to be sure of filling the exhibit and then the best of the leftovers, (including some young blooms in case of an extra-hot day) are placed in separate cars. Then we retire to bed to snatch a few hours sleep.

We meet at our rendezvous at 5.30 a.m. and, all being well, off we go in convoy for the show (oh yes, we have had our breakdowns and other mishaps! One year the van we had been promised was there all right, but the gate was padlocked, so my son climbed over to see whether the keys were in the ignition and then cut through the chain holding the padlock, all the time expecting the law to pounce on us and ask awkward questions).

It is important to allow plenty of time for staging so that you can take things easily. When all the buckets have been unloaded a colour scheme is worked out (this is where sorting into colours beforehand pays dividends). Drapes are staged first and paper is put down on top of them in case of any spillage of water. The ladies generally work on the set in stockinged feet to save marking the drapes. Material for the bowls and baskets is staged and the height of each is checked for uniformity. They are then placed in position and viewed from all angles, opinions of individual team members being noted. I almost forgot to mention that we take it in turns to go to breakfast and have a rest.

Having staged the blooms we then watch that no roses become blown before the time of judging, and that all is in order. Any individual blooms which do blow are, of course, replaced from the younger blooms held in reserve.

As we have been staging exhibits for the Society for twenty years we have made some very good friends among rival Societies and the camaraderie is wonderful. We talk of the trials and tribulations of the growing season and also about our families in a really friendly atmosphere.

The bell goes for all exhibitors to leave the hall; we wish each other the best of luck and retire for a rest and to await the verdict of the judges. The fact that over the past twenty years Worcester Park has not been out of the first four in the Franklin Dennison Class and has won the Hereford Centenary Cup six times in a row, is at least evidence that our methods produce results.

To stage for a Society you have to put aside personal glory and be proud that your Society is renowned for the quality of its exhibits. If we have a successful show, on my return I try to notify all the donors of blooms and the pleasure it gives them to think that their blooms have helped to put the Society on the map makes up for all the hard work, planning and long hours spent staging.

I sincerely hope that other Affiliated Societies will be helped by this article and will be induced to stage in the Franklin Dennison Class, for the motto of our Society is "Share what you know, show what you grow".

Members are invited to write to the editor, indicating which five articles they liked best in this edition of *The Rose Annual,* and placing them in order of preference. They are also asked to state which, if any, of the regular features they find of little interest and to suggest subjects for papers they would like to see in future editions.

Articles for *The Rose Annual* should be submitted to the editor by the end of August, addressed to him at The Royal National Rose Society's Offices, Bone Hill, Chiswell Green Lane, St. Albans, Herts. They should be the author's own work, should not have been accepted by any other publication and should be typed in double spacing or, if hand-written, the lines should be well spaced. Black and white photographs of good definition, featuring items of general interest to members, are also welcomed.

# The Rose Analysis

## L. G. TURNER

The last occasion on which a comparison of the Rose Analysis Tables was made after the passing of a decade was in 1964; therefore it seems appropriate to make a similar comparison this year. Bearing in mind that during the last ten years no fewer than 2,700 new varieties have passed through the trial ground, over 200 of which have received awards and possibly even more than that have been introduced into commerce, one could reasonably expect a complete change in the varieties listed.

In fact, a number have stood up to the test of time and still hold a place—even if somewhat lowly in some instances. In the Tables for Specimen Blooms, 'Peace', 'Perfecta', 'Pink Favourite', 'Silver Lining', 'Anne Letts' and 'Rose Gaujard' are still listed and in the tables for General Garden Cultivation, 'Peace', 'Josephine Bruce', 'Rose Gaujard', 'Pink Favourite', 'Silver Lining', 'Prima Ballerina' and 'Perfecta' remain. The virtues of 'Peace' have been extolled by every horticultural writer and most gardeners over the years; the fact that it has appeared in the Rose Analysis Tables since 1949 (when many of our present day exhibitors were in short trousers!) is surely another outstanding achievement to the credit of this great variety. The Floribunda Table produces fewer survivors, 'Queen Elizabeth', 'Allgold', 'Iceberg' and 'Circus' being the only ones.

Once again, however, there are no startling changes in the tables compared with 1973 beyond the exclusion of 'City of Belfast', 'News', 'Orange Silk' and 'Copper Pot' from the Audit of Newer Floribunda varieties because of the date of introduction, and of 'Fred Gibson', 'Bonsoir', 'Peer Gynt' and 'Red Queen' from the Audit of newer hybrid teas, for the same reason, and also 'Ginger Rogers', which failed to qualify. Of all these only 'Copper Pot', 'Orange Silk' and 'Ginger Rogers' have failed to make the grade in the main analysis.

The exhibitors of Specimen Blooms favour 'Grandpa Dickson' this year with 'Red Devil' as runner up. 'Pink Favourite' continues to hold a place in the top part of the tables.

There are also changes at the top of the General Garden Tables with 'Wendy Cussons' and 'Piccadilly' being preferred to 'Fragrant Cloud' and 'Peace'. 'Super Star' also drops from 4th and 5th to 12th and 9th in the South and North Tables respectively; evidently its susceptibility to Mildew is now influencing the votes.

The returns for the climbers of all types are very similar to last year and one can only presume that the reason for this is that climbers are not replaced so often as bush roses. However, we have seen one or two quite attractive varieties in the trials and perhaps within a year or two some of the newer ones, such as 'Compassion' and 'Dreaming Spires', will find their way into the Tables.

The number of voters this year is 61–37 in the South and 24 in the North—to whom the Publications Committee expresses its thanks for so conscientiously carrying out the task. Over the years the number of members who can devote time to this exercise has decreased, and to ensure the true value of the analysis is maintained for the future it is important that we have some new volunteers. Any member who has over 30 varieties in reasonable quantities is welcome to take part, particularly those whose main interest is in garden display rather than exhibition.

## THE ROSE ANALYSIS
### AUDIT OF NEWER ROSES—FLORIBUNDAS

*This table includes only varieties introduced in this country since 1 January 1969*
(Maximum points possible—621)

| Position | Number of points | NAME | Introduced | COLOUR |
|---|---|---|---|---|
| 1 | 460 | Anne Cocker | 1971 | Dutch vermilion |
| 2 | 391 | Stephen Langdon | 1969 | Deep scarlet |
| 3 | 389 | Molly McGredy | 1969 | Rose red, reverse silver |
| 4 | 371 | Megiddo | 1970 | Scarlet-red |
| 5 | 283 | Rob Roy | 1971 | Scarlet-crimson |
| 6 | 278 | *Michelle | 1970 | Salmon pink |
| 7 | 277 | *Pineapple Poll | 1970 | Orange yellow, flushed red |
| 8 | 272 | Esther Ofarim | 1971 | Orange, red and yellow |
| 9 | 265 | Picasso | 1971 | Carmine, silvery reverse |
| 10 | 249 | Kerryman | 1970 | Cream deepening to pink |
| 11 | 215 | Lively Lady | 1969 | Vermilion |
| 12 | 178 | Topsi | 1972 | Glowing orange-scarlet |
| 13 | 154 | Southampton | 1972 | Apricot-orange |
| 14 | 64 | Korbell | 1972 | Salmon–orange |
| 15 | 61 | Korp | 1972 | Signal red, scarlet reverse |

* Most fragrant

## FLORIBUNDA ROSES

*This table includes only varieties introduced in this country before 1 January 1969*
(Maximum points possible—1281)

| Position | Number of points | NAME | Introduced | COLOUR |
|---|---|---|---|---|
| 1 | 1038 | Iceberg | 1958 | Pure white tinged pink in bud |
| 2 | 1037 | Evelyn Fison | 1962 | Vivid red with scarlet shading |
| 3 | 855 | Queen Elizabeth | 1955 | Clear self pink |
| 4 | 809 | *Elizabeth of Glamis | 1964 | Light salmon |
| 5 | 777 | City of Leeds | 1966 | Rich salmon |
| 6 | 731 | Pink Parfait | 1962 | Medium pink, yellow base |
| 7 | 606 | Allgold | 1956 | Unfading golden yellow |
| 8 | 592 | *Orange Sensation | 1960 | Light vermilion |
| 9 | 513 | City of Belfast | 1968 | Bright red |
| 10 | 505 | *Escapade | 1967 | Magenta with white reverse |
| 11 | 500 | *Arthur Bell | 1965 | Yellow to creamy yellow |
| 12 | { 490 | Orangeade | 1959 | Bright orange-vermilion |
| | 490 | Lilli Marlene | 1959 | Scarlet-red |
| 14 | 482 | *Dearest | 1960 | Rosy salmon |
| 15 | 471 | Paddy McGredy | 1962 | Carmine, lighter reverse |
| 16 | 428 | Dorothy Wheatcroft | 1960 | Bright orient red |
| 17 | 365 | Anna Wheatcroft | 1959 | Light vermilion |
| 18 | 363 | Sea Pearl | 1964 | Pale orange and pink, with yellow |
| 19 | 361 | News | 1968 | Beetroot red shading to purple |
| 20 | 339 | Irish Mist | 1967 | Orange-salmon |
| 21 | 323 | Europeana | 1963 | Deep crimson |
| 22 | 314 | Redgold | 1967 | Golden yellow edged cherry red |
| 23 | 275 | Violet Carson | 1963 | Soft pink, silvery reverse |
| 24 | 272 | Circus | 1955 | Yellow, pink and salmon |

## AUDIT OF NEWER ROSES—HYBRID TEAS

*This table includes only varieties introduced in this country since 1 January 1969*
(Maximum points possible—823)

| Position | Number of points | NAME | Introduced | COLOUR |
|---|---|---|---|---|
| 1 | 665 | *Alec's Red | 1970 | Cherry red |
| 2 | 435 | *Mullard Jubilee | 1970 | Cerise pink |
| 3 | 411 | City of Bath | 1969 | Deep pink, paler reverse |
| 4 | 404 | Elizabeth Harkness | 1969 | Off-white to creamy buff |
| 5 | 390 | National Trust | 1970 | Red |
| 6 | 382 | Red Planet | 1970 | Crimson |
| 7 | 354 | City of Gloucester | 1970 | Yellow shaded gold |
| 8 | 311 | *Mala Rubinstein | 1971 | Pink |
| 9 | 296 | *John Waterer | 1970 | Deep rose red |
| 10 | 274 | Alexander | 1972 | Vermilion |
| 11 | 251 | Bob Woolley | 1970 | Peach pink, apricot base, lemon reverse |
| 12 | 196 | Embassy | 1969 | Light gold, veined and edged carmine |
| 13 | 180 | Troika | 1972 | Light apricot to orange |
| 14 | 148 | Tenerife | 1972 | Coral-salmon, peach reverse |
| 15 | 146 | Typhoon | 1972 | Coppery orange-salmon |

* Most fragrant

## HYBRID TEA ROSES PRODUCING LARGE SPECIMEN BLOOMS SUITABLE FOR EXHIBITION

*This table includes only varieties introduced in this country before 1 January 1969*
(Maximum points possible—504)

Northern counties

| Position | Number of points | NAME | Introduced | COLOUR |
|---|---|---|---|---|
| 1 | 436 | Grandpa Dickson | 1966 | Yellow, fading to creamy yellow |
| 2 | 429 | *Red Devil | 1967 | Scarlet, reverse lighter |
| 3 | 409 | *Royal Highness | 1962 | Soft light pink |
| 4 | 386 | Pink Favourite | 1956 | Deep rose pink |
| 5 | 366 | Perfecta | 1957 | Cream, shaded rose red |
| 6 | 326 | *Fragrant Cloud | 1964 | Geranium lake |
| 7 | 309 | *Ernest H. Morse | 1965 | Rich turkey red |
| 8 | 293 | *Red Lion | 1966 | Deep cerise pink |
| 9 | 265 | Peace | 1947 | Light yellow edged with pink |
| 10 | 241 | Gavotte | 1963 | Light pink with silvery reverse |
| 10 | 241 | Memoriam | 1960 | White, tinted pale pink |
| 12 | 236 | Stella | 1959 | Carmine shading to cream |
| 13 | 226 | Princess | 1964 | Vermilion |
| 14 | 223 | *Bonsoir | 1968 | Peach pink, deeper at base |
| 15 | 222 | Isabel de Ortiz | 1962 | Deep pink with silver reverse |
| 16 | 219 | Fred Gibson | 1968 | Amber yellow to apricot |
| 16 | 219 | Chicago Peace | 1962 | Phlox pink, base canary yellow |
| 18 | 209 | *Wendy Cussons | 1959 | Cerise flushed scarlet |
| 19 | 192 | Norman Hartnell | 1964 | Deep cerise |
| 20 | 162 | Red Queen | 1968 | Cherry red |
| 21 | 154 | Honey Favourite | 1962 | Yellowish pink, base yellow |
| 22 | 146 | *Silver Lining | 1958 | Pale rose with silver reverse |
| 23 | 116 | *Super Star | 1960 | Pure light vermilion without shading |
| 24 | 106 | Charlie's Aunt | 1965 | Cream, heavily suffused rose |

## SOME ROSES FOR INDOOR DECORATION

| NAME | Introduced | COLOUR |
|---|---|---|
| *Super Star | 1960 | Pure light vermilion without shading |
| *Ernest H. Morse | 1965 | Rich turkey red |
| Pascali | 1963 | White |
| *Fragrant Cloud | 1964 | Geranium lake |
| Mischief | 1960 | Coral-salmon |
| *Wendy Cussons | 1959 | Cerise flushed scarlet |
| Grandpa Dickson | 1966 | Yellow fading to creamy yellow |
| Queen Elizabeth | 1955 | Clear self pink |
| *Blue Moon | 1964 | Silvery Lilac |
| *Sutter's Gold | 1950 | Light orange shaded red |
| Peace | 1947 | Light yellow edged pink |
| Virgo | 1947 | White |

* Most fragrant

## HYBRID TEA ROSES PRODUCING LARGE SPECIMEN BLOOMS SUITABLE FOR EXHIBITION

*This table includes only varieties introduced in this country before 1 January 1969*
(Maximum points possible—777)

Southern counties

| Position | Number of points | NAME | Introduced | COLOUR |
|---|---|---|---|---|
| 1 | 677 | Grandpa Dickson | 1966 | Yellow, fading to creamy yellow |
| 2 | 648 | *Red Devil | 1967 | Scarlet with lighter reverse |
| 3 | 536 | Pink Favourite | 1956 | Deep rose pink |
| 4 | 490 | *Ernest H. Morse | 1965 | Rich turkey red |
| 5 | 467 | *Royal Highness | 1962 | Soft light pink |
| 6 | 466 | Fred Gibson | 1968 | Amber yellow to apricot |
| 7 | 464 | Gavotte | 1963 | Light pink with silvery reverse |
| 8 | 402 | *Red Lion | 1966 | Deep cerise pink |
| 9 | 397 | Perfecta | 1957 | Cream, shaded rose red |
| 10 | 390 | *Wendy Cussons | 1959 | Cerise flushed scarlet |
| 11 | 386 | *Fragrant Cloud | 1964 | Geranium lake |
| 12 | 375 | Memoriam | 1960 | White tinted pale pink |
| 13 | 343 | Peace | 1947 | Light yellow edged with pink |
| 14 | 319 | *Bonsoir | 1968 | Peach pink, deeper at base |
| 15 | 308 | Isabel de Ortiz | 1962 | Deep pink with silver reverse |
| 16 | 281 | Princess | 1964 | Vermilion |
| 17 | 262 | *Silver Lining | 1958 | Pale rose with silver reverse |
| 18 | 239 | Honey Favourite | 1962 | Yellowish pink, base yellow |
| 19 | 229 | Stella | 1959 | Carmine, shading to cream |
| 20 | 187 | Charlie's Aunt | 1965 | Cream, heavily suffused rose |
| 21 | 183 | Rose Gaujard | 1958 | White, flushed rich carmine |
| 22 | 162 | Anne Letts | 1953 | Pale pink with paler reverse |
| 23 | 160 | Norman Hartnell | 1964 | Deep cerise |
| 24 | 144 | Chicago Peace | 1962 | Phlox pink, base canary yellow · |

## REPEAT FLOWERING CLIMBERS

(Maximum points possible—660)

| Position | Number of points | NAME | Introduced | COLOUR |
|---|---|---|---|---|
| 1 | 525 | Handel | 1965 | Cream, edged rose pink |
| 2 | 506 | Danse du Feu | 1954 | Orange-scarlet |
| 3 | 455 | *Golden Showers | 1957 | Golden yellow |
| 4 | 440 | Pink Perpêtue | 1965 | Clear pink with carmine pink |
| 5 | 302 | Schoolgirl | 1964 | Orange-apricot |
| 6 | 291 | *Zéphirine Drouhin | 1868 | Bright carmine pink |
| 7 | 285 | Parkdirektor Riggers | 1957 | Blood red |
| 8 | 257 | Casino | 1963 | Soft yellow, deeper in bud |
| 9 | 246 | *Maigold | 1953 | Bronze yellow |
| 10 | { 234 | *New Dawn | 1930 | Pale flesh pink |
|  | 234 | Mermaid | 1917 | Primrose yellow |
| 12 | 226 | Royal Gold | 1957 | Deep yellow |

The following varieties may also be recommended: *'Aloha', 'Bantry Bay', *'Copenhagen', 'Dortmund', 'Galway Bay', 'Hamburger Phoenix', 'Parade', 'Raymond Chenault', 'Swan Lake', 'Sympathie' and 'White Cockade'.

* Most fragrant

## HYBRID TEA ROSES FOR GENERAL GARDEN CULTIVATION
*This table includes only varieties introduced in this country before 1 January 1969*
(Maximum points possible—504)

Northern counties

| Position | Number of points | NAME | Introduced | COLOUR |
|---|---|---|---|---|
| 1 | 434 | Piccadilly | 1960 | Scarlet, yellow reverse |
| 2 | 416 | *Ernest H. Morse | 1965 | Rick turkey red |
| 3 | 415 | *Wendy Cussons | 1959 | Cerise, flushed scarlet |
| 4 | 413 | *Fragrant Cloud | 1964 | Geranium lake |
| 5 | 395 | Peace | 1947 | Light yellow edged pink |
| 6 | 359 | Mischief | 1960 | Coral salmon |
| 7 | 356 | Pink Favourite | 1956 | Deep rose pink |
| 8 | 351 | Grandpa Dickson | 1966 | Yellow, fading to creamy yellow |
| 9 | 328 | *Super Star | 1960 | Pure light vermilion without shading |
| 10 | 274 | Chicago Peace | 1962 | Phlox pink, base yellow |
| 11 | 264 | *Prima Ballerina | 1958 | Deep pink |
| 12 | 250 | Diorama | 1965 | Apricot yellow, flushed pink |
| 13 | 231 | King's Ransom | 1961 | Rich pure yellow |
| 14 | 228 | Rose Gaujard | 1958 | White flushed rich carmine |
| 15 | 204 | Stella | 1959 | Carmine shading to cream |
| 16 | 164 | Pascali | 1963 | White |
| 17 | 158 | *Whisky Mac | 1967 | Bronze-yellow and orange |
| 18 | 142 | Perfecta | 1957 | Cream, shaded rose red |
| 19 | 108 | *Josephine Bruce | 1952 | Deep velvety crimson scarlet |
| 19 | 108 | *Silver Lining | 1958 | Pale rose with silver reverse |
| 19 | 108 | Gavotte | 1963 | Light pink with silvery reverse |
| 22 | 104 | *Duke of Windsor | 1968 | Orange-vermilion |
| 23 | 96 | Fred Gibson | 1968 | Amber yellow to apricot |
| 24 | 85 | Peer Gynt | 1968 | Yellow, flushed pink at edges |

## WICHURAIANA CLIMBING AND RAMBLING ROSES— SUMMER FLOWERING
*Suitable for pergolas and fences*

| Position | Number of points | NAME | Introduced | COLOUR |
|---|---|---|---|---|
| 1 | 473 | *Albertine | 1921 | Salmon opening to coppery pink |
| 2 | 362 | Paul's Scarlet Climber | 1915 | Bright scarlet crimson |
| 3 | 311 | American Pillar | 1902 | Bright rose with white eye |
| 4 | 285 | Emily Gray | 1916 | Rich golden buff |
| 5 | 248 | Excelsa | 1909 | Bright rosy crimson |
| 6 | 244 | Dorothy Perkins | 1901 | Rose pink |
| 7 | 231 | *Albéric Barbier | 1900 | Yellow to creamy white |
| 8 | 230 | Chaplin's Pink Climber | 1928 | Bright pink |
| 9 | 211 | *Dr. W. Van Fleet | 1910 | Pale flesh pink |
| 10 | 182 | Crimson Shower | 1951 | Crimson |
| 11 | 176 | *Sanders' White | 1915 | White |
| 12 | 113 | Crimson Conquest | 1931 | Deep scarlet, white base |

* Most fragrant

## HYBRID TEA ROSES FOR GENERAL GARDEN CULTIVATION

*This table includes only varieties introduced in this country before 1 January 1969*
(Maximum points possible—756)

Southern counties

| Posi- tion | Number of points | NAME | Intro- duced | COLOUR |
|---|---|---|---|---|
| 1 | 548 | *Wendy Cussons | 1959 | Cerise flushed scarlet |
| 2 | 546 | *Fragrant Cloud | 1964 | Geranium lake |
| 3 | 524 | Pink Favourite | 1956 | Deep rose pink |
| 4 | 516 | *Ernest H. Morse | 1965 | Rich turkey red |
| 5 | { 508 | Peace | 1947 | Light yellow edged pink |
|  | { 508 | Grandpa Dickson | 1966 | Yellow fading to creamy yellow |
| 7 | 416 | Piccadilly | 1960 | Scarlet, yellow reverse |
| 8 | 386 | Mischief | 1960 | Coral-salmon |
| 9 | 364 | Rose Gaujard | 1958 | White flushed rich carmine |
| 10 | 354 | *Prima Ballerina | 1958 | Deep pink |
| 11 | 335 | King's Ransom | 1961 | Rich pure yellow |
| 12 | { 324 | Pascali | 1963 | White |
|  | { 324 | *Super Star | 1960 | Pure light vermilion without shading |
| 14 | 319 | *Red Devil | 1967 | Scarlet with lighter reverse |
| 15 | 248 | Fred Gibson | 1968 | Amber yellow to apricot |
| 16 | 239 | Perfecta | 1957 | Cream, shaded rose red |
| 17 | 229 | *Bonsoir | 1968 | Peach pink, deeper at base |
| 18 | 220 | Gavotte | 1963 | Light pink with silvery reverse |
| 19 | 206 | Diorama | 1965 | Apricot yellow flushed pink |
| 20 | 201 | *Silver Lining | 1958 | Pale rose with silver reverse |
| 21 | 195 | *Blessings | 1967 | Light coral pink |
| 22 | 194 | Chicago Peace | 1962 | Phlox pink, base yellow |
| 23 | 170 | Stella | 1959 | Carmine shading to cream |
| 24 | 151 | *Josephine Bruce | 1952 | Deep velvety crimson scarlet |

## SHRUB ROSES—REPEAT FLOWERING

| NAME | COLOUR | Height in feet |
|---|---|---|
| *Chinatown | Yellow, sometimes tinted pink | 6 |
| *Fred Loads | Vermilion–orange | 5–6 |
| *Penelope | Creamy salmon | 5 |
| Joseph's Coat | Yellow, orange and red | 5–6 |
| Nevada | Pale creamy white, sometimes with pink | 6 |
| Ballerina | Pink with white eye | 4 |
| *Cornelia | Pink with yellow base | 5–6 |
| Heidelberg | Bright red | 5–6 |
| Bonn | Orange-scarlet | 6 |
| Kassel | Scarlet red | 6 |
| Elmshorn | Light crimson | 5 |
| Dorothy Wheatcroft | Orient red with deeper shades | 4–5 |

* Most fragrant

'SNOWLINE' (floribunda)
Raised by N. D. Poulsen, Denmark
TRIAL GROUND CERTIFICATE 1970
See 1971 *Rose Annual*, page 177

'MALAGA' (climber)
('*Danse du Feu*'×'*Hamburger Phoenix*')ד*Copenhagen*'
Raised by Sam McGredy IV
TRIAL GROUND CERTIFICATE 1971
*See 1972 Rose Annual, page 178*

## CLIMBING AND RAMBLING ROSES FOR SPECIAL PURPOSES

| Position | NAME | Introduced | COLOUR |
|---|---|---|---|
| | *Suitable for walls or closeboard fencing* | | |
| 1 | Danse du Feu | 1954 | Orange scarlet |
| 2 | Pink Perpêtue | 1965 | Clear pink with carmine pink |
| 3 | Handel | 1965 | Cream edged rose pink |
| 4 | Mermaid | 1917 | Primrose yellow |
| 5 | *Maigold | 1953 | Bronze yellow |
| 6 | *Albertine | 1921 | Salmon opening to coppery pink |
| 7 | Parkdirektor Riggers | 1957 | Blood red |
| 8 | Royal Gold | 1957 | Deep yellow |
| 9 | *Golden Showers | 1957 | Golden yellow |
| | *Suitable for open fences* | | |
| 1 | *Albertine | 1921 | Salmon opening to coppery pink |
| 2 | *New Dawn | 1930 | Pale flesh pink |
| 3 | Danse du Feu | 1954 | Orange scarlet |
| 4 | *Maigold | 1953 | Bronze yellow |
| 5 | Pink Perpêtue | 1965 | Clear pink with carmine pink |
| 6 | Paul's Scarlet Climber | 1915 | Bright scarlet crimson |
| 7 | Parkdirektor Riggers | 1957 | Blood red |
| 8 | American Pillar | 1902 | Bright rose with white eye |
| 9 | Emily Gray | 1916 | Rich golden buff |
| | *Suitable for pillars* | | |
| 1 | Handel | 1965 | Cream edged rose pink |
| 2 | *Golden Showers | 1957 | Golden yellow |
| 3 | Danse du Feu | 1954 | Orange scarlet |
| 4 | Casino | 1963 | Soft yellow, deeper in bud |
| 5 | Pink Perpêtue | 1965 | Clear pink with carmine pink |
| 6 | *Zéphirine Drouhin | 1868 | Bright carmine pink |
| 7 | Joseph's Coat | 1963 | Yellow, orange and red |
| 8 | Royal Gold | 1957 | Deep yellow |
| 9 | Schoolgirl | 1964 | Orange-apricot |

## SHRUB ROSES—SUMMER FLOWERING ONLY

| NAME | COLOUR | Height in feet |
|---|---|---|
| Canary Bird | Rich yellow | 6 |
| *Frühlingsgold | Clear light yellow | 6 |
| R. moyesii | Deep red | 8–10 |
| Frühlingsmorgen | Deep pink to yellow, maroon stamens | 6 |
| R. rubrifolia | Pink, foliage tinted mauve and grey | 6 |
| Golden Chersonese | Yellow | 8 |
| R. hugonis | Yellow | 5 |
| *Celestial (Alba) | Pure pink | 5 |
| *Mme. Hardy | White | 6 |
| R. gallica versicolor | Crimson striped pink and white | 4 |
| *Maiden's Blush (Alba) | Warm pink shading to cream pink | 5 |
| Charles de Mills | Purple crimson shading to maroon | 4–5 |

* Most fragrant

## REPEAT FLOWERING ROSES FOR HEDGES
### *Up to 5 ft*

| Position | NAME | Introduced | COLOUR |
|---|---|---|---|
| 1 | Iceberg | 1958 | Pure white tinged pink in bud |
| 2 | Queen Elizabeth | 1955 | Clear self pink |
| 3 | *Chinatown | 1963 | Yellow sometimes tinted pink |
| 4 | Peace | 1947 | Light yellow edged pink |
| 5 | *Fred Loads | 1967 | Vermilion orange |
| 6 | Dorothy Wheatcroft | 1960 | Orient red with deeper shades |
| 7 | *Penelope | 1924 | Creamy salmon |
| 8 | Ballerina | 1937 | Pink with white eye |
| 9 | Masquerade | 1950 | Yellow, pink and red |
| 10 | Frensham | 1946 | Deep scarlet crimson |
| 11 | *Super Star | 1960 | Pure light vermilion |
| 12 | Scarlet Queen Elizabeth | 1963 | Orange scarlet |

## REPEAT FLOWERING ROSES FOR HEDGES
### *Over 5 ft*

| Position | NAME | Introduced | COLOUR |
|---|---|---|---|
| 1 | Queen Elizabeth | 1955 | Clear self pink |
| 2 | *Fred Loads | 1967 | Vermilion orange |
| 3 | *Chinatown | 1963 | Yellow, sometimes tinted pink |
| 4 | Uncle Walter | 1963 | Scarlet with crimson shading |
| 5 | Joseph's Coat | 1963 | Yellow, orange and red |
| 6 | *Golden Showers | 1957 | Golden yellow |
| 7 | Nevada | 1927 | Pale creamy white, sometimes with pink |
| 8 | Heidelberg | 1958 | Bright red |
| 9 | *Zéphirine Drouhin | 1868 | Bright carmine pink |
| 10 | Bonn | 1949 | Orange scarlet |
| 11 | Roseraie de L'Haÿ | 1901 | Purplish crimson |
| 12 | Kassel | 1958 | Scarlet red |

## WEATHER RESISTANT ROSES—HYBRID TEAS

| NAME | Introduced | COLOUR |
|---|---|---|
| Peace | 1947 | Light yellow edged pink |
| *Ernest H. Morse | 1965 | Rich turkey red |
| Grandpa Dickson | 1966 | Yellow, fading to creamy yellow |
| Mischief | 1960 | Coral salmon |
| Piccadilly | 1960 | Scarlet, yellow reverse |
| *Wendy Cussons | 1959 | Cerise flushed scarlet |
| Rose Gaujard | 1958 | White, flushed rich carmine |
| Pink Favourite | 1956 | Deep rose pink |
| Stella | 1959 | Carmine, shading to cream |
| *Super Star | 1960 | Light vermilion without shading |
| *Fragrant Cloud | 1964 | Geranium lake |
| Chicago Peace | 1962 | Phlox pink, base canary yellow |

* Most fragrant

## WEATHER RESISTANT ROSES—FLORIBUNDAS

| NAME | Introduced | COLOUR |
|---|---|---|
| Evelyn Fison | 1962 | Vivid red with scarlet shading |
| Iceberg | 1958 | Pure white tinged pink in bud |
| Queen Elizabeth | 1955 | Clear self pink |
| Allgold | 1956 | Unfading golden yellow |
| Lilli Marlene | 1959 | Scarlet red |
| Orangeade | 1959 | Bright orange vermilion |
| Dorothy Wheatcroft | 1960 | Orient red with deeper shades |
| *Elizabeth of Glamis | 1964 | Light salmon |
| Paddy McGredy | 1962 | Carmine, lighter reverse |
| *Orange Sensation | 1961 | Orange vermilion |
| Europeana | 1963 | Deep crimson |
| City of Leeds | 1966 | Rich salmon |

## MINIATURE ROSES

*Mostly of about 6–9 in. in height, rarely more*

| Position | NAME | COLOUR |
|---|---|---|
| 1 | Baby Masquerade | Yellow and red |
| 2 | Rosina | Sunflower yellow |
| 3 | Coralin | Coral red to orange red |
| 4 | Pour Toi | White, tinted yellow at base |
| 5 | Starina | Orange scarlet |
| 6 | New Penny | Salmon, turning pink with age |
| 7 | Cinderella | White, tinted carmine |
| 8 | Easter Morning | Ivory white |
| 9 | Little Buckaroo | Bright red |

## HISTORICAL (OLD GARDEN) ROSES

*This table is restricted to varieties introduced prior to the Hybrid Tea and which are particularly suitable for use in a garden of average size.*

| NAME | Classification | Introduced | COLOUR |
|---|---|---|---|
| Rosa Mundi (R. gallica versicolor) | Gallica | Before 1800 | Crimson, striped pink and white |
| *Mme. Hardy | Damascena | 1832 | White |
| Cécile Brunner | Hy. china | 1881 | Pale pink |
| *Cardinal de Richelieu | Gallica | Before 1840 | Maroon purple |
| *Celestial | Alba | — | Pink |
| *Mme. Isaac Pereire | Bourbon | 1881 | Purplish crimson |
| *Tuscany | Gallica | — | Deep maroon |
| *Mme. Pierre Oger | Bourbon | 1878 | Cream shaded pink |
| *Charles de Mills | Gallica | — | Purplish crimson to maroon |
| Maiden's Blush | Alba | — | Warm pink to cream pink |
| *Boule de Neige | Bourbon | 1867 | Creamy white |
| *De Meaux | Centifolia | 1814 | Pink |

* Most fragrant

# OLD ADAM'S LAMENT
### (On hearing a song)

My love were like a red, red rose
When she and I were wed.
But now she'm like a thorny briar;
The grafted rose is dead.

I dig my roses in the spring
And prune 'em three buds 'igh;
But I can't cultivate my wife,
She'm spracklier than I.

Her shoots do wrastle left and right
And scrat I night and day.
Wherever I do put my foot
'Tis always in the way.

If I could plant she in the earth
And tie a stake to she,
Come June next year I'd have her back
Just like she used to be.

I'd cut the trump'ry (all bar one,
The burliest one that grows),
I'd slit 'er bark and graft a bud
From my old sweet red rose.

Then come the summer (if I'm spared)
Come sun and good warm rain,
I'd see my missus bursting forth
A red, red rose again!

J. C. B.

# LETTER FROM HITCHIN

By the look of the plants we sent out, our customers ought to have a wonderful show in 1974. We are very grateful for the orders received, and will continue to do our best to justify the confidence shown by many rosarians, whether beginners or very experienced.

1973 proved a wonderful year for us, and a fine haul of Trophies and Medals rewarded our efforts at the Shows. Pride of place, as always, goes to the Society's Championship Trophy, which we won in the summer for the 39th time. We shall really celebrate when we can make it 40, which will be as soon as Mr Mattock and other friends permit! It was a pleasure to receive the premier award at the Autumn Show as well as the Summer, and we privately thought our Autumn exhibit was the most beautiful we have ever staged at that show.

Our new Roses collected another dozen awards. The Edland Medal for Fragrance went to *Compassion*, an orange pink climber. It was the first time a Climber had taken the Edland Medal, and who can deny that of all Roses, fragrance is most welcome and appropriate in a climber around the doors and windows?

*Alexander* won a Gold Medal in Germany; and *Escapade* became an All German Rose Selection – two high honours indeed. The Germans consider that *Escapade* is one of the best Roses for associating with other garden plants. It seems that Harkness varieties are well liked in Germany, because we also won 6 Silver Medals there in the summer. *Southampton*, *Busy Lizzie*, *Dr Barnardo* and *Princess Chichibu* were among the recipients. We also won Certificates from Holland and New Zealand.

Then in September came the news that the Society had decided to award us the Queen Mary Commemoration Medal, for our work breeding Roses. The pleasure of this was all the greater for finding Alec Cocker and other friends had been similarly honoured.

As always, it is a pleasure to grow Roses, show them and breed them; to meet our customers and rose friends at the nursery, the Shows, or through their letters. And to enjoy the activities of the Society, whereby all these pleasures seem to be the more worthwhile. Long may all good Rose folk continue!

R. Harkness & Co. Ltd,  
The Rose Gardens,  
Hitchin, Herts.  
Tel. 0462 4027

ISOBEL HARKNESS  
JACK HARKNESS  
PETER HARKNESS

# LATEST INTRODUCTIONS FROM HARKNESS

## COMPASSION (Harkness, 1973)

*The First Climbing Rose to receive the Edland Medal for Fragrance*

*Colour:* Light salmon pink, generously shaded orange as it opens.

*Habit:* Vigorous to 10 feet or so, repeat blooming, abundant dark green foliage.

*Form:* Double Hybrid Tea form, average 39 petals, medium size.

*Fragrance:* Very fragrant, a great asset in a Climbing Rose.

*Uses:* Walls, fences, pillars.

*Awards:* Edland Medal for Fragrance; Trial Ground Certificate.

*Parentage:* White Cockade × Prima Ballerina.

*Price:* £1. Please order early; this variety is also obtainable from The British Council for the Rehabilitation of the Disabled, to help their funds. We already have a lot of orders carried over from last year, so Compassion is likely to be sold out before Christmas again.


## YESTERDAY (Harkness, 1974)

*A little Shrub Rose of unique character and pleasing fragrance*

*Colour:* Rose pink to lilac pink, young and old flowers agree together delightfully.

*Habit:* Bushy and low, with graceful shoots arising, usually 2–4 feet; abundant small shiny leaves, turning dark and burnished in the Autumn. We can think of hardly any variety which is in flower so continuously.

*Form:* Small semi-double flowers, average 13 petals, opening flat, with stamens that stay yellow a long time; very charming, in character.

*Fragrance:* There is a pleasing scent; especially enjoyable if you cut some and have them in the house.

*Uses:* For beds, groups, associating with other garden plants; Yesterday is very easy to fit into your garden, it should be a godsend to garden designers. Also extremely rewarding to cut, and an excellent Rose for growing in pots or containers.

*Awards:* Certificate of Merit (RNRS); Award of Merit (RHS).

*Parentage:* (Phyllis Bide × Shepherd's Delight) × Ballerina.

*Price:* £1. Stock of this variety is limited. If you like the Old Garden Roses, this one should please you.


James Cocker & Sons Ltd,
Whitemyres,
Lang Stracht,
Aberdeen.
Tel. 33261

R. Harkness & Co. Ltd,
The Rose Gardens,
Hitchin,
Herts.
Tel. 0462 4027

# LATEST INTRODUCTIONS FROM COCKER

## BURMA STAR (Cocker 1974)

*An Apricot yellow Floribunda, with fascinating growth*

*Colour:* Bright apricot yellow, holding clear as the flower develops.
*Habit:* Vigorous upright bush around 4 feet, putting out long shoots later in the year. Can be used as Floribunda or Shrub, by either pruning or retaining the shoots as required. Abundant bright green foliage.
*Form:* Hybrid Tea type, very regular high centred flowers.
*Fragrance:* Not strong, but there is a very pleasant scent.
*Uses:* Beds, borders, or as a shrub.
*Awards:* Will be eligible the first time in 1974.
*Parentage:* Arthur Bell × Manx Queen.
*Price:* 70p. This variety has been named for the Burma Star Association, and we are very honoured to pay this tribute to the men and women who did so much to defend their country in the East.

## CAIRNGORM (Cocker 1973)

*Brilliant jewel of a Floribunda, upright, strong grower*

*Colour:* Orange-red and yellow, very bright; gives a massive show of colour.
*Habit:* Vigorous, upright bush to around 4 feet. Very easy and free growing, with ample bright dark green foliage.
*Form:* Full flowers (average 37 petals) of average Floribunda size, pretty H.T. form. Trusses are very large, and the flowers produced very evenly, giving an impressive display.
*Fragrance:* Slightly fragrant.
*Uses:* An excellent bedding rose, it was one of the healthiest in its time under trial in St Albans.
*Awards:* RNRS Trial Ground Certificate.
*Parentage:* (Highlight × Colour Wonder) × Arthur Bell.
*Price:* 70p. And we believe this Scottish jewel will be found more than value for money.

James Cocker & Sons Ltd,
Whitemyres,
Lang Stracht,
Aberdeen.
Tel. 33261

R. Harkness & Co. Ltd,
The Rose Gardens,
Hitchin,
Herts.
Tel. 0462 4027

# Your garden has many visitors...

## Not all of them are welcome

### 40,000,000 Fungus Spores

In the soil and floating about in the air just waiting to cause you problems.

Black spot and mildew on roses, powdery mildew, grey mould and scab. Spray your plants and trees with new multi-purpose Murphy Systemic Fungicide and see them come clean. Available in handy sachet packs.

### Masses of Moss

Moss can choke your lawn and make your paths and drives slippery and dangerous. Clear it up with New Super Moss Killer and Lawn Fungicide. It also controls the three major lawn diseases.

*Figures based on conservative population estimate of infestation in 1/12 acre garden.*

## Murphy

**Murphy Chemical Limited,**
Wheathampstead, St. Albans, Herts. AL4 8QU
Tel: Wheathampstead 2001 (STD Code 058 283)

213

**THE QUEEN MARY COMMEMORATION MEDAL**
for outstanding contribution in the raising of new
roses by British hybridists

was

awarded in 1973 to:

# JOHN SANDAY
## (ROSES) LTD.
### for
## ALMONDSBURY ROSES

The award is the happy outcome not only of our own efforts, but due in no small measure to the valued encouragement of our many friends in the growing and showing of our roses throughout the country and to whom we offer our warm thanks.

This year we bring you:

**1. LIFEBOAT JUBILEE** introduced to celebrate the 150th anniversary of the Royal National Lifeboat Institution.

**2. 'FRED FAIRBROTHER'** – our tribute to one of the great Rosarians of our day.

Both the above fully described and pictured in our comprehensive new catalogue free on request in May, including our award winning introductions.

Please Note: Plants of 'Fred Fairbrother' will be in very limited supply in 1974.

# JOHN SANDAY (ROSES) LTD.
Over Lane, Almondsbury, Bristol, BS12 4DA

216

Anderson's
fragrant Scottish roses
from Royal Deeside

The North's Premier Nursery
where we concentrate on
growing fragrant roses.

Our Free
Catalogues are
now available.

WHISKY
MAC

We grow almost two million rose bushes
annually therefore if you wish the choice of
the best in the rose world send now for our
free 58 page catalogue with 76 colour
illustrations.

Select from over 175 varieties

from **£3·50**

per dozen + 35p c & p

# First choice for top rose growers

No one knows how many awards have been won through the help of these two well-known 'aids to perfection'.

## Toprose

Toprose, the top rose fertilizer, is based on the well-proven Tonk's formula, but with added extras to give top quality blooms on prolific plants.

## Du Pont Benlate*

And, of course, for disease control Benlate is at the top of every rose grower's list. This first systemic fungicide for roses goes *inside* the leaf to prevent and cure mildew and blackspot.

## Pan Britannica Industries Limited
Britannica House, Waltham Cross, Herts.

*Benlate is a Registered Trademark of E. I. Du Pont de Nemours & Co. (Inc.)

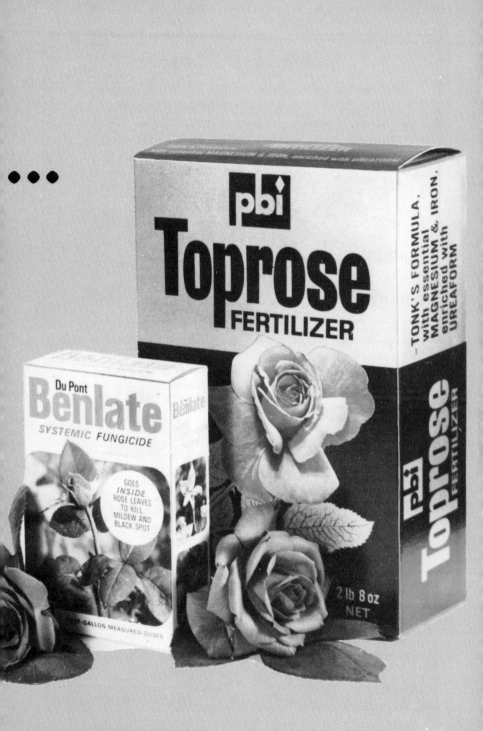

# Hamburg's Love

Another new Rose from TIMMERMANS' ROSES. A fragrant orange-yellow Floribunda, strong growing, with very broad leaves. This  Rose was christened in Hamburg during the International Horticultural Show last Summer.

If you missed out on TENERIFE, we have a good stock for Autumn 1974. You will find a colour picture in this issue.

*Write for free catalogue, or see this and other varieties at:*

## TIMMERMANS' ROSES
## WOODBOROUGH, NOTTINGHAM NG14 6DN
### TELEPHONE LOWDHAM 2393

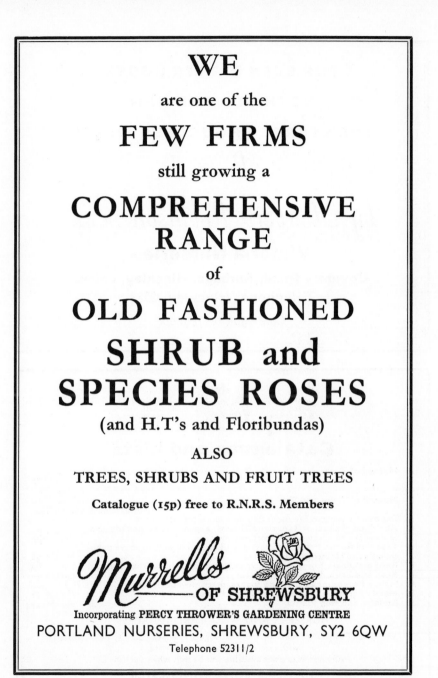

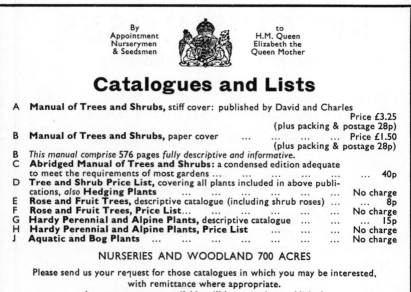

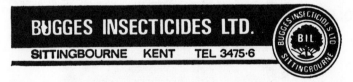

# SPECIALLY RECOMMENDED FOR ROSES
## AND ENDORSED BY LEADING ROSE GROWERS

# PHOSTROGEN

## is Britain's <u>most</u> economical, most widely used, all purpose garden plant food

### *Because...*

★ IT SAVES YOU the need to buy one plant food for root feeding and another for foliar feeding — it is highly successful for both, also as top dressing and for use with soil-less composts and for hydroponics.

★ IT SAVES YOU the need to buy separate plant foods for different subjects — it is a scientifically balanced all-purpose plant food — excellent as a starter solution for seeds and seedlings, for flowers, vegetables, shrubs, lawns and even established trees.

★ IT SAVES YOU a great deal of money — over 8 gallons of PHOSTROGEN solution for just one penny, according to the size of pack you buy.

★ IT SAVES YOU worry about impoverished soils — it is a scientific soil restorer derived from a formula for growing plants without soil.

★ IT SAVES YOU waiting time — it works fast, showing a noticeable improvement after just one application.

★ IT SAVES YOU labour — you just water it in at the rate of one level teaspoon to a two gallon watering can — no smell, no trouble.

**PHOSTROGEN**
the wonder soluble
**PLANT FOOD**

for root and foliar feeding
● simple to use
● very economical
● immediate results

PHOSTROGEN
9p MINI CARTON
makes 34 galls.
20p STANDARD CARTON
makes 114 galls.
40p ECONOMY CARTON
makes 274 galls.
£2.25 DUAL-PURPOSE
POLYTHENE BUCKET
makes 1,826 galls.
PHOS-tro-TABS
25p CARTON
of 220 tablets.
*Recommended retail prices including 10% V.A.T.*

# PHOS (TRO) TABS
## The modern PLANTOIDS
### containing PHOSTROGEN

Based on the outstandingly successful PHOSTROGEN formula, these unique plant food tablets are a balanced diet for vigorous and healthy growth.

★ Specially beneficial for all houseplants, window boxes and individual subjects in garden or greenhouse.
★ Simple, easy, clean and safe to use.

**Obtainable from:**
Woolworth Stores, Gardening Departments of Boots and Timothy Whites, and most leading stores, horticultural shops, seedsmen and garden centres.

**FREE:**
"All about PHOSTROGEN" —Booklet No. 10 for general garden use. Booklet No. 11 for soil-less culture and hydroponics.

# PHOSTROGEN LTD., CORWEN, MERIONETH LL21 OEE.

226

227

# New from Harry Wheatcroft

## Sir Harry Pilkington

A glorious, intense carmine red Hybrid Tea rose of medium height and very free flowering. Given the name of the great glass magnate as a retirement present by the Australian division of Pilkington Brothers.

## Did you order Topsi last year?

## Peggy Netherthorpe

Named after the wife of Lord Netherthorpe retiring chairman of Fisons. The long slender Hybrid Tea buds of this beautiful rich pink rose grow on a tall robust vigorous bush.

My new red dwarf floribunda Topsi was so much in demand last year that literally thousands of orders had to be unfilled, I must apologise to frustrated Topsi buyers, particularly as its showing this year in my garden confirmed what a sensational rose it is, but as with all small roses we can only increase stocks slowly. I can only ask you to order early this year.

In addition to these two magnificent roses, we offer, for the first time, Lady Helen, a delightful clear pale pink H.T. of medium growth and, of course all the recent introductions and established favourites from my catalogue. If you are not on my list send for a copy today.

HARRY WHEATCROFT GARDENING LTD. EDWALTON, NOTTINGHAM. NG12 4DE TELEPHONE 211231

Our new Floribunda rose for 1974–75 is a seedling X Firecracker of medium height yet simply weighed down with trusses of 'Persian Rose' flowers each containing an average of 30 petals and $4\frac{1}{2}$ inches across. The weight of flowers and the continuous flowering habit has forced upon us its name "ABUNDANCE". The flowers are lit up at a distance with a background of dense dark green foliage. This rose can be yours for only 60p.

A rose we put into commerce three years ago is not selling half as well as it should do; that gorgeous deep copper bronze **H.T. WHISKY GILL.** This and all our latest award winning varieties such as **EGYPTIAN TREASURE, ORIENTAL GLAMOUR, MEGIDDO** and **MARTIAN GLOW** are in our latest catalogue for 1974–75, available free on request.

---

# GANDY'S (ROSES) LTD. Dept. R.70

**North Kilworth, Lutterworth, Leicestershire LE176 HZ.**

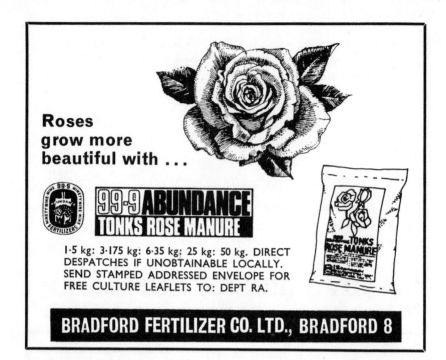